Imperial Crime and Punishment

Imperial Crime and Punishment

THE MASSACRE AT JALLIANWALA BAGH
AND BRITISH JUDGMENT, 1919–1920

Helen Fein

The University Press of Hawaii ☿
Honolulu

Manufactured in the United States of America

Designed by Roger Eggers

Library of Congress Cataloging in Publication Data

Fein, Helen, 1934–
   Imperial crime and punishment.

   A revision of the author's thesis, Columbia University, 1971.
   Bibliography: p.
   Includes index.
   1. Amritsar, India—Massacre, 1919. I. Title.
DS480.5.F4   1977   954'.03'5   77-2930
ISBN 0-8248-0506-2

To my guides to Amritsar,
Mrs. Bandhari, Professor Datta, and Mr. Sethi,
who clung to truth and offered apples,
chapati, and tea in friendship

Contents

Preface

This book tries to explain how groups condone, legitimate, and authorize violence toward other groups which would be punished as criminal acts if committed against their own members. The origin of such violence is related to types of power structures that make such crimes more likely.

Collective violence—which has also been called racial, religious, or communal violence—has reached epidemic scope in this century. If we believe that all groups should enjoy the same right to live, exercise civil rights, and maintain their own collective identity, violence victimizing any of them because of their identity must be regarded as a scourge. But despite its prevalence, there are few signs we have learned much about how it occurs or can be checked. Since the mass extermination of European Jewry during World War II, we have seen genocide or widespread massacre against distinct groups practiced without external check in southern Africa, Brazil, Burundi, India, Indonesia, Lebanon, northern Ireland, Nigeria, Pakistan, and Uganda. Doubtless, the list is incomplete.

Social theorists, however, have not developed a coherent explanation of collective violence nor always discriminated it from mass political violence that may serve as a means of petition or sign of express grievances. Analysis of collective violence has been divided arbitrarily by disciplinary borders, regions in which cases occur, and topical contexts. Therefore, we have discrete case studies of communal violence in south Asia, American violence, internal war, colonial conflicts, violence related to tribal and national integration and to race relations, and war between nations. This book does not attempt to review or codify such analyses nor survey the writings of the nineteenth-century theorists who offered explanations of the genesis of group violence in class or group conflict. It draws upon but recasts deductions from one major theoretical line, conflict theory, with two seminal sources: Georg Simmel, interpreted by Lewis Coser, and Karl Marx, as revised by Ralf Dahrendorf.[1] Little systematic use of such propositions has been made, except Allen Grimshaw's use of Simmel in his classic study of American race riots.[2]

What has been overlooked (or unstressed) by many conflict theorists (and other sociologists) is the essentially repressive nature of collective violence—the deliberate injury of any and sometimes all members of the tribe, race, or community accused of the crimes of one member, or some members. Or accused simply of being the other. "Racism" is sometimes casually invoked as an explanation, but few examine how and why people classify others as members of different races and whether such classification in itself is thought to imply their right to injure members of the other category. However, we know that groups of different characteristic physical types often live together peacefully and that people of the same hue frequently kill one another, discriminating the other by religious, ethnic, or cultural signs.

One approach to understanding collective violence that has been neglected is to appreciate it as crime and punishment simultaneously: it is objectively a crime against the victims but is understood by its perpetrators as a punishment. The fact that pogroms, lynchings, and colonial massacres are crimes that have usually gone unpunished is so well known that to comment on it is to risk criticism for elaborating the commonplace. The class perpetrating the crime often claims the victims deserved this punishment for a criminal act alleged to have been committed by one or more of them against the class of the perpetrators. Sometimes these punishments are frankly acknowledged by the aggressors to be reprisals or revenge. In other cases, such violence is frequently accounted for by perpetrators as acts of self-defense, and the blame is cast on the victim for provoking them. How are we to explain this? Shall we explain it simply by unmasking it as an ideological cover-up or an accounting device to evade legal sanctions by the perpetrators?

Simply negating the truth-value of their claims may blind us from new discovery. Although many sociologists believe that taking the viewpoint of the actor whose behavior is to be explained is a useful method of discovery, for a sociologist to acknowledge that collective violence may be not only accounted for but intended as punishment is to invite censure as a sympathizer with the oppressors. Identification with the oppressed thus may become an ideological blindfold preventing us from understanding the significance of people's own accounts of their acts simply because we disapprove of them.

How does understanding collective violence as acts of punishment enable us to understand why they occur and reoccur? The theorist who best explained the functions of repressive punishment for the community and the need for vengeance was Emile Durkheim.[3] Durkheim explained how repressive sanctions— punishment designed deliberately to injure the offender—restored the unity of a community based on mechanical solidarity, likeness of role, belief, habit, and sentiment. An injury against one is an injury against all until it is expiated.

This work extends Durkheim's theory on the relation of group solidarity to crime and punishment to show how a social order based on membership in racial, ethnic, religious, or national groups tends to produce class crimes and class solidarity. Each class is excluded from the universe of moral obligation of the other, so that offenses against the other are not recognized as crimes. Although crimes against members of the dominant class by members of the class dominated are understood by the dominant class to be crimes against all of its members, they recognize no obligation toward the dominated class that impels them to punish their own crime toward the dominated. This theory, elaborated in Chapter 1, explores the paradoxes of the crime-punishment–crime cycle and how it can be manipulated.

One advantage of such a generalizing line of analysis is that it can be extrapolated to explain diverse situations including warfare against civilian populations, internal war, communal conflicts in plural societies, and colonial violence. Seldom have students of warfare related the social license to kill foreign nationals to the assumptions emergent in civil war. The essential assumption allowing people to kill is the same—the enemy must be defined as outside the universe of moral obligation. Just as the nation becomes the boundary of the universe of obligation in war, the class, race, or tribe becomes the boundary of the universe of obligation in collective conflicts within the state.

To argue that such an explanation is plausible cannot prove or disprove it. One way to test it is to analyze the difference between those who condoned crimes toward a subordinated class and those who condemned them in a social order based on the collective domination of people of one nation and race by those of another. Colonialism offers an array of examples and English imperial history a choice of well-documented massacres. The massacre of April 13, 1919 at the Jallianwala Bagh gives us a unique opportunity to prove this assumption because of the subsequent debate it engendered.

Jallianwala Bagh has resonated in the memory of Indians for over a half a century. By official estimate, 379 Indians attending an unlawfully convened but peaceful political rally were killed by the orders of Brig. Gen. Reginald E. Dyer: Indian contemporaries alleged that there were 1,000 to 1,500 deaths, and a census counted over 500 victims. A. J. P. Taylor calls the massacre "the worst bloodshed since the Mutiny, and the decisive moment when Indians were alienated from British rule."[4] No event in modern British history occurring in the United Kingdom or its white colonies has compared to it in loss of lives as a consequence of firing against civilians. The Peterloo massacre had claimed about 11 lives. Across the Atlantic, British soldiers provoked into firing on Boston Commons had killed five men and were accused of deliberate massacre. In response to the self-proclaimed Easter Rebellion of 1916 in Dublin, the British had executed sixteen Irishmen.

Although we shall see later that the massacre at Jallianwala Bagh was not an isolated or exceptional event but a prototypical instance of a repressive collective punishment practiced by the

British in black and Asian colonies, this was not a means of social control of natives sanctioned by the British. Dwelling on the massive and sudden violence at Jallianwala Bagh ought not to obscure what it did not represent. It was not the consequence of a taken-for-granted campaign of cultural genocide and collective expropriation, as was the massacre against Native Americans at Wounded Knee in 1890. There has never been any substantive proof that it was calculated by the British-appointed imperial government of India, as were many pogroms in Russia calculated and arranged by the czarist regime.[5] Collective violence had not become an institutionalized means of social control in India as it had in the United States between 1890 and 1900, during which decade an average of two blacks were lynched weekly. Nor was there any evidence of a plot or any intention to destroy the Indian people, as the Germans attempted to destroy the Jewish people (with help of many friends and bystanders) during World War II.

Because it was a clear and well-documented violation of explicit British rules regulating the use of firepower against civilians, the Amritsar massacre is especially suitable for analysis and was recognized as such at the time. It called for evaluation precisely because Dyer's act—ordering firing without warning into a dense seated crowd—was an extraordinary one not anticipated by his superiors. His absolution by the bureaucracy was post facto. Had Dyer been an officer obeying orders, there would never have been a parliamentary debate on the meaning of the massacre. However, it cannot be regarded as an aberration in terms of British-Indian relations. Rather, it was a potentiality endemic in the class division created by the empire as racial solidarity and polarization between the races intensified in the half-century before 1919.

This work places the massacre in the context of imperial history and examines it as a paradigm of confrontation between two classes, divided in this case by race, nation, and religion as well as by power. The analysis of this crime is uniquely accessible because of the accounts produced by the Government of India's Hunter Committee and the Indian National Congress subcommittee established to investigate the Punjab disorders. They record the evidence from the executioners and the victims respectively. The biracial and binational Hunter Committee Report also merits investigation to show the function of such riot reports and how such committees are constituted to cope with breakdowns of class relations. We can profitably examine its workings to understand, too, why they fail—in this instance, the majority and minority, splitting on the racial and national axis, issued separate conclusions. The Hunter Committee's Majority and Minority Report and the Congress Report are analyzed to test the proposition that the critical link in punishment is labeling an act a crime. The analysis illustrates how the assumptions, mode of logic, and final evaluations of each committee fit the class of the men rendering judgment.

The Majority Report of the Hunter Committee was the basis for the decision by the Government of India to remove General Dyer from his post—this action was, as Winston Churchill, the secretary of state for war, told the House of Commons in July 1920, the lightest sanction that could have been employed. The Government of India's censure of Dyer's action, reaffirmed subsequently by both the British Cabinet and the Army Council, provoked motions by Dyer's defenders in both Houses of Parliament in July 1920, passage of which would have symbolically condemned the government's sanction, thus condoning Dyer's action and the imperial policy it was recognized to represent. The motion passed the House of Lords that the government's conduct of the Dyer case was "establishing a precedent dangerous to the preservation of order in the face of rebellion." The debate records give us an opportunity to explore how people are exonerated or rewarded for acts committed against others that would be labeled and punished as crimes if committed against members of their own class. The key hypothesis developed here is that punishment of an offender depends on the inclusion of the victim in the universe of moral obligation of the class rendering judgment. This hypothesis was developed both deductively, by extrapolating Durkheim's theory of crime and punishment, and inductively, by reading the debates on the Dyer sanction; then it was tested by examining how well it explains the vote cast by speakers in that debate.

The focus is upon comparisons of British judgment, for the British were ultimately the judges. And it was their judgment that reiterated to Indians they could be violated with impunity. The comparisons are not intended to diminish the dignity of the

victims as human beings—comparison is both irrelevant and ir-
reverent in weighing the pain to the survivors of lives cut down
and wasted. Some, seeking to commemorate the victims, have
cast them in mythical terms as martyrs or freedom fighters. I do
not believe that ordinary men such as those who attended the
protest meeting at Jallianwala Bagh on 13 April 1919, not believing they were taking an extraordinary risk by their own accounts,
need have their collective biography rewritten in order to confirm
their dignity. The right to be, to enjoy elementary human rights,
is a postulate I think most readers will grant. Where dominant
classes do not grant them we must learn how to establish or defend these rights.

Acknowledgments

This book is a revision of my doctoral dissertation in the Department of Sociology at Columbia University (1971), "Imperial Crime and Punishment: A Study of the Sanctioning of Collective Violence in the Punjab, 1919." I am indebted to my advisor, Sigmund Diamond, for his criticism, his patience, his demand for precision in expression, and his disdain for sociological flatulence. Needless to say, the concepts elaborated, conclusions, deviations from the straight and narrow path, and adaptations in style and content since that time are my own.

I am also grateful to Charles Kadushin of Teachers College for his advice on methodology and organization and to Leonard Gordon of Columbia University for his aid in exploring Indian historical sources.

V. N. Datta, author of *Jallianwala Bagh,* the definitive historical study of the massacre, was most gracious and exceedingly helpful in answering my questions on discrepancies in the original sources. I would also like to express my thanks to Professor Datta for his kind hospitality to me in Kurukshetra.

Anne Weiss, who coded the debates with me, made a unique

contribution to the dissertation. I am deeply grateful to her for the intelligence, curiosity, tenacity, and patience she brought to a task gratuitously assumed.

Eugene Irschik of the Department of History at the University of California at Berkeley read the dissertation and offered valuable advice on revision and reorganization.

I am indebted to my husband, Richard J. Fein, for criticism of style and syntax and also for spiritual and material sustenance while this book was being written. Not only did he help me cast the principal characters mentally in a screen extravaganza; he also took me to Amritsar in 1971 to observe the setting for myself. To my daughters, Marsi and Miriam, I owe thanks for time off and whatever wit I have left.

Primary Source Notation

In order to simplify the text, conventional footnoting was abandoned in favor of symbols for the following primary sources. Citations in the text include source and page.

HC   Hunter Report: *Parliamentary Papers* (Commons), 1920, vol. 14 (*Reports,* vol. 6), Cmd. 681, "Report of the Committee Appointed by the Government of India to Investigate the Disturbances in the Punjab, etc."

DC   District Report: *Parliamentary Papers* (Commons), 1920, vol. 14 (*Reports,* vol. 6), Cmd. 534, "District Accounts Submitted by the Government of the Punjab."

INC   Indian National Congress Punjab Subcommittee, *Report of the Commissioners,* 2 vols. (Bombay: Karnatak Press, 1920).

PDC   *Parliamentary Debates* (Commons), 5th series, vol. 131 (28 June 1920–16 July 1920).

PDL   *Parliamentary Debates* (Lords), 5th series, vol. 41 (6 July 1920–16 August 1920).

CHAPTER 1
Crime, Punishment, and Class Solidarity

Crime brings together upright consciences and concentrates them.
                                                    —Emile Durkheim

The volcanic eruptions of history—war, revolution, and genocide—have always drawn the attention of both historians and theologians. But until recently the dominant trend in western sociology focused on the continuity of social systems, drawing especially on Emile Durkheim (1858–1917), who was concerned with explaining how the bonds characterizing different states of society create solidarity. Durkheim articulated his explanation in *The Division of Labor in Society,* first published in 1893. Hidden within Durkheim's theory is a potential explanation of the genesis of collective violence which I shall explicate and amplify in this essay. I draw upon Durkheim because his theory claimed to comprehend how the punishment of crime preserves solidarity. This seems like an appropriate departure point in a century which has institutionalized crime on such a grand scale.

Durkheim conceived of social evolution as the history of societies evolving from earlier tribal societies based on *mechanical solidarity,* or likeness. In such societies, members usually performed the same function, held the same beliefs, and acted out the same rituals in worshipping the same gods. Modern societies resulting from the division of labor he contrasted with this earlier type as being characterized by *organic solidarity*: citizens were bound together by cooperative relations presuming interdependence but assuming the greater development of individual personality and conscience as their roles became more various and self-conceptions individuated. Less conformity of belief and opinion was expected in such a society, and fewer differences were held to be critical by all. Whereas in societies bound by mechanical solidarity, any violation of the core beliefs of the society was a threat to the society, and hence was punished as criminal, in societies bound by organic solidarity, freedom of thought and expression in religion was enjoyed because likeness of belief was no longer regarded as a necessity.

However, all societies were characterized by a *common conscience,* a shared body of values, rules, and corresponding sentiments. Sanctions against crime were not simply a means of social control—punishments deterring future violations of the rules—but an indicator of the type of solidarity integrating the society. Societies with a differentiated division of labor were likely to use *restitutive sanctions,* measures compelling the violator to make good for the losses he had caused his victim, whereas societies based on mechanical solidarity typically employed *repressive sanctions,* punishment designed to injure the violator, and were more likely to classify failure to conform to group beliefs and practices as a crime. Biblical injunctions providing payment for the loss of another man's sheep over which one was guardian are an example of a restitutive sanction; the injunction specifying one shall stone a blasphemer is a repressive sanction.

Punishment was identified by Durkheim as the specific social act which expiates the blow to the common conscience, renewing the shared sense of lawful reality. Crime creates a sense of dissonance, drawing people together on the basis of the common denominator. In Durkheim's words: "As for the social character of this reaction, it comes from the social nature of the offended sentiments. Because they are found in all consciences, the infraction committed arouses in those who have evidence of it or who learn of its existence the same indignation. . . . Crime brings together upright consciences and concentrates them."[1]

Although the domain of beliefs constituting the common conscience diminishes in states of organic solidarity, it does not disappear. Durkheim stressed continually that exchange was not the basis of relatedness in any society. Contract relationships, typical of states of organic solidarity, presupposed the existence of mutual trust among partners, trust which was itself based on the preexisting "community of like beliefs and sentiments."[2] Solidarity, then, preceded the division of labor, which itself produced a new type of solidarity. One may plausibly infer that such similarities of usages, beliefs, and work roles which Durkheim assumes to have existed were associated with racial and ethnic homogeneity characteristic of tribes who have not traveled from their place of origin or have not intermarried with others encountered in their journeys.

Durkheim, while acknowledging that population concentration was likely to thrust dissimilar people into economic cooperation, did not assess the influence of racial or ethnic diversity on solidarity, although he commented, in terms of the international division of labor, that "for one people to be penetrated by another, it must cease to hold to an exclusive patriotism and learn another which is more comprehensive."[3] Nevertheless, he implicitly accepted that the largest unit within which people are bound to one another is the nation-state, assuming society to be coextensive with the community which arose from the original collectivity.

But society does not always coincide with community, and nationality does not automatically correspond to citizenship. This gap in Durkheim's theory or glossing over the kaleidoscopic composition of contemporary societies might be attributed to his own preoccupation with problems raised by the industrial revolution and immersion in a particular historic period—one in which nation-states based on linguistic unity over a common territory were liberating themselves from foreign domination or consolidating feudal principalities in Europe. Problems of settler societies—the United States, Canada, Australia, New Zealand, South Africa—were far off and then peripheral to European intellectual attention. Eastward, beyond Germany, the checkerboard distribution of linguistic-ethnic groups interspersed and overridden by foreign sovereigns had not arrived at the center of European diplomatic concern as they did after World War I with the breakup of the Austro-Hungarian and Russian Empires.

Thus Durkheim did not anticipate the problems arising both from imperialism and from the enclosure within the modern nation-state of sizable national minorities (which resemble post-

World War II problems arising from decolonization in Africa and Asia). Modern nationalist movements have evoked consciousness among majorities and minorities that they are governed by strangers. Reacting to this, peoples in Europe who had been free might support movements for autonomy, liberation, and reintegration with the "fatherland," leading to irredentist movements, foreign intrigues, and wars. Similarly, in postcolonial Africa the overlapping and mismatching of tribes within new nation-states based on lines of colonial administration has engendered civil wars and genocidal persecutions.

Within the state, domination by a foreign society commonly leads to a political order in which the dominant collectivity rules over the subject collectivity. A similar situation is produced in homogeneous societies by the importation of slaves and the subjugation of indigenous peoples as in the settler societies. Since classes are based on and identified by specific identities—racial, religious, linguistic, ethnic—the name of the collectivity to which they belong itself becomes the name of the political class.[4] Jew, Indian, Maori, Negro, Pole, and Saxon have been the names of subject classes ranked below governing classes within systems of ethnic stratification. A class in this sense is based not on economic opportunity or possession of resources (land or capital) but on control over the structure of authority.

How can one observe the existence of political classes? Political rank or rights are indicated by which class may bear arms under command for the state, command men bearing arms, possess arms as citizens, hold public office, vote for officeholders, and exert power over incumbent officials. We recognize a political order implicitly when we speak of second-class citizens. Let us set up an ideal or limiting type by assuming that the governing class has absolute rights to rule, administer, judge, and execute judgment over a subject class which is powerless. Let us also assume that the more power the governing class has, the less power the subjects have.

We need not assume, as Ralf Dahrendorf does, that an authority structure always divides people into two antagonistic classes in order to distinguish between the governing and the governed or those with rights and the rightless.[5] When class is determined by peoples' collective identity we have a system of ethnic stratification. Modern western history before the twentieth century has largely been the history of social classes and estates without rights demanding their share of rights and authority by winning liberty from and representation within the state. The twentieth century has been a century of nations and groups emancipating themselves from ethnic stratification systems and creating new ones to oppress others.

To simplify discussion, the dominant collectivity (which may be a racial, religious, national, or ethnic group) in a system of ethnic stratification will be referred to from now on as a governing class and the subordinated collectivity as a subject class. These may correspond to the division between the landed and landless class or owners and workers because the law, established by the governing class, opens opportunities for some to acquire wealth and resources and restricts it for others. The law can guarantee new types of property and contract commitments for the governing class while restraining the subject class from institutionalizing and protecting their property or organizing themselves as workers. Political class and economic class do not always correspond, however, especially when one focuses on marginal subject classes who may be imported or tolerated because they perform economic functions needed by the governing class—overseas Chinese, Indians, and Jews are cases of such marginal subject classes who may be rightless but (temporarily) well-to-do. As they have often discovered, riches cannot be guaranteeed without rights, and at times neither can their lives.

Classes arising from the division of ownership, such as landlords and tenants, usually create conditions of exchange in which the ability of the lower class to bargain with the higher class is grossly unequal: Alvin Gouldner has aptly termed exchanges under such conditions cases of *exploitation.*[6] Without presuming that authority is always antagonistic and indivisible, we may note that when the division of powers between the governing and subject class is grossly unequal, a governing class can usually ensure obedience by raising the sanctions for disobedience so high the subject has scarcely any choice but to conform simply to survive. Just as exchange in a situation of inequal resources and scarcity produces exploitation, the demand for obedience in a situation of gross inequality of power produces *oppression,* assuming that the subject has no other state to which to flee. By calling attention to political class which produces oppression, we focus on an order which defines life-chances (and death-chances) more ubiquitously than does social class.

The likelihood of an ethnic stratification system becoming oppressive is greater than that of other political class systems because of the governing class's inability to identify with the subject class. Within any order, the more that lines of social cleavage converge, the greater probability there is of violent conflict.[7] A threat from below is likely to cause the governing class to make higher demands for obedience.

While political classes within settler societies and empires are patently based on the ranking of two nations (British/Indian, French/Algerian), the metaphor of two nations has been applied to classes issuing from economic stratification as well. Durkheim concluded that the forced division of labor based on such a class system could not lead to solidarity: "Inversely, we may say that the division of labor produces solidarity only if it is spontaneous and in proportion as it is spontaneous. . . . Labor is divided spontaneously only if society is constituted in such a way that social inequalities exactly express natural inequalities."[8]

Durkheim, then, believed that a class system which arbitrarily assigns people to different classes without regard to their natural capacity for achievement could not create solidarity among them. To be sure, his vision was not singular. Marx had proclaimed the necessity and certainty of class conflict in the Communist Manifesto of 1848; Disraeli had diagnosed the existence of "two nations" in 1845 *(Sybil)*.

Where two nations coexist in one state as governing and subject classes, the subject class is unlikely to accord legitimacy to the rule of the governing class because there is no solidarity between them. If the belief in a state's legitimacy erodes, rule must depend increasingly on coercion. Without solidarity, neither tradition, legality, nor charisma can operate to refute the subjects' perception of their domination as illegitimate.[9]

STRATIFICATION AND THE COMMON CONSCIENCE

How does class stratification based on collectivity membership (ethnic, national, religious, or racial criteria) affect the development of the common conscience?

One might reason that if there is little solidarity between classes, leading to discord over norms, the common conscience will be attenuated and the need for punishment will lessen; society will tend toward an anarchic or anomic state. But a governing class cannot afford to tolerate anarchy or the unpredictability of social relationships. Let us begin with another assumption as a point of departure. The coexistence of collectivities first encountering each other as strangers or enemies in a political order is usually based on the ability of one to enforce its domination over the other rather than on trust. Their coexistence leads to greater discrimination between members of one's own class as against the other class, or heightened "consciousness of kind."[10] The common conscience is then limited to one's own kind, members of one's class, excluding the other class from the *universe of obligation*—the range of persons and groups toward whom basic rules or "oughts" are binding. They are the people who must be taken into account, to whom obligations are due, by whom we can be held responsible for our actions. If that universe corresponds to the boundaries of the social system, it can be described as a morally inclusive universe; if it corresponds to the membership group or class, it is an exclusive universe.

The common conscience does not exist in the ether but in the minds of members of any society; it is not eternal but transmitted and mutable. Identification is the mechanism through which new human beings introject the common conscience, internalizing both specific norms—rules—and the expectations of the "generalized other." If one is socialized not to see members of the other class as "significant others" or is segregated from reciprocal relations with them, the universe of obligation will correspond to one's own class."[11] But obligations cannot be unilaterally disclaimed by the subjects. Members of the subject class may be consciously tutored by parents, guardians, and teachers to internalize the expectations of the dominant class so that they can play out behaviors expected of them even before they are personally exposed to the governing class. Therefore, they are more likely to include the governing class within their universe of obligation than the other way around.

Durkheim, distinguishing between imperatives of morality derived from philosophical systems and the rules which are actually employed in a given society, held that "there is no rule where there is no obligation."[12] This criterion has direct implications for the distribution of justice (or injustice, as the case usually is). To demonstrate this, one must assume that the occurrence of an offense—a violation of a legal code—can be proved independently of whether it has been socially recognized, labeled, and indicted as a crime.

Assuming that judges are representative of their class of origin, if that class has been socialized to accept obligations only toward peers within the class one may expect less capacity to identify with members of the other class than with peers toward whom one is obligated. Assuming that judges are chosen from the governing class, there should be greater need to expiate crimes against members of the governing class than against the subject class. Thus the judge is induced to mete out severer penalties to offenders against victims of his own class than offenders against subject class victims. The predicted likelihood of unequal sanctions or "oppressive class justice" when the judge is of a higher class than the accused is illustrated in Table 1. When the judge is of the same class as the victim, inequity is reduced by liability to the same punishment in a like situation; this state (portrayed in Table 2) might be called "equal repressive justice." Table 3, which one might characterize as the "defendant's peer group permissive justice," starts with the judge belonging to the class of the accused. One could conclude that if heavier sanctions deter crime, repressive justice is more likely to reduce interclass crime than is peer group justice.

Although hypothetical alternatives (Tables 2 and 3) which eliminate the asymmetry of sanctions do exist, they are unlikely to be institutionalized in an ethnically stratified society. Given the need of the governing class to monopolize legal authority to retain its control, these alternatives are unacceptable.

To illustrate what inequities in sanctions would be expected from the governing class having the exclusive right to judge within a polity where classes are characterized by mechanical solidarity, their universes of obligation excluding the other, let us extrapolate the judgments that would be made in Table 1 to such a polity—British India between 1857 and 1919—as in Table 4.[13]

The judgment on meting out sanctions is only one of many points in the judicial process at which inequities can occur. In fact, injustice or inequity of outcomes may result from any phase of lawmaking, law enforcement, judgment, and administration; some of the substantive issues and mechanisms involved are noted in the outline on page 10.

Table 1 Predicted Relative* Sanctions Meted Out to Accused When Class of Judge is Higher Class (Oppressive Class Justice)

Class of victim	Class of accused	
	High	Low
High	Standard sanctions	Heavier sanctions
Low	Lighter sanctions	No prediction

Table 2 Predicted Relative* Sanctions Meted Out to Accused When Class of Judge is Same As Victim (Equal Repressive Justice)

Class of victim	Class of accused	
	High	Low
High	Standard sanctions	Heavier sanctions
Low	Heavier sanctions	Standard sanctions

Table 3 Predicted Relative* Sanctions Meted Out to Accused When Class of Judge is Same As Accused (Defendant's Peer Group Permissive Justice)

Class of victim	Class of accused	
	High	Low
High	Standard sanctions	Lighter sanctions
Low	Lighter sanctions	Standard sanctions

*Parity in all cases is indicated by whether the hypothesized sanction is equal to, greater than, or less than the standard sanction which the judge would award to an accused of his own class violating a victim of his own class.

Table 4   Sanctions Expected against Persons
Accused of Crimes If Judge is from
the Governing Class

Accused	Victim	Penalty of accused is higher if
Britisher	Indian	
Britisher	Britisher	Victim is British
Indian	Britisher	
Indian	Indian	Victim is British
Britisher	Indian	
Indian	Indian	No expectation
Britisher	Britisher	
Indian	Britisher	Accused is Indian

1. Lawmaking: Which class's conventions and rules are incorporated into the law? How are conflicts between classes' sacred
precepts and practices resolved? To what extent are each class's
folkways or life-styles regulated? Are the groups' own legal institutions and ceremonies authorized, ignored, or prohibited?

2. Law enforcement: Which class administers enforcement and
who is allowed to exercise police functions? Do enforcement modes
—permissive, preventive vigilance, or punitive apprehension—
depend on the status of the enforcing officer, the complainant, or
the accused? Is the likelihood of a victim's protection, and the apprehension, detention, bail, and physical punishment of the accused, contingent on the class status of the victim and the accused?

3. Judgment: Which classes appoint judges and from which are
juries selected? To whom are they responsible for their decision or
failure to decide? Is the likelihood of indictment, exoneration, or
further prosecution a function of the class status of defendants and
victims? Does the length of penal sentence or severity of other sanctions depend on class status?

4. Administration: Which class's representatives control penal
organizations and surveillance systems? How is the likelihood of
discharge and future apprehension related, directly or indirectly, to
the class of the prisoner?

THE CRIME–PUNISHMENT–CRIME CYCLE

An ethnically stratified society is not only prone to punish the same
offenses inequitably but also to generate crimes of violence against

its members. An increase in class consciousness among members of the subject class represents a threat to the state which guarantees the domination of the governing class. Now, Durkheim reasoned that threats to any governmental organ were punished most severely because that organ represented the defense of the authority of the common conscience. In a stratified society, the state represents an embodiment of rules believed imperative by the governing class. Since the governing class has more to lose from disorder and is more competent to maintain both physical control and symbolic systems essential to preserving the authority structure, one would expect a high level of class consciousness among the governing class at an earlier period. The subject class's self-organization as a "class for itself"[14] develops dialectically from experiences imposed by the governing class.

While the collectivity with which subjects identify may be their tribe, to the settler their identity becomes increasingly generalized or abstracted: they are now "Indians" or "natives" or "blacks," viewed alike administratively. Because the subject class is inferior in terms of power and visibly differentiated often by physical characteristics, these likenesses can come to be perceived as stigmata. If the stigmata they share are irreversible—such as skin color—alternatives to organization (such as individuals rising to the governing class) are unfeasible. In such a society, the development of political organizations and class consciousness by the subject class should lead to even heightened levels of class consciousness by the governing class, weakening interclass ties based on paternalism.

The self-organization of the subject class leads to political challenges. Such challenges may be violent or nonviolent, depending on the resources of both classes, their size, and ideologies justifying or inhibiting violence. Since the liberties essential to political self-organization have been and may again be defined as crimes, protesters from the subject class are likely to be viewed as criminals whether they select nonviolent or violent means of protest. These restrictions on organization are likely to provoke real violence; when a class is unorganized, mass protest is likely to incite spontaneous violence which, in turn, provokes official violence in response. Whether crimes are unilateral or bilateral depends on the ties between classes, belief systems restraining self-defense or violent offense, what weapons are at the subject class's command, and how much violence they anticipate their threat will provoke. If the latent state of illegitimacy becomes expressed by the subject class, crimes against the state which oppresses them may be rationalized as necessary and right. Crimes against the state which have been espoused for ideological motives include terrorist activities—assassination, kidnapping, bombing, taking hostages—as well as outright rebellion. However, crimes are not only enacted because they are instrumental to achieving liberation, revolution, or power. Besides expiating the sense of violation, crime serves also to join conspirators, either temporarily or permanently, by bonds of intimacy which few relationships produce. Radical theorists have speculated that crime may play a unique role among oppressed classes: participation in criminal acts creates a new solidarity, pledging the initiates to a society not yet born or in exile and forbidding them individual reentry to the present polity.[15] There is no return from the underworld of political crime (unless one becomes an agent of the governing class) without revolution.

Crimes against the state by the subject class are, in effect, crimes against the governing class or dominant ethnic collectivity. And crimes against the dominant collectivity are crimes against the governing class. How can that class be expected to expiate a threat to one and all? Crimes against a group united by mechanical solidarity trigger a need for repressive sanctions—vengeance. The psychodynamics of such collective behavior are based on primitive logic: collective punishment assumes collective attribution of responsibility for violations. The symbolic offense is generalized to the whole class and punishment is displaced on any member of the offending class. Given this demand for vengeance (that Durkheim assumes), the offended—assuming they are the dominant group—may execute the punishment collectively without recourse to law or fear of legal sanctions, a mode of collective behavior which Durkheim assures us precedes but is continuous with the evolution of specialized executive organs for penalizing crime.

Given the need for punishing violations against their members, such punishments visited upon the subject class would trigger the same cycle of collective punishment if their rage were not held in check by fear, repressed or opposed by a commitment to nonviolence. If either fear or such a commitment becomes less inhibiting, a political crime wave becomes more likely.

No longer, then, ought we to define punishment as the consequence of crime. Each punishment may be a new crime which has as its function an associated punishment (crime) committed in retribution for the first crime (punishment). In the eyes of the victimized class, each punishment (received) is a crime and each of their crimes (committed) is a punishment. Departing from Durkheim, one could say that the "function" of punishment is to produce new crime and the "function" of crime is to legitimate punishment. What kinds of findings are explained by this insight? Reviewing the research on collective violence, that is, violence directed against groups or arbitrarily selected members of groups because of membership in a racial, ethnic, or religious group, one notes that with surprising regularity a crime is alleged to have been committed by a member of the group before he (or they) is attacked. Stanley Lieberson and Arnold Silverman, who studied the precipitants of American race riots between 1913 and 1963, have shown that two-thirds were set off after an alleged crime by a member of the race being attacked. They note in puzzlement that "applying Durkheim's typology, we observe that many of the immediate precipitants were acts that call for repressive sanctions. . . . Repressive sanctions are normally administered under penal law by courts in the U.S. . . . Although the immediate precipitants were highly inflammatory, we may still ask why a riot occurred rather than the normal processes of arrest, trial, and punishment."[16] Rather than ask why such a punishment was necessary, they might have queried why such a charge was necessary. What unique function did it serve? To which one might reply: What better justifies punishment than crime?

That is to say, crime is a necessary (if not sufficient) condition to invoke punishment. One cannot infer deductively whether it is a precipitating factor or an accounting factor derived during or after such punishments were instituted. Seeking the underlying causes of race riots, Allen Grimshaw found that American urban race riots (before 1960) resulted from "reactions of the dominant group to real or perceived assaults upon the accommodative structure."[17] In the period he studied, this ordinarily meant that whites tried to prevent blacks from rejecting their subordination, from getting "out of place." Certain crimes symbolize insubordination in many cultures; rape of a female from the dominant class by a male from the dominated class is a crime since in an ethnic or racial order which is also patriarchal, men from the dominant class have exclusive rights over women of their class and may also have rights over women from the dominated class, but men from the dominated class have no rights over women from the dominant class. Their rape—the forcible domination of women of a dominant class—is thus an existential challenge of their subordination by dominated men who are appropriating the property of their masters by seizing their women.

This is not to say that collective violence is always preceded by or provoked by the violations of the other. When a class recognizes themselves to be threatened, the allegation of a crime by the other legitimates collective violence to put them in their place. Although violations may trigger spontaneous violence, often the association between them may be accounted for (or may be used to account for) underlying causes of class and communal conflict.

Collective violence is not always preceded by the victims' challenge to the structure of accommodation. Pogroms against Jews have traditionally been incited by charges of ritual murder or desecration of the host, charges propagated until modern times within societies in which Jews were characterized by the dominant churches as guilty of the greatest crime of history, deicide. That such crimes as ritual murder, based on the false assumption that Jews needed Gentile blood for baking Passover matzoth, were spurious did not mean that alleged violators in a climate of hysteria could not be found to confess to them. Among societies in which such beliefs were shared, there was both a perceptual ground and, often, a collective tradition of pogroms which enabled governments to foment such pogroms purposefully. Otto Dahlke describes how such charges against the Jews were sanctioned by the Russian government in Kishinev in 1903 to divert attention from indigenous sources of unrest.[18] The publication (tolerated by government censors) of the Jews' alleged crime was abetted by police who participated in rioting leading to the pogrom. More recently, the fraudulent *Protocols of the Elders of Zion*—the master plan of a nonexistent directorate of the Jewish people for world domination—was used, Norman Cohn has shown, as a "warrant for genocide" by the Nazis who aimed (and succeeded) at mass murder of the Jews of Europe.[19]

It has been widely observed, in accord with Simmel's proposition, that conflict with an external enemy ordinarily unifies communities while suppressing class conflict and intergroup antagonisms.[20] Many commentators have suggested, like Hannah Arendt, that Nazism unified people on the basis of racial solidarity, offering a counter to class solidarity.[21] To create an ideology unifying the Germans, the myth of a pure Aryan race to which the German people belonged and a counter-race, a subhuman enemy which polluted their blood, was developed, both explaining their troubles —accounted for by the presence of the enemy—and making them aware of their likeness to each other. The Jew—traditionally vilified as Christ killer, communist, cosmopolitan, criminal, capitalist —was indispensable as the enemy. Thus anti-Semitism was not an aberration: it was integral to the logic and success of Nazi ideology and legitimated their later violence. Lewis Coser, explicating Simmel, has noted that groups (and communities and nations, one may add) which need enemies in order to exist will find them, whether a threat is present or not.[22] One can see how the dialectic of class solidarity and crime and punishment can be consciously manipulated by defining membership itself in the class targeted for destruction as a crime, rendering that group subject to genocide.

To reinterpret Durkheim to comprehend the experience of the twentieth century, one could say that the function of punishment is no longer to expiate crime but to create crime. If the passion of offended morality was extreme, reaction to the crime could not be contained by the juridical system: the victims are compelled, by Durkheim's logic, if the intensity of prescribed sanctions do not correspond to the passion of the reaction, to retaliate extralegally. In Durkheim's words:

> Punishment, thus, remains for us what it was for our fathers. It is still an act of vengeance since it is an expiation. What we avenge, what the criminal expiates, is the outrage to morality. . . .
> All that we can say is that the need of vengeance is better directed today than heretofore. The spirit of foresight which has been aroused no longer leaves the field so free for the blind action of passion.[23]

How could one anticipate that the state would itself legalize murder, institutionalize the death machine bureaucratically, and decree the duty justified by the outrage of the victims' mere existence?

REFLECTIONS AND REVISIONS ON DURKHEIM

Durkheim anticipated that the division of labor would produce greater respect for the individual, assuming that the common conscience became more universalistic as division of labor advanced:

"There is even a place where it is strengthened and made precise; that is the way in which it regards the individual. As all the other beliefs and all the other practices take on a character less and less religious, the individual becomes the object of a sort of religion."[24]

Karl Mannheim was less sanguine, observing that democratization led not to universal valuation of individualism, but accentuated consciousness of group differences initially.[25] Mannheim was pessimistic about the increase of destructive power arising from the division of labor, which advanced bureaucracy in government, business, the military, and education. Modern bureaucracies routinize the obedience of many persons, each performing the role assigned him or her and not questioning the ends of their actions. While Durkheim recognized that growth of the scope of government followed from the increase of the division of labor, he ignored the implications of bureaucy which would typify the organs of government. Mannheim foresaw that the newer "instrumental" rationality appropriate to such bureaucracies, which instigated one to ask only what is the best method to do what has to be done, could multiply irresponsibility as more people became schooled in technique, indoctrinated to view themselves as tools who did not question what were the objectives of their actions, but were obligated only to follow orders.[26] When killing can be routinized and the victims made invisible, all that the staffs that serve the death machine need do is follow their orders, performing their ordinary jobs, in the bureaucracies organizing the crime. Max Weber, who best analyzed the essentials of bureaucracy, perceived modern society becoming an "iron cage."[27] But he did not anticipate that the cage would become an elevator, descending mechanically to crush the members excluded from the universe of obligation.

This is not meant to argue that the bureaucratic organization of society is in itself the cause of genocide. Collective violence has occurred in every form of social organization. But bureaucracy may facilitate the accomplishment of genocide, assuming the necessary preconditions: the victim has been first excluded from the universe of obligation.

Amplifying Durkheim, I have proposed that a political class system based on ethnic collectivities—one folk, one race, one tribe —generates a mechanical solidarity among class members which causes the common conscience to be constricted to one's own kind.

Thus the universe of obligation becomes one's own class. The ideology of exclusive obligation, group superiority, and singular destiny may be the product of the class structure or the class structure may be a product of the ideology. Ideologies of racial supremacy or group exclusiveness such as "Aryanism" based on a mystique of blood have been exploited to create class systems which enforce obligations solely to the master race and systematically generate violence against other races defined as inferior or less than human. In either case, the proximate cause of collective violence is the exclusion of the other from the universe of obligation.

A REVISIONIST THEORY OF CRIME AND PUNISHMENT

To enable the reader to judge whether anything new and of value (barring neologisms) has been added, I conclude by listing what has been accepted from Durkheim and adapted. Definitions, postulates, and implications of my own are printed in italic type. The following four propositions are restatements from Durkheim's *Division of Labor in Society:*

1. All societies based on organic solidarity are societies developed from homogeneous societies in which a previously existent state of trust united members.
2. These societies underlie modern states in which the common conscience persists, although its solidarity function is increasingly replaced by that of the division of labor.
3. Punishment is the defensive response activated by any violation of the common conscience. All violations and only violations of the common conscience activate punishment of the violator. (Acts which do not activate punishment are not violations of the common conscience.)
4. Insofar as the common conscience is incorporated into specialized organs in modern states, legal prescriptions and proscriptions correspond to its moral imperatives. Deviation from such imperatives is recognized as crime. Activation of the criminal sanction against crimes corresponds to punishment for violations of the common conscience.

Some additional propositions are specified below:

5. *The common conscience predicates both substantive norms and the range of persons and groups toward whom such norms apply—the universe of obligation.*

6. *The universe of obligation may be coextensive with the social system or limited to the membership group or class: the former is referred to as an inclusive and the latter an exclusive universe.*

7. *Because the division of labor cannot create solidarity between persons whose roles are arbitrarily assigned, classes based on ranking of ascribed attributes distinguishing collectivities (skin color, for example) are classes characterized by exclusive universes of obligation.*

8. *If persons are not defined within the universe of obligation, then offenses against them are not violations of the common conscience. Therefore, offenses against persons (and groups) outside the universe of obligation will not activate criminal sanctions.*

Some elementary observations and further inferences regarding labeling and the social accounting of action follow:

9. Classes of action may or may not be socially defined as crimes.

10. All crimes are offenses.

11. Acts may be empirically classified by their existential status and by their socially determined juridical status. If a crime is generically defined by observable characteristics, and an instance has been observed, then one may classify it as an offense independently of whether that instance has been socially recognized and labeled as crime.

12. Only acts which are socially recognized and labeled as crime can activate criminal sanctions. Acts which are not violations of the common conscience are acts which are not socially recognized and labeled as crimes.

This leads to the following consequences:

13. *Offenses against persons outside the universe of obligation will not be socially recognized and labeled as crime.*

14. *Assuming judges to be representative of their class of origin, the ability of judges to identify with the victim of an offense depends on the victim's inclusion within the judge's universe of obligation. This causes differential likelihood of punishment of the*

accused offender, contingent upon the status of both victim and offender, leading to the inequities depicted in Tables 1 to 4.

15. *Collective violence is a punishment of a crime—actual or alleged—generalized against the class of the accused.*

16. *All punishments which are generalized against individuals not committing violations are offenses against those individuals.*

17. *Collective violence is an offense not recognized as a crime by members of the class perpetrating it.*

18. *Offenses not socially recognized and labeled as crimes are offenses against persons outside the universe of obligation. (Converse of proposition 13.)*

19. *Collective violence is an offense against a class whose members are outside the universe of obligation.*

The next three chapters describe the events in Amritsar and the Punjab between 10 April 1919 and June 1919, the Indian political class order since 1857, and the immediate causes of the 1919 disorders in the Punjab. Then I proceed to the testing and illustration of propositions 8, 13, and 14 by analyzing the evaluation and judgment of the Amritsar massacre and Punjab terror. But before we can fully understand the crime-punishment cycle emerging in Amritsar in 1919 (Chapter 2), we must understand the rising national consciousness among Indians, aroused reactively by the exclusive solidarity of the British governing class (Chapter 3) and why the Rowlatt Bills—measures intended to check political crimes— served to trigger the confrontation between them (Chapter 4).

The Massacres in Amritsar and Punjab Terror of 1919

It was no longer a question of merely dispersing the crowd, but one of producing a sufficient moral effect, from a military point of view, not only on those who were present, but more specially throughout the Punjab.
— Brig. Gen. Reginald E. Dyer

On 13 April 1919, Brig. Gen. Reginald E. Dyer strode through the narrow entryway to the Jallianwala Bagh in Amritsar (Punjab province), a dirt quadrangle ordinarily used as a dumping ground hemmed in by brick buildings with few arched exits, and ordered the fifty Indian tribesmen with him to fire into a crowd of between 15,000 and 25,000 natives gathered illegally for a protest meeting. Without any warning to the seated people listening to speakers, playing cards, and chatting with friends, they began firing and continued for about ten minutes, ceasing momentarily and redirecting their fire, under Dyer's order, to aim at the thickets of bodies scrambling toward the wall in panic. Leaving only sufficient ammunition from their 1,650 rounds to be prepared against ambush on their route back to the police station, Dyer then led his soldiers out of the Jallianwala Bagh, taking no action either to aid the injured or dispose of the dead. Initial Indian estimates of the dead ranged up to 1,500: a house-to-house census later showed that 530 were reported killed.

As well as the firing at the Jallianwala Bagh, General Dyer

was also remembered for his Crawling Order. This edict forced all Indians passing through the street on which a Miss Sherwood had been accosted on 10 April to crawl on all fours. His Flogging Order authorized public whippings of suspects in that case without trial. These two orders were typical of many issued by officers ruling in the Punjab under martial law (decreed in districts of the province on 15 April), prescribing public humiliation and rituals of abasement toward British officers or civilians, such as salaaming, saluting, and descending from vehicles in their presence. There were numerous other documented cases of physical punishment and torture, described later in this chapter.

But had it not been for the massacre, General Dyer's name surely would not have become an issue, a public symbol, a flag, and later an epithet—"Dyerism." To his contemporaries, the meaning and motive of Dyer's act seemed clearer than they have to certain historians. Most British historians have concentrated exclusively on explaining how the firing occurred, as if it were a singular event and as if Dyer had not intended to do exactly what he did. They assess the sincerity of Dyer's motives in terms of the threat he perceived in Amritsar in those days. Exploring the contradictory defense statements made under threat of incriminations, the after-dinner remarks indicating boastfulness or penitence, and the physical symptoms displayed by Dyer after the firing has been a singularly vacuous academic exercise, considering that Dyer clearly asserted what his motives were in his response to the commander in chief of the Indian Army's request for a written account. In his report of 25 August 1919, he wrote the following:

> I fired and continued to fire till the crowd dispersed, and I considered that this is the least amount of firing which would produce the necessary moral and widespread effect it was my duty to produce if I was to justify my action. If more troops had been at hand the casualties would have been greater in proportion. *It was no longer a question of merely dispersing the crowd,* but one of producing a sufficient moral effect, from a military point of view, not only on those who were present, but more specially throughout the Punjab. [HC: 112]

All evidence shows that neither General Dyer's reasoning nor his motives were unique: the same motives were exhibited by other officers in the Punjab during martial law (without producing an equivalent number of corpses, it is true). However, it was

Dyer's action at Jallianwala Bagh that was credited by Lt. Gov. Sir Michael O'Dwyer of the Punjab with saving the situation and preventing further rebellion.[1]

The Amritsar massacre may be seen as the last assault in a cycle of collective self-defense by British and Indians. It was a response to the first modern race riot in India, which itself was sparked by British response to the first threatened use of mass nonviolence by Gandhi. This movement was a response to a perceived British assault on Indian freedoms signified by the Rowlatt Bills, which were a response to previous Indian criminal conspiracy against the raj (British rule). To escape from this regression of motives and perceptions, one must examine the Indian understanding of British intentions and the motives of the actors as they understood them.

Before beginning such a quest, let us inquire whether the massacre at Jallianwala Bagh was, as Winston Churchill put it in the Commons debate of July 1920, "an episode . . . without precedent or parallel in the modern history of the British Empire. . . . It is an extraordinary event, a monstrous event, an event which stands in singular and sinister isolation" [PDC: 1725].

COLONIAL MASSACRES AS RECALLED IN 1920

That massacres were perpetrated by both sides during the Indian Mutiny of 1857 with similar intent—to display vengeance—has been well documented, although the recognition of collective violence on the British side was suppressed because of the double standard employed by British historians, Edward Thompson tells us.[2] However, although retaliation was allowed by British officers, reprisals were not authorized by the government in London. Earl Curzon of Kedleston, former viceroy of India (1899–1905), recalled in the House of Lords in 1920 how that demand was rejected:

> On that occasion in India there was a Governor-General who was fiercely assailed because he preferred justice to wrath, self-restraint to resentment, and clemency to vengeance. In the end of the year 1857, when the Mutiny was over, the European public of Calcutta and Bengal drew up a petition to the Queen in which—expressing their dissatisfaction with the manner in which the Governor-General had discharged his duties, and speaking of the blindness, weakness, and incapacity of his Government—they prayed Her Majesty to mark her disapproval of the policy pur-

sued by the Governor-General by directing his recall. This is one
of the passages in their Petition—

"The only policy by which British rule and the lives, honour,
and properties of your Majesty's Christian subjects in this country can in future be secured, is a policy of such vigorous repression and punishment as shall convince the native races of India—
who can be influenced effectually by power and fear alone—of
the hopelessness of insurrection against British rule, even when
aided by every circumstance of treachery, surprise, and cruelty."

words not unlike some of those which we have heard in the
past few weeks. What has become of the authors of that memo-
rial? Are they counted as the saviours of India? . . . I hope that
in arriving at the decision which you will reach to-night, you will
all be imbued with the spirit, and will profit by the example, the
never-to-be-forgotten example, of the Illustrious Canning. [PDL:
367-368]

The images of Canning and his critics, the benign administra-
tor versus the "man on the spot," continue to be the point and
counterpoint themes reiterated in imperial history. After the 1872
attack at Maler Kotla (Punjab) by the Kukas—a militant Sikh
revivalist movement—the local officials, conceiving it to be the
beginning of a rebellion, had sixty-five prisoners believed to be
responsible for the uprising blown out of a cannon and one
hacked to pieces within the next three days without benefit of
trial, despite orders insisting on the necessity of a trial. The action of Deputy Commissioner Cowan, approved by the Punjab
government, was promptly disapproved by the Government of
India, which removed Cowan from office (with a pension) and
transferred his superior, who had directly supported him.[3]

Members of both houses in 1920 recalled, too, the debate on
the Jamaica Rebellion of 1865. After the rebellion had been put
down and further military intercession had been rejected by
Governor Eyre, over 400 blacks—arbitrarily selected by officers—
were slain, 600 flogged, and 1,000 of their huts burned, according to John Stuart Mill and Mr. Buxton, the first two chairmen
of the Jamaica Committee (see Appendix C). Governor Eyre was
removed from office by the crown; the accused civil and military
officers were brought before Jamaican courts and an outside
court-martial by the British government, and Governor Eyre
himself was prosecuted by Mill and his associates.[4]

One of General Dyer's frankest defenders in 1920, Brigadier
General Surtees, compared the present debate with the one on
Jamaica in Commons:

Many Members of this House, if they do not remember, as I do,
are still cognizant of the facts of the Jamaica Rebellion in 1865,
which rebellion was put down properly and most strongly by
Gov. Eyre. Gov. Eyre was persecuted by John Bright and John
Stuart Mills *[sic]* in the same way as Gen. Dyer is being
persecuted by certain individuals, and on that occasion Sir John
Pakington, speaking in Debate on this House, said:
> "He acted in full pursuance of the belief that the handful of
> Europeans who inhabited that island was not safe from attack by
> the 400,000 half-civilised and infuriated negroes."

I think something similar to that was on Gen. Dyer's mind.
[PDC:1776]

Other "Europeans" were to write of their fears during the
time they spent in isolated but protected enclaves—fortresses,
hospitals—testifying how grateful they were to General Dyer. But
what had provoked such fears and caused the military to se-
quester them before 13 April 1919?

THE ANTI-ROWLATT BILL CAMPAIGN

Before World War I, the Indian Nationalist movement represented by the Indian National Congress (INC) had been split by
a division between the "extremists," who sought independence
by violent means, and the "moderates" (later termed Liberals),
who espoused "constitutional" methods of advance toward becoming a self-governing colony. Concurrently, a schism had
developed between the INC and the leadership of the Muslim
community, which insisted on separate electorates and a quota of
public positions as against a general electorate and free competition between individuals. However, in 1916 these divisions were
compromised by a new agreement between the INC and the Muslim League that pledged cooperation toward joint goals. Their
expectations were expanded by the promise of the secretary of
state for India, Edwin Montagu, in 1917 that His Majesty's
Government and the Government of India were committed to
"the gradual development of self-governing institutions with a
view to the progressive realisation of responsible government in
India as an integral part of the British Empire."[5]

Shortly after that, the Government of India appointed a special committee headed by Judge Rowlatt to investigate and
recommend methods of dealing with revolutionary conspiracies
and political crimes. The government had been plagued with

assassination, bombings, and burglary for the preceding twenty years, chiefly in Bengal: these were usually committed by dedicated young men of the respectable classes who were organized in small semireligious sects or *dal*. During the war official fears were heightened by the appearance of the Ghadr Party, an avowedly revolutionary party based on Sikh emigrants from the Punjab who had settled in North America. The Defense of India Act, a wartime measure enabling the government to detain men without trial, had effectively curtailed such activities as well as their taken-for-granted liberties of speech, movement, and the press; but the act was soon to expire. In 1919, Judge Rowlatt's committee reported its findings (Chapter 4) and recommendations. They recommended two laws: the first curtailed the right to jury trial, authorized what amounted to house arrest, proscribed circulation of seditious material, and authorized far-sweeping powers in event of a declared emergency; the second (never enacted) made even possession of such material illegal.

The reaction of Indian politicians of all factions was uniformly negative—they saw such restraints on their freedoms as a negation of British willingness to trust them ultimately to their own governance. The British governing class saw Indian objections as obstructionism, indicating that Indians probably could not be trusted, if granted greater self-government, to protect British interests. The Legislative Council of the Government of India passed the Rowlatt Act on 21 March 1919, against the advice of twenty-two of the twenty-three Indian members of that council.

Gandhi, who had recently emerged as one of the leaders of the Indian National Congress, called upon Congress committees and other groups to prepare people to register their mass opposition nonviolently by observing a hartal—a religious ritual of fasting and desisting from daily business which became the Indian version of the general strike. The hartals were in general peacefully observed in northern India, with few instances of coercion (such as crowds pressing vendors to close shop). British provincial officials in Amritsar commented on the amity between Hindus and Muslims during those days of preparatory organization.

Amritsar had been the center of Congress organization in the Punjab since 1917; and the All-India Congress convention accepted the local organization's bid to convene there for their annual meeting in December 1919. Successful public meetings to mobilize the people for a hartal were held on 29 March and 3 April 1919. Similarly, successful and complete nonviolent hartals were held on both 30 March and 6 April without any evidence of "enforcement" being noted by local officials. On 30 March, a mass meeting was held in Jallianwala Bagh, the first of its kind in that arena, which was estimated to have been attended by 30,000 to 35,000 people.

The spirit manifested during these hartals was enthusiastically nationalist but not anti-British: the deputy commissioner, Miles Irving, recalled being greeted in the street by the band playing "God Save the King." Hindu-Muslim unity was reinforced by the joint celebration of a Hindu holiday, Ram Naumi Day, on 9 April, during which day the winding traditional public procession was joined by many Muslims, some of them dressed as Turks.[6]

This successful organization was credited by the government to two local leaders, Dr. Satyapal and Dr. Kitchlew: the former was a medical doctor and the latter a lawyer who had spent his undergraduate years at Cambridge. Both were advocates of communal unity and had obtained popularity by their championship of mass causes; Dr. Satyapal had led a successful protest against the railway's previous refusal to sell platform tickets at Amritsar, and Dr. Kitchlew was involved in both the Home Rule and Pan-Islamic movement. The Punjab was better organized than ever before in terms of its participation in the nationalist movement both because of a positive asset of astute local leadership consciously articulating bonds between communities and because of a negative pull—the dominating role of its lieutenant governor, Sir Michael O'Dwyer. O'Dwyer had expressed contempt publicly for the aspirations of the educated class, denied earlier requests for token representation of Indians in his administration, and vigorously curbed the press. He was a militant believer in the imperialist ideology that justified a firm hand.

Gandhi had publicly committed himself to violate the press law in order to perform symbolic civil disobedience against the Rowlatt Act since it could not be violated automatically but could only be invoked by the government. He was due to enter the Punjab, and the government feared that arresting him at a public meeting would provoke a riot. They could, and did, forbid him to speak; but they knew he would refuse to heed the injunction as it violated his conscience, so they forcibly detained him from entering the Punjab on 9 April. The government extended its original order to allow provincial governments to ban other movement speakers in order to prevent the eruption of public disorder.

Satyapal and Kitchlew were banned from making public addresses by the government's edicts on 29 March and 4 April respectively. Satyapal did not disclose this at the mass meeting of 30 March, and both he and Kitchlew continued to lead the movement, preparing plans at private meetings.

The Congress Committee had changed its decision (not to call a second hartal) unexpectedly on 5 April, although it had previously informed Deputy Commissioner Irving that there would be no hartal on 6 April. This led Irving to address a letter to his superiors on 8 April, "much perturbed by the proof," exhibited by the decision to hold the second hartal, of the power and influence of the two leaders. He hinted that there was a conspiracy behind it:

> Who are at the bottom of this I cannot say. The Congress party are at the Outer circle. They passed a resolution against a strike and promptly came to heel when Kitchlew ordered it. . . . Kitchlew himself I regard as the local agent of very much bigger men. Who those are can only be guessed by their rage at the Rowlatt Acts which strike at the roots of organised anarchic crime. [HC: 19–20]

At the same time the Government of India decided to prevent Gandhi from entering the Punjab, provincial goverments were authorized to act similarly. The government of the Punjab ordered the deportation of Kitchlew and Satyapal from Amritsar, whisking them away in a private car (disguised as a hunting party) on the morning of 10 April without any public notice as to which authority had ordered their deportation, where they were going, and how long they would be gone.

Crowds gathered soon and the shops began shutting down in the Hall Bazaar near the carriage bridge. Official strategy, agreed on the previous evening when planning the deportations, was to hold expected crowds back from the civil lines.

The civil lines divided the walled and densely populated native city with its claustrophobic bazaars, where merchants rolled out their bolts of cloth from rectangular holes in the side of winding lanes, from the white suburb with its spacious lawns, officials' bungalows, British social clubs, government buildings, and fort. Entry to the British precinct depended on access to three bridges. But ordinarily, British bankers and merchants worked in the city and native servants and workers were employed beyond the bridges—the sectors were interdependent and movement was open.

The crowd milled around the bridge leading to the deputy commissioner's bungalow, demanding to see Irving. Evidence regarding the character and intent of this crowd is directly conflicting. The Congress Report asserts that "it was a crowd of mourners—bareheaded, many unshod, and all without sticks . . . on its way . . . to plead for the release of its loved ones" [INC: I,48]. The Hunter Committee states that the crowd was "excited and angry" but "had not as yet resolved upon anything" [HC: 9]. Both could be true: the observer's sensitivity to recognizing or sniffing out danger depends on his apprehension. Cues that Indians might perceive as expressions of righteous indignation would likely be seen as menacing signs of hostility to the British. However, both sources agree that the crowd did pass and ignore British civilians on their way to the carriage bridge.

Upon reaching the carriage bridge, the crowd surged forward, agitating the horses until the mounted soldiers posted there as pickets retreated beyond the bridge. The soldiers fired upon orders, after being pelted with paving stones. This pattern was repeated at least twice: the British pickets were powerless before a crowd estimated at one time to be as large as 40,000. They fired in order to carry out their instructions to block the human tide from flowing over the bridge. Before the second firing, two Indian lawyers attempted to persuade the crowd to retreat (after explaining their intention to the soldiers), but their pleading was rendered useless when the soldiers opened fire without warning directly behind them at great risk to these peacemakers. The second firing is estimated to have killed twenty to thirty Indians. The crowd turned.

Within the next four hours, two banks were set afire after three of their English managers were killed, their bodies left to be consumed in the pyres of kerosene-drenched furniture. The manager and assistant of the National Bank were saved because their Indian employees helped to hide them. The banks, post office, and railway yard were looted soon after. One off-duty soldier (an electrician) and a railroad guard were also killed. But the incident most often repeated in England was that of Miss Sherwood, a "missionary lady" dragged from her bicycle, attacked and beaten, but saved by the parents of one of her pupils. An English woman doctor—who allegedly had made derogatory remarks about the Indians who had been shot—was sought by hostile crowds but escaped with the aid of her Indian servants.

Several buildings were also ignited, most of which stood in direct line from the bridge which was the scene of the last police confrontation. According to the Hunter Report, there were two Christian edifices burned, and an attack on a missionary girls' school was frustrated only by police intervention. Apart from this incident, the police made no attempt to intervene at any vital point; this avoidance was reciprocal, as the crowd made no attempt to burn the police station.

The Amritsar riot of 10 April was afterward construed by General Dyer and others as part of a rebellion because a race riot was not a recognized event. It triggered a chilling fear among the colonial class that anyone might be killed now because of his or her nationality or race, evoking the mutiny syndrome of hatred and dread. No single assassination or revolutionary conspiracy before that time was comparable. Anybody, they could understand, could become a target because of the role they played; but in this case the crowd seemed to have selected their victims at random. The symbolic assault was more radical because of the attack on Miss Sherwood. Although there was no evidence to support this, as late as 1930 a British journalist in India familiar socially with the colonial class reports that they still talked of Miss Sherwood's rape.[7] Americans are familiar with how the allegation of rape of a white woman served as a justification for lynching: such an assault—white women being the highest form of property of the governing class—represents an attack on the whole system of domination.

To the Indian rioters, burning British victims must have been viewed as collective retaliation for the British soldiers shooting twenty to thirty unarmed Indians. (The Hunter Report is very casual as to the figure, indicating little administrative concern at the time over counting the victims.) That is, it was a retaliation, if the shooting provoked the mob rampage. But, at this point, there is a critical disagreement between sources and among historians as to whether the second shooting preceded or succeeded the beginning of the mob's rampage in the city. The Hunter Report declares that the banks were burned before the shooting. Witnesses and circumstantial evidence are inconclusive but seem to me to support the Congress Report's contention that the confrontation did provoke the rampage; this conclusion gains credibility from the British officials' initial willingness to negotiate with the two pleaders at the footbridge.[8]

THE RESTORATION OF "LAW AND ORDER"

While the mob killed five British residents of Amritsar and burned and looted banks and post offices, the English women and children (along with some older British men and Indian Christians) were gathered together and evacuated to the fort beyond the civil lines. By nightfall, 560 soldiers had arrived; they were supplemented by 300 more on the next day, 11 April. Their commander was instructed to take whatever means necessary to restore order so that civilian authority might function again.

General Dyer was dispatched to Amritsar on 11 April and similarly given complete authority by Deputy Commissioner Irving. The city within the walls was believed by the authorities to be held by the mob; however, no incidents were reported when the troops marched through on 12 April led by Dyer, who arrested about a dozen of the suspected ringleaders of the mob. It was recalled that people spat on the ground and muttered nationalist slogans as the soldiers marched by. Sometime on 12 or 13 April the city's electricity and water supply were deliberately cut off by the authorities, admittedly to punish the people.

Tense negotiations were recalled between British officials and Indian representatives, usually lawyers, for families seeking to bury their dead who had been shot at the bridge on 11 April. The deputy commissioner reported handing a notice to these representatives forbidding public processions and advising that such gatherings would be fired on if necessary. General Dyer issued a similar edict on 12 April, but there is no evidence that it was ever proclaimed or published. That edict also warned inhabitants that if any acts of property damage or violence were committed in Amritsar, "it will be taken for granted that such acts are due to the incitement in Amritsar city and offenders will be punished according to military law."[9]

The following morning, 13 April, General Dyer marched

through the city with the civil and police officials, pausing at
nineteen places to have an Indian crier read the following proclamation in Urdu and Punjabi translation, catching people's attention by beating a drum:

> It is hereby proclaimed to all whom it may concern that no per-
> son residing in the city is permitted or allowed to leave the city in
> his own private or hired conveyance or on foot without a pass
> from one of the following officers. . . .
>
> No person residing in Amritsar city is permitted to leave his
> house after 8:00 P.M.
>
> Any person found in the streets after 8:00 P.M. is liable to be
> shot.
>
> No procession of any kind is permitted to parade the streets in
> the city or any part of the city or outside of it at any time. Any
> such processions or any gathering of four men will be looked
> upon and treated as an unlawful assembly and dispersed by force
> of arms if necessary.[HC: 28]

Perusal of the map of sites at which the order was proclaimed
confirms the Congress Report's assertion and the Hunter Committee's assessment that awareness of the ban could not have
been general; the Hunter Committee estimated that no more than
10,000 (out of 160,000) could have heard it [HC: 199]. Dyer
himself indicated no interest in whether or not the inhabitants
had heard his warning.

Shortly after the general's edict had been delivered, two men
went round the city with a counterproclamation, banging on an
empty tin can to announce that a meeting would be held in the
Jallianwala Bagh that afternoon at 4:30; they promised that
Kanheya Lal, a respected lawyer who had presided over earlier
protest meetings, would preside and that letters from Kitchlew
and Satyapal would be read. According to Datta, the Hunter
Committee testimony shows that "people's fears of official intervention were allayed by the assurance that Dyer's proclamation was a mere bluff."[10]

THE FIRING AT THE BAGH

Returning from his rounds, General Dyer was informed of the
meeting called for at the Jallianwala Bagh. The general affirmed
that he did nothing until after 4 P.M. Upon being informed at
that time that the meeting had begun, he marched to the Bagh
with fifty armed Gurkhas (Indian tribesmen) and two armored

cars with machine guns. To his dismay, he found he could not get the cars through the entrance. Then, posting his soldiers on the mound overlooking the squatting assembly, he gave the order to fire into the crowd without a word of warning addressed to that audience. They fired into the crowd without hesitation. He directed their fire into the midst of bodies clogging the exits toward which people ran.[11] After they had fired almost 1,650 rounds of ammunition, General Dyer turned his soldiers round and left the Bagh.

Because of the immediate panic, the absence of relatives or friends, and later the fears of being shot (if one returned) for curfew violation, many more persons than the 200 to 300 who received local treatment in Amritsar were left to lie wounded in the dirt of the Bagh that night. Rattan Devi told the Congress investigating committee of her attempt to retrieve the body of her husband:

> I was in my house near Jallianwala Bagh when I heard shots fired. . . . I got up at once as I was anxious because my husband had gone to the Bagh. . . . There I saw heaps of dead bodies and I began to search for my husband. . . . By this time it was 8:00 o'clock and no one could stir out of his house because of the curfew order. I stood on, waiting and crying. At about eight-thirty a Sikh gentleman came. . . . I entreated the Sikh gentleman to help me in removing my husband's body to a dry place, for that place was overflowing with blood. He took the body by the head and I by the legs and we carried it to a dry place and laid it down on a wooden block. I waited up to 10:00 P.M. . . . Then I started toward Katra again and saw an old man. I repeated the whole of my sad story to him. He took pity on me and asked the men to go with me. But they said that it was 10:00 o'clock and that they would not like to be shot down. . . . So I went back and seated myself by the side of my dead husband. Accordingly I found a bamboo stick which I kept in my hand to keep off dogs. I saw men writhing in agony and buffalo struggling in great pain. A boy of about twelve years old, in agony, entreated me not to leave the place. . . . I asked him if he wanted any wrap and if he was feeling cold I could spread it over him. He asked for water, but water could not be procured at that place. . . .
>
> I was all alone the whole night in a solitary jungle. Nothing but the barking of dogs, the braying of donkeys and the groans of the wounded was audible.[12]

Indian estimates of the total number of persons who died from that fusillade vary from 530 to 1,500.[13] The former figure, established by a house-to-house census conducted by an Indian social service organization, exceeds the 379 who were reported to the Hunter Committee, possibly indicating the reluctance of Indians to apply to the government of the Punjab, notwithstanding the possibility of compensation (later received). Many more must have been seriously wounded or maimed because of the absence of medical aid and the numbers hit by the same bullet when the fire was directed toward the thickets of people stumbling over each other in panic.

INTIMATIONS OF CONSPIRACY

Hans Raj, the organizer of the meeting at Jallianwala Bagh, was considered by contemporaries to have misled people into attending that gathering, both because he knew of Dyer's proclamation and because he had announced the presence of a noted leader whose name would draw people and who had attended previous protest meetings. That gentleman, however, had never been asked to speak.

When, shortly before Dyer's appearance, an airplane flew over the Bagh, Raj soothed the flurry of concern in the audience:

> As some people began to move away Hans Raj stood up on the platform and urged the crowd to be seated and not to worry. He told the people that the "Government will never fire." After a while he waved his handkerchief, and Dyer and his soldiers appeared. Hans Raj then stepped down from the platform and disappeared in their direction on the pretext of having a talk with them. Immediately after this the shooting began. Hans Raj had already left the meeting.[14]

Witnesses also testified before the Congress hearings that Indian Criminal Investigation Division (CID) agents had been seen in the Bagh speaking to Raj while he was preparing for the meeting; other agents warned their friends not to go to the Bagh that day and hid in nearby houses where they could observe the sight.

Hans Raj, himself accused of "sedition" and "waging war," turned "approver" (accuser) for the government on 23 April 1919, saving his own life. This fact, as well as the previous evidence, leads Datta to accept the theory asserted in the *Bom-*

bay Chronicle of 15 July 1920—that Raj "was 'in active touch with the police' and that a death trap had been laid by 'police underlings' to help the authorities 'teach a lesson to the citizens of Amritsar.' "[15] Unpublished Government of India documents in the Home Department show that Deputy Commissioner Irving denied that Raj was a police agent before 23 April 1919. Nevertheless, the weight of the evidence of previous police contact and Raj's immediate disappearance suggest there must have been complicity, if not conspiracy, with General Dyer. Since Dyer had spoken to police officers in Irving's absence and Irving admitted that his own exhaustion during this period precluded his taking responsibility, it is possible Irving never knew of it.

Dyer's biographer states that Dyer believed he could fight the rebels only if he got them out of the winding streets where they could dodge his forces; he had to "get them somehow out in the open."[16] After hearing at 1 P.M. that a meeting was to be held in the Bagh at 4:30, he took no steps to post pickets, publish his proclamation there, or deny entry to the Bagh by any physical barrier; however, police agents went there and spoke to Raj.[17] Although Dyer drove there with the police superintendent and deputy superintendent, Mr. Plomer and Mr. Rehill, he marched on ahead so neither of them was at his side when he gave the order to fire.

Datta notes that it was unusual for a brigadier general to attend to such a mission as dispersing an unlawful meeting himself. He conjectures that Dyer "did not entrust anyone else with the command of the column because he was aware that they would not order the soldiers to open fire immediately. Probably Dyer was determined to teach the 'rebels' a lesson and he could scarcely give such a risky and gruesome assignment to a subordinate."[18] Dyer's own testimony before the Hunter Committee seems to confirm Datta's interpretation of the general's motive.

RESPONSE THROUGHOUT THE PUNJAB

The news of Gandhi's arrest and the deportations of Dr. Kitchlew and Dr. Satyapal spread quickly to other cities and the satellite towns and villages located along the western and northern circuits of the railway line. Before 10 April both large cities and about half the towns and villages mentioned in the District

Reports had observed hartals against the Rowlatt Act. These hartals were usually organized by a local Congress Committee, the Arya Samaj, or a group of local lawyers. After the news spread, hartals were renewed or organized in communities where they had either previously failed or had not been initiated. Students were reported to be particularly active in spontaneous attempts to close down shops.

Crowd violence usually occurred in two ways. When police confronted moving demonstrations with a limit to their progress or attempted to reopen shops, as they had previously done in Delhi, bricks and stones were thrown at them. This might provoke shooting. The most common violation was against government property—post and telegraph offices were looted and frequently lines were cut. Symbolic violence and "inflammatory" leaflets were examined by the Hunter Committee (usually out of context), but the only acts of personal violance against Britishers outside Amritsar were the killing of two British officers traveling through Kasur who had begun discharging their pistols to ward off a gathering crowd—they soon found themselves without ammunition.

There is evidence (see Chapter 4) that the mobilization of a town or city during the anti-Rowlatt Bill campaign before 10 April made later violence less likely. This is not to imply that potential rioters were inhibited by Gandhi's message—far fewer understood him than revered him even then—but that confrontations were inhibited by the very fact protest was organized and leaders were acknowledged. Where leadership was removed as in Amritsar and Indian police made no attempt to control the crowd, a futile confrontation occurred. Where there was no evidence of prior leadership and no police presence, as in Kasur, the mob took British lives with impunity. Where there was active leadership and a reliable police presence, as in Lahore, no violence was reported (except for stoning the cavalry and beating up an Indian police spy caught in a public meeting) despite persistent confrontations.

THE ADVENT OF MARTIAL LAW

To deter further disorders, the government marched a moving column of troops around the affected districts: "After the

restoration of order in the town Kasur, a moveable column proceeded along the railway line via Patti to Amritsar and returned
the same way. Accompanied by a European Magistrate, it made
a certain number of arrests, and in some cases took 'hostages'
from villages which were known to contain bad characters; no
floggings were inflicted" [DC: 32].

To stop the crowds attacking the railway stations and burning
other buildings, the government dispatched two airplanes; one
bombed and the other machine-gunned people from a low
altitude. Their targets included the Khalsa High School and
villagers returning home to a village two miles outside Gujranwala. Indeed, it was the kindergarten era of aerial bombardment;
there were only twelve killed and twenty-four wounded because
most of the bombs did not explode. The pilot's testimony led the
Hunter Committee's majority as well as its minority and the
Congress Subcommittee to question the selection of targets, but
the majority exonerated him while the Indian members of the
minority and the Congress Subcommittee condemned the act
[HC: 49, 130, 134; INC: I, 108].

Martial law was maintained in five out of twenty-nine districts
of the Punjab between 15 April and 11 June 1919 upon the request of Lieutenant Governor O'Dwyer, whose request in May
for its continuation was questioned but ultimately granted by the
Government of India. These districts were the borders of a
closed society coordinating law, police, the press, and the
schools. O'Dwyer admitted before the Hunter Committee that
his desire to prolong that rule was motivated by his intention to
prevent demonstrations while the trials of those accused of
organizing, inciting, and participating in crimes during the
disorders of April were held. Both the Hunter Report and the
Congress Report are confined to events in these five districts:
Amritsar, Lahore, Gujranwala, Gujrat, and Lyallpur.

The system created summary courts administered by one or
three officers and Martial Law Commissions, the latter of which
could impose the death penalty without appeal. Flogging was
more often the penalty: out of 120 instances, flogging was executed publicly in 65 cases. While flogging was legal under the
Criminal Code, it had not been traditional to administer it with a
cat-o'-nine-tails.

A total of 569 persons were sentenced for crimes committed during the disorders (which included public addresses judged to have incited sedition), 108 of whom were sentenced to death and 265 to "transportation for life." Although most of these sentences were commuted by a royal proclamation in December 1919 issued just before the Congress convention in Amritsar, during the period of martial law, eighteen Indians were publicly hanged before a direct protest from Congress President Motalil Pandit Nehru moved the governor general of India to prohibit that form of execution.[19] Edwin Montagu, secretary of state for India, responding to a question from Colonel Wedgwood in Commons on 3 May 1921, stated that there were still eighty-six prisoners in Punjab jails who had been convicted during the disorders.

The quality of justice meted out by those summary courts and the commissions lies somewhere between that reportedly administered by American police (before the *Miranda* v. *Arizona* decision of the Supreme Court in 1966 made it mandatory to inform those arrested of their rights and threw out of court station-house confessions secured under other conditions) and that routinely practiced by dictatorships which, lacking the ideological means to compel conformity, rely on torture instead. For this reason, scant attention has been paid in this study to the "findings" of such courts of conspiracies to wage war and similar conclusions, but much has been paid to the *means* of producing such findings.

Although the right of defense was not suspended, severe restrictions were placed upon Indian lawyers; for example, all lawyers outside the Punjab were prohibited from entering that province, which effectively served to overwhelm those within. In addition, lawyers were forbidden the right to practice in some towns and the right to travel to defend clients in others. Lawyers defending political cases were intimidated by feared loss of future government privileges and by being followed by CID agents after they took such cases. Courtroom defense became a sham because clients could seldom consult their lawyers before the case was tried, and usually had no idea when it would be called up. Complaints of judges' bias and reporters' failure to record examination unfavorable to the accuser were also registered.

CASE-MAKING

Many corroborating reports of Indian witnesses tell of attempts to extort or coerce them to produce false evidence, either to arrest offenders for unsolved crimes or to confirm the cases against other prisoners. These witnesses were threatened that if they failed to cooperate, they would be framed, beaten, jailed indefinitely, or tortured. In a number of towns, children and teenagers were induced to give false testimony (admitted later to the Congress Committee), becoming "approvers" (accusers) for the administration. In other towns, *badmash* ("hooligans") were used systematically as approvers.

While there is no evidence that those who refused to invent such testimony were framed systematically, they were likely to be beaten or held for long periods. During the reign of martial law, over 600 persons were detained or arrested without being charged or tried. Of the 573 for whom data are available on length of detention, we find that 91 (or 15.9 percent) were imprisoned from four weeks to seventy-nine days, 134 (23.4 percent) were jailed for fourteen to twenty-eight days, 108 (18.8 percent) were jailed for seven to thirteen days, and 240 (41.9 percent) were jailed for less than one week.

In some cases, the military wanted specific persons framed; in others, they were apparently satisfied to indict randomly selected culprits in order to make their case. The case of Dr. Mahmood is one of the former type:

> Dr. Maqbool Mahmood, High Court Vakil, who at the risk of his life, it will be remembered, tried, on the 10th April, to turn away the crowd near the bridge, was later on arrested by a Sub Inspector, was taken to the police station and was prompted to say "I could and would identify the murderers of Robinson and Rowland." I informed the police that I had already sent a written statement to them and that I had stated that I could not recognize any body. This statement was then brought to me and I was then asked to tear it off with my own hands and to submit a fresh statement giving the names of those whom they had found out as culprits. I refused to comply with the demand and some threats were flung at me. However, I was subsequently allowed to leave. [INC: I, 67]

Sometimes the threats were followed by torture. The tortures imposed in Amritsar under General Dyer's regime exceeded cases elsewhere. One witness, Quolam Qadir Toopgar, reported that after being beaten for refusing to point out looted property (of which he pleaded ignorance), his hands were tied with his turban and he was suspended from a tree for ten minutes, along with eight or nine other men. But he saw worse fates: "I saw Perra Gujar lying flat on the ground and a Havaldar, whom I know by face, pushed a stick into his anus in the presense of Sub-Inspector Amir Khan. He cried piteously all the time, but the police showed no mercy. For full 3 days and nights we were not allowed any food, during which period we were subjected to police torture. I was released after 5 days" [INC: I, 71]. This punishment was meted out to at least two other persons (one of whom died shortly thereafter) and was confirmed by an additional eight witnesses.

The object of torture in Amritsar was to frame Dr. Kitchlew and Dr. Satyapal, the deported leaders. The most intense coercion was that described by Gholam Jilani, a Muslim imam and deedwriter who helped organize the Muslim participation on Ram Naumi Day in Amritsar, clearly indicates this. Arrested three times without being informed of any charges—"but that I must try to get rich and prominent persons arrested"—he was removed from the jail and beaten unconscious. This treatment was repeated until he agreed to cooperate with his captors. Then he was told he must name Dr. Kitchlew and Dr. Satyapal and swear he had paid the boys who dressed in Turkish garb on Ram Naumi Day money to participate. Although he retracted his statements before the judges in Amritsar and Lahore, they overlooked his retractions while he was taken into another room and threatened with either being hanged or framed in a bank murder case unless he went back in and signed the necessary papers. Jilani suffered serious illness between harassment and torture [INC: II,180–186].

Muslim testimony may have been sought especially to make a political case of conspiracy against the nonviolent leadership. Such a case would attempt to demonstrate that Hindu-Muslim unity was contrived and specious, thus impugning the belief that events before 10 April were signs of widespread dissatisfaction among all classes and communities.

THE NATURE OF MARTIAL LAW

Governing officers instituted curfews, price controls, and traditional prohibitions of public meetings and processions; however, some rather novel types of social control were introduced which need further description.

The following orders specified the collective obligations owed by Indians as a class to Britishers:

1. The Crawling Order (Amritsar)
2. The Salaaming Order (Amritsar, Gujranwala)
3. The Saluting Order (Wazirabad)
4. The Descending Order (Lahore)
5. All males made to sweep or do sanitary work (Malawakal, Sheikupura)
6. Lawyers made menials (Constable Order in Amritsar)
7. Indemnities exacted for damages and taxes levied for support of troops (Akalgarh, Gujranwala, Hafizabad, Manianwala, Sheikupura)
8. Vehicles commandeered (Lahore)
9. Crops or shop inventories confiscated (Nawan Pind, Sheikupura, Wazirabad)

These were ritualized duties imposed on all Indians regardless of what they had done, but there were also individual and collective punishments that were ordered, including the following:

1. Public flogging (Amritsar, Lahore)
2. "Freak" punishments—as the Hunter Committee put it—such as rubbing a prisoner's nose in the dirt (Kasur, Nizambad, Ramnagar)
3. Forced marches of students (Lahore)
4. Schoolboys or whole populations forced to sit or stand in the sun (Hafizabad, Sangla Hill, Wazirabad)
5. Students deprived of scholarships, fined, or expelled (Lahore)
6. Villagers prevented from cutting crops (Chuhar Kara)

All the actions described in the two preceding lists were legal under martial law. But there were extralegal acts as well:

1. Extortion (general)
2. Looting (Chuhar Kara, Nawan Pind, Sangla Hill, Sheikupura, Wazirabad)
3. Torture of prisoners (Amritsar, Wazirabad)

4. Verbal abuse (Manianwala)

5. Threats of bombing houses (Lahore), of burning houses (Chuhar Kara, Sheikupura), of shooting (Sheikupura), and of choking (Wazirabad)

6. Burning of property (Kasur)

Ordinances and punishments inflicting degradation or compelling deference as a duty might be enacted against specific Indians violating other ordinances but were also prescribed wholesale, regardless of violations. Examples of the former are Captain Doveton's "fancy punishments." Doveton readily admitted that if Indians failed to salaam (bow) before Europeans, instead of trying them for the offense he made prisoners in Kasur skip rope and compelled them to touch their noses to the ground. He denied, however, that he had them whitewashed. This effect, it appears, was merely a by-product of ordering them to lift limestone. The pain of public floggings added injury to degradation in Amritsar and Lahore.

Compulsory obligations toward British officers were, in effect, *rituals of abasement:* natives were forced to reaffirm their low status by performing traditional gestures of deference. Orders compelling saluting, salaaming, or descending from vehicles in front of British officers were promulgated in Amritsar, Gujranwala, Lahore, Ramnagar, and Wazirabad. Martial Law No. 7, the Saluting Order, illustrates their manifest purpose:

> We have come to know that Gujranwala District inhabitants do not usually show respect to the gazetted commissioners, European Civil and Military officers of His Imperial Majesty, by which the prestige and honour of the Government is not maintained. Therefore, we order that the inhabitants of Gujranwala district should show proper respect to these respectable officers, whenever they have occasion to meet them, in the same way as big and rich people of India are respected.
>
> Whenever any one is on horseback or is driving any kind of wheeled conveyance, he must get down. One who has opened or got an umbrella in his hand should close or lower it down, and all these persons should salute with their right hand respectfully. [HC: 90]

The much discussed Crawling Order of General Dyer differs from these only in that it was confined to a particular street which had assumed symbolic significance. Dyer's order, in force between 19 and 24 April (later disapproved by Lieutenant Governor O'Dwyer), compelled all persons in the street where Miss Sherwood (the "missionary lady") had been attacked to crawl on all fours if they ventured out between 6 A.M. and 10 P.M. And since General Dyer's Curfew Order was simultaneously in effect, they could not go out between 10 P.M. and 6 A.M.

A platform was also set up at one end of the street for public flogging, supposedly intended solely for Miss Sherwood's attackers. Fifty persons, mainly residents, were affected by the Crawling Order and more may have been deprived by the absence of sweepers, water carriers, and doctors who refused to enter the lane. Other indignities were suffered by a blind man, a banker, and a teacher who were kicked and threatened with a bayonet while crawling. To complete the symbolism: "Whilst the crawling was being enforced, sacred pigeons and other birds were shot. The Pinjarapole, a sacred house for the care of animals which was just at one end of the lane, was defiled. The wells in the lanes were polluted by the soldiers easing themselves near them" [INC: I, 63].

These acts were complemented by collective punishments which, although they were physically demanding, were more humiliating than laborious since dirty work in India is reserved for those low in caste or below the caste system (then untouchables) and is considered polluting. In Sheikupura, all men were compelled to perform the work of coolies and street cleaners.

Perhaps the most outstanding case of collective punishment was the forced student marches in Lahore. After finding one poster deemed treasonable on the walls of the Sanatam Kharma College, the British arrested all males and marched them three miles to the fort (some carrying bedding), where they were interned for two days. To prevent such occurrences at neighboring colleges, Colonel Johnson, the officer in charge, ordered roll calls of students to be taken four times a day, which meant that the medical college students had to walk sixteen miles daily. After that, the deputy commissioner ordered the college council to pick out ringleaders for punishment; the council took this to mean that some students must be selected, and did so arbitrarily. Shortly thereafter the administrators were informed that the punishments were inadequate; they were increased. Finally, the commanding officer officially notified the colleges of their quota—how many students were to be expelled, "rusticated for a year," deprived of their scholarships, temporarily suspended, and punished in other ways—which they had to fulfill if they were to remain open. Similarly, in Wazirabad and Sangla Hill schoolchildren were forced to attend roll calls, as was the whole male population of Nawan Pind.

TERROR AND PUNISHMENT

What was the purpose and effects of these martial law acts? Contemporaries recognized them as examples of "deterrents," "terrorism," "chastisement," "Prussianism"—their judgments revolve around the essential nature of punishment. How do we recognize terror other than by sensing we are terrified (or empathizing with the victim's dread)? While definitions and ideologies abound, the most common denominator that we sense among all circumstances is the arbitrary or categorical choice of victims. A useful definition is that of E. V. Walter, who distinguishes between punishment, terror, and warfare. Terror, he asserts, is violence used deliberately as a means of social control by instilling irrational fears; under civil conditions, it stops short of destroying the party terrorized because its object is not destruction: "A segment of the group may be destroyed to instill terror in the rest, but the group is not wiped out."[20]

Walter defines punishment as a response to a transgression of a recognized norm, duly imposed and limited by legal institutions: he also insists that to qualify as punishment, acts must be calculated to increase the probability of obeying the law. For a response to be a punishment, "there must be a way of being innocent." Terror is not contingent upon any previous action of the victim.

Using this definition, it becomes clear that these reprisals were instances of terror, as was the firing at Jallianwala Bagh. General Dyer was explicit in his report of 25 August 1919 as to his motives for firing at the Jallianwala Bagh: he was intent on "producing a sufficient moral effect . . . throughout the Punjab."

The Hunter Committee's cross-examination established that he took no steps to stop the meeting, post notices, or consult with leaders during that afternoon [HC: 112–113]; nor did he allege belief that sufficient notice had been given when he ceased his morning round: "I did not think anything. When it was too hot to walk in the city I took the nearest route out.'' The General not only affirmed that no warning had been given and that he was impeded from taking in armored cars with machine guns only by the size of the opening, but he asserted baldly that ''I had made up my mind that I would do all men to death if they were going to continue the meeting.''[21] When asked directly if his idea ''was to strike terror,'' he reiterated the motives he had described on 25 August: ''Call it what you like. I was going to punish them. My idea from the military point of view was to make a wide impression.''

Dyer consistently rejected following up any leading questions that contained partial exonerations of his behavior (such as the possibility he might not have been heard giving warning). Moreover, he denied that he believed he was being attacked or would have been attacked; and he admitted that he could have dispersed the crowd if he had given warning:

> A. *Dyer* Yes: I think it quite possible that I could have dispersed them perhaps even without firing.
>
> Q. *Committee member.* Why did you not adopt that course?
>
> A. I could disperse them for some time, then they would all come back and laugh at me, and I considered I would be making myself a fool.[22]

In George Orwell's essay ''Shooting an Elephant,'' that same fear is captured by a young policeman in Burma, gifted with the ability to separate his inner voice from his role:

> And suddenly I realized that I would have to shoot the elephant after all. . . . Here was I, the white man with his gun, standing in front of the unarmed native crowd—seemingly the leading actor of the piece; but in reality I was only an absurd puppet pushed to and fro by the will of those yellow faces behind. . . . A sahib has got to act like a sahib . . . to trail feebly away, having done nothing—no, that was impossible. The crowd would laugh at me. And my whole life, every white man's life in the East, was one long struggle not to be laughed at.[23]

General Dyer's testimony fits well with the description recorded of him by Nehru, the first prime minister of India:

> Towards the end of that year (1919) I traveled from Amritsar to Delhi by the night train. The compartment I entered was almost full and all the berths, except one upper one, were occupied by sleeping passengers. I took the vacant upper berth. In the morn-

ing I discovered that all my fellow-passengers were military officers. They conversed with each other in loud voices that I could
not help overhearing. One of them was holding forth in an aggressive and triumphant tone and soon I discovered that he was
Dyer, the hero of Jallianwala Bagh, and he was describing his
Amritsar experiences. He pointed out how he had the whole town
at his mercy and he felt like reducing the rebellious city to a heap
of ashes, but he took pity on it and refrained.[24]

The use of terror was consistent with the officers' conviction
that they, the British, were in a state of war with the Indians,
who could no longer be regarded indulgently, like children, but
must be treated sternly as enemies. The officer who demonstrated in Sheikupura how the machine guns worked—"and told
that those persons would be made the targets of these very
machines, if they rebelled against the Sirkar [government]
again"—must have presumed this: he chose to declare that warning after a state proclamation advising and requesting cooperation [INC: I, 143]. The day after the Amritsar massacre, General
Dyer reportedly had this to say to a meeting of local residents
called by the civil officials: "You people know well that I am a
sepoy and a soldier. Do you want war or peace? If you wish for
war the Government is prepared for it, and if you want peace,
then obey my orders and open all your shops; else I will shoot.
For me the battle-field of France or Amritsar is the same" [INC:
I, 50]. Colonel O'Brien is recalled to have delivered a similar
message in Wazirabad stressing the government's authority to
burn any house to the ground [INC: I, 112].

Occasionally these threats were combined with explicit racist
abuse, as in the case of Bosworth Smith, who called together the
people in the town of Manianwala in order to condemn the
lawyers. He paraded before them a barefooted and handcuffed
police inspector who was to be deported to Burma for his
disloyalty and was to forfeit his pension, according to Smith.
Witnesses testified that

> he then advised the people generally. He said that they were all
> *"Suar log"* (swine) and *"Gandi Makhi"* (contemptible flies),
> *"sab ek rang ka"* (all of one colour), inasmuch as they had
> rebelled against the *Sirkar* by the closing of their shops. He told
> them that they never should listen to the pleaders, who always
> cheated them, but go for advice to their Lambardars, Zaildars,
> Tahsildars and Deputies. [INC: I, 143–144]

Other officers believed, as did General Dyer, that terror was justified because all Indians were potential rebels and thus enemies. Thus, they veered between violence intended to repress disorder, violence to retaliate for past insubordination, and seeming random violence. Colonel Johnson, for instance, threatened to destroy all property (excepting temples only) within a fifty-yard radius from the point at which a bomb exploded in Lahore [HC: 121]. Their belief that all Indians were enemies persuaded them it was logical to shoot at Indians regardless of what they were doing: if the Indians were not attacking them today, they were planning to attack tomorrow.

The commander of the armored train who was accused of firing indiscriminately told the Hunter Committee how he knew (although there were no signs of milling) from people's vaguely discerned everyday actions (mounting a horse) that his victims were planning to attack. This line of reasoning was carried even further, to its ultimate sophistry, by Colonel Carberry, accused of bombing a high school boarding house and some villages outside Gujranwala:

> Q. Your object seems to be to hit or kill more people of that crowd, although they had begun to disperse, and were running away after the bombs were thrown?
>
> A. I was trying to do it in their own interest. I also realised that if I tried to kill people, they would not gather again and do damage.
>
> Q. The idea being to have a sort of moral effect?
>
> A. Quite right. [INC: I, 108]

This is not to say that terror was the only function of such punitive measures. The few reported cases of torture were not random but calculated to coerce specific individuals (because their high status might give their accusations credibility) into framing a case against others who would be tried for crimes committed during the disorders or for planning the disorders. Such convictions would clearly exonerate the government of the Punjab from responsibility for the disorders and legitimate their previous actions.

The looting and extortion cases, by contrast, seem to have been motivated by petty gain rather than collective ends.[25] Obviously, martial law opens up opportunities for officers that do not occur on a regular basis during their career. The officers' demands served to degrade, if not terrify, their victims by emphasizing to them their own impotence, as in the following case:

> Basant Ram was arrested along with 25 others on the 19th May. He and the others were released on the 22nd May, without any statements having been taken from them. He says, "During the period of arrest, the police did not permit us even to answer calls of nature, unless we paid something. We paid Rs. 2 daily for this very purpose." [INC: I, 125]

Cases are recorded in which that privilege was forbidden without granting prisoners the opportunity to pay for it.

Terror, whether a spontaneous invention (as was the case of the British military in the Punjab) or a bureaucratic staple of totalitarian regimes, is designed to terrify. Hundreds of Indian witnesses whose testimony is printed in the Congress Report inform us that they were, indeed, terrified during those months of 1919.

CHAPTER 3
Prologue to Collective Violence in India, 1858–1919

A young artillery officer put the present popular feeling in a nutshell. He said: "I know nothing of politics, but I do know that if a nigger cheeks us we must lick him."

—Philip Woodruff

Do not circumscribe your vision like a frog in a well; get out of the Penal Code, enter into the lofty atmosphere of the Shrimat Bhagavad Gita and then consider the actions of great men.

—B. G. Tilak

Before we can understand what people expect of each other, we must inquire how their relations are ordered. What classes and communities do they belong to and to what extent do they identify with those in similar positions or with those above them? What benefits can the governing class in a racial or ethnic order of domination promise the subject class and what means do they have to compel obedience? Who may make the rules and how are they applied to each class? What commitments or interests will make the powerful fulfill or retract their promises? What interests, myths, and other beliefs sustain the loyalty of the subjects?

One may readily observe that an imperial order always contains the germ of its own dissolution. When people are divided by national identity into a governing class and a subject class, the subjects, if they become conscious of their class interest, ought to challenge the basis of their subordination. When the governing and the governed are divided by race, creed, and culture simultaneously, the likelihood of conflict is even greater. Racism is a postulate of likely ideology that can rationalize such a division on behalf of the governing class, but it is a problematic credo because it cannot be expected to evoke much loyalty among the governed. How does the governing class cope with the challenge? Quite likely such a challenge will be made criminal. Let us see how class consciousness emerges and provokes further polarization of race relationships—and what crimes and punishments each class produces and receives as previous accommodations are tested.

To understand the emerging limits of British rule after 1857, one must understand how Indians came to regard themselves as a political class—regardless of internal class, communal, and caste cleavages—united by their common subordination to British rule. This chapter describes the interplay between communal self-consciousness and competition and the emerging national class consciousness of Indians as an oppressed entity. Both class and communal consciousness evolved from coalitions and conflicts with the British raj. The development of the twentieth-century mass nationalist movement is related to the ability of elites to agree on common goals transcending communities.

Although there had not been a decade since the mutiny (or rebellion) of 1857 without peasant riots, revolts inspired by messianic religious movements, student demonstrations, urban riots and terrorist bombings and assassinations, these incidents were localized and usually easily suppressed, except for the revolutionary movement emerging in the last decade of the nineteenth century. Some nonviolent peasant movements, as well as riots, caused the British to legislate on behalf of the peasants to appease their discontent. Not until the second decade of the twentieth century was the British raj challenged by a concerted drive for self-government on the part of the Indian political elite. However, the governing class had been organized since 1857. Because they came to govern, they were always conscious of being a class, and justified their role by belief in their right to rule. This belief was reinforced by their isolation both from the Indians and from London, the source of their authority.

THE STRUCTURE OF EMPIRE

The British who ruled India were responsible both to the Government of India through each provincial government and to an administration in London (the India Office) created by the

British Cabinet. The Cabinet appointed the highest executive of the Government of India, the viceroy of India, who was responsible to the secretary of state for India in the India Office. The secretary of state was answerable to Parliament, which was the final arbiter adjudicating the claims of the Indian bureaucracy, the Government of India, Indian natives' associations, and the classes of Indians aspiring to serve that government. The dual responsibility of Parliament and the Government of India is signified by the conventional attachment and ordering of the names of both the secretary of state for India and the viceroy to the historic reforms passed during their tenure, such as the Morley-Minto reforms and the Montagu-Chelmsford reforms in the period under discussion. In which direction did the line of imperial hierarchs turn Indian rule after the rebellion?

BRITISH GOALS AND IDEOLOGY

Before the mutiny, administrators had a variety of opinions regarding the benefits of westernization and its political consequences. The middle position, represented by the "Liberal Tory view" of such governors as Metcalfe, Munro, Malcolm, and Elphinstone, looked toward western innovation and the eventual independence of their progeny in the spirit of benign paternalism. Malcolm wrote:

> Let us proceed on a course of gradual improvement, and when our rule ceases, as cease it must (though probably at a remote period) as the natural consequence of our success in the diffusion of knowledge, we shall as a nation have the proud boast that we have preferred the civilisation to the continued subjection of India. When our power is gone, our name will be revered; for we shall leave a moral monument more noble and imperishable than the hand of man ever constructed.[1]

The founding of an Indian university system modeled after that of the British, recommended by Lord Macaulay in 1839, was a genuine response to the governors' perception, which agreed with that of educated Hindu reformers, that modern literature and science were superior to prescientific lore. Josselyn Hennessy refutes the charges of many later Indian nationalists that such a system was superimposed on India. She notes that the emerging middle classes "eagerly *sought* the alien culture" and cites Pannikar's opinion that Macaulay's minute, divested of its "narrow prejudices against Hindu civilization . . . was . . . the most beneficently revolutionary decision taken by the British."[2]

Before the mutiny, the British did not nourish an active desire to educate a class which might replace them; but they were not preoccupied with obsessive fears of Indian disloyalty as they were after that event. Their fears and their determination to continue governing India led most of them to repudiate that earlier benevolent paternalism and evolve an ideology of British rule legitimating autocracy and recognizing the British raj as a despotic regime based on the superior racial qualifications of the British to rule. This view was best articulated by James Fitzjames Stephens, an English lawyer who had served on the Viceroy's Council in India (1869–1872) and returned to England to publish *Liberty, Equality, Fraternity,* a manifesto of the school Thomas Metcalf calls "authoritarian liberalism."[3] Stephens' view on the Government of India were concisely expressed in a letter to *The Times* (London) on 1 March 1883 attacking the Ilbert Bill:

> It is essentially an absolute Goverment founded, not on consent, but on conquest. It does not represent the native principles of life or of government, and it can never do so until it represents heathenism and barbarism. It represents a belligerent civilization, and no anomaly can be so striking or so dangerous as its administration by men who, being at the head of a Government founded on Conquest, implying at every point the superiority of the conquering race . . . and having no justification for its existence except that superiority, shrink from the open, uncompromising, straight-forward assertion of it, seek to apologize for their own position, and refuse, from whatever cause, to uphold and support it.

Stephens believed that the Indian people were "ignorant to the last degree" and "steeped in idolatrous superstition"; the British role should not be to prepare them to rule but solely to keep law and order, enforcing the law of contract.[4] His conclusions were reached by another philosophical route by Sir Henry Maine, his successor on the Viceroy's Council. Maine, best known to sociologists for his analysis of social evolution as a process from status to contract relations, concluded that India was not fit for self-government because the predominant type of social relation was founded on status, best exemplified by the caste system.

Stephens' and Maine's justifications for autocracy were buttressed by the new racial doctrines appearing in mid-century, which were purportedly derived from scientific evidence. The combination of racialism, legitimation of autocracy, and the fears transmitted to British administrators since the mutiny transformed the benevolent paternalism of some previous governors to a manifestly hostile guardianship in which the guardians hoped in vain to arrest their wards' maturity. To justify their position, the imperial governing class had to assert the unfitness of Indians to govern, unless they were to admit their dominion was motivated solely by their need for power, profits, and privilege—a scarcely idealized self-image. This may explain their emphasis on what Metcalf calls the "myth of oriental stagnation" and their antagonism to the "educated classes," evident in memoirs, correspondence, and British literature about India.[5]

The governing class interpreted signs of disorder routinely as the product of "agitators" devising "conspiracies" to exploit the ignorant masses rather than indications of grievance or strain. They maintained that the vast majority of Indians were content to submit to the British raj, which had brought order and tranquility to the Indian subcontinent as well as just arbitration of the conflicting claims of classes, castes, and religious communities. This cluster of ideological tenets constituted the axioms of empire still shared by the imperial class in 1919.

INDIANS IN ADMINISTRATION

While the British governing class which actually administered Indian provinces and districts was intent upon retaining British rule, which they believed could not be entrusted to the natives, the imperial policymakers in London intermittently stressed the necessity of co-opting some natives into administration. The Royal Charter Act of 1833 had forbidden proscription of any position on a racial basis, and such bans were reiterated by later legislation of Parliament. Nevertheless, despite this promise, the Government of India successfully resisted attempts to open the ranks of the governing class to Indians during the post-mutiny period. The Government of India refused to implement laws enabling them to appoint Indians without examination (1870) or allowing simultaneous civil service examinations to be held in India as well as London (1893); and they never appointed the maximum number of native Indians they were permitted to assign to civil service posts without examination.

With a few significant exceptions, Liberal viceroys or viceroys appointed by Liberal Cabinets were no more likely to pursue an egalitarian policy—supporting the creation of equal opportunities for Indians or a just share of the positions available as a matter of right for its own sake—than were their Conservative counterparts. They were, however, more willing to make structural changes to accommodate the "moderate" faction of the Indian educated class interested in posts and politics. Both Liberals and Conservatives in the ninteteenth century expected that the British would continue to rule India indefinitely. Most Conservatives, unlike the Liberals, did not expect that British rule could ever be legitimated by popular assent, so they were less favorable toward moves to co-opt a native elite into higher administrative roles.

Until 1917, the most liberal of imperial hierarchs were committed only to opening up the class of higher-ranking administrators (the Indian Civil Service) to educated natives who would then be responsible to the British raj. They intended to create a class of bureaucrats—not a political class which would govern the Indian people and be responsible to them for their activities. This did not mean that Indians could not be consulted on policy questions: it was agreed that they might serve an advisory function.

Indians were first appointed as nonofficial representatives to the Governor General's Council in 1861 but were forbidden the right to criticize the policy of the executive or to ask questions. Reforms to rectify those restrictions first proposed in 1888 were lethargically eased through both Houses of Parliament and became law in 1892. These reforms expanded both the central and the provincial Legislative Councils by increasing the number of nominated nonofficial (native) representatives, some of whom were permitted to be elected from designated corporate bodies. The councils were allowed to make inquiries but not to pass resolutions regarding the budget or other questions; the governor general continued to have the ultimate veto on legislation.

The Morley-Minto reforms of 1909 did not alter the consultative role of these councils but legally mandated, rather than merely allowed, the election of Indians as representatives of constituencies; some of these were chambers of commerce and universities and others were communal electorates such as Muslims of a region. The governing personnel could be ranked into an elite of governors who were politically appointed by London, a higher-ranking corps of officials and bureaucrats who were tenured and permanent residents of India, and a lower-ranking stratum of functionaries such as subinspectors, tax collectors, and government clerks who served the bureaucracy in less authoritative roles. The elite was closed to Indians until the appointment of Lord Sinha to the Executive Council in 1909, and the lower stratum was virtually closed to Englishmen by the last decade of the nineteenth century. Most positions in the higher-ranking class were held by the civil service. Was this class open to Indians?

THE INDIAN CIVIL SERVICE

The Indian Civil Service, while legally open to competition by all subjects in 1853, was effectively closed out of competition by many mechanisms—examinations were held only in London, the age limit was manipulated to discourage Indian applicants who could afford and dared to make the journey, and the subjects excluded all oriental tongues except Sanskrit and Arabic. The number of Indian candidates grew from seven in 1870 to twenty-six in 1914. However, the chances of Indian applicants to pass did not increase between 1870 and 1910, although the chances of British applicants rose steadily during that period.[6] Using H. L. Singh's and Philip Woodruff's estimates of the total number of Indians in the civil service in 1909 and 1919, one finds they held 5 percent of all the positions in 1909 and 6 percent in 1919.[7]

The Indian National Congress petitioned continuously for an equal chance to compete from its first convention in 1885 onward. This plea was opposed by Sir Syed Ahmed Khan, a prominent nineteenth-century Muslim spokesman and government employee who foresaw that Muslims would enjoy inferior chances of success in a contest based on English literacy.

Parliament finally obliged the aspiring university-educated Indians by passing an act in 1893 which enabled examinations to be held simultaneously in both countries; but the viceroy, Lord Lansdowne, refused to enforce it. His letter explaining that rejection claimed that the groups the government desired to advance would not be selected by examination: "It would exclude the most valuable and capable assistance which the British Government could obtain from natives of India, in the Sikhs, Muhammadans, and other races accustomed to rule and possessing exceptional strength of character, but deficient in literary education."[8]

Between the premise of nondiscrimination (which several viceroys were told or realized would not be publicly abrogated by parliament) and the implied promise of equal opportunity for natives, there were few deeds; nevertheless, the gateway to aspiration had been opened.

How did the Government of India resolve the conflict between its public promise and its private desire for a closed service into which only their Anglo-Saxon peers might enter? Two divisions of service were created. Initially, these were the covenanted (or higher) service and the unconvenanted service; later, they were replaced by the imperial and provincial civil services. The top stratum was virtually closed to the natives and the bottom one to Britishers. Legally, entry to the covenanted service was to be open to Indians by nomination, so that a fixed ratio of the total could be co-opted without examination in accord with certain statutory rules. But that maximum was never reached during the period under consideration.[9]

RACE SOLIDARITY AND JUSTICE

The British governing class was less anxious to keep Indians out of the judiciary than the executive branch of government, because they could not foresee any significant challenge to their authority from admitting Indians to those roles. However, the admission of Indians into the judiciary through the civil service led to the possibility that they might judge Europeans, a situation which would contradict the Europeans' legal privilege of being tried by white magistrates only (1872). Contradictions between this privilege and the need to rationalize judges' roles in terms of the legal jurisdiction of their courts led Lord Ripon, the most liberal of Liberal viceroys, to forward legislation to London in 1882 which clarified the magistrates' duties by making all subjects equally subject to their jurisdiction. This proposal, drafted as the Ilbert Bill, evoked overwhelming opposition from the European community in India, especially the planters. Anil Seal reports that:

> A European and Anglo-Indian Defense Association was formed. . . . There was wild talk of a white mutiny, of packing the Viceroy off to England by force, of getting the European Volunteer Corps to disband. . . . The cry of "our women in danger" revived fears and passions latent since the Mutiny. They were not confined to India. In England, too, the controversy evoked an outspoken attack on liberal policy towards India and an uncompromising assertion of the doctrine of racial superiority.[10]

The bill was finally altered to grant Europeans the right to trial by a jury consisting of at least 50 percent Europeans, accepting the assertion of the Eurasian and Anglo-Indian Association that "it cannot be contended that they [the natives of India] are the peers or equals of Englishmen."[11] The Bombay government noted in its report of 1883-84 that "during the past two years, nearly one hundred natives had been killed by European soldiers, most of whom had escaped the punishment they deserved."[12]

Lord Curzon was vexed during his viceroyalty (1899-1905) by the failure of juries to punish Europeans who maliciously wounded or killed natives either out of personal pique (sometimes randomly vented) or desire to retaliate for some previous crime of an Indian:

> I grieve to say that, since I came to India, I have not found a single man among "the better class," to whose feelings you think that we might safely appeal, who either shares my views, or could be relied upon to back them, at the cost of clamour or unpopularity. They all admit privately that the occurrence of these incidents is regrettable . . . [but] contend that the blame rests with the Natives (which I certainly in my experience, have not found to be the case): and as for the judicial scandals—well, they shrug their shoulders and smile.[13]

Philip Woodruff, writing from the perspective of an ex-civil servant, believes that the attitude of the guardians toward their wards had become less paternalistic and benevolent and increasingly withdrawn and hostile after the mutiny. He attributes the increase in racial hostility to the emergence of a class of educated Indians from whom deference could not be automatically expected by the sahib: "There was a feeling in the air summed up in a sentence overheard. . . . A young artillery officer put the present popular feeling in a nutshell. He said: 'I know nothing of politics, but I do know that if a nigger cheeks us we must lick him.' "[14]

Norman Barrier, relying on Curzon's unpublished statistics of racial assaults of British officers against Indians, notes that such assaults declined in the Punjab during the first decade of the twentieth century but racial antagonism and Indian sensitivity to attacks had increased. As nationalist newspapers such as the *Panjabee* arose, openly voicing their distrust, the British found themselves increasingly under public attack for *zulum* ("racial injustice").[15]

The British did not view Indians as one racial mass, however. They recognized differences between Indian "races," castes, and communities and expressed decided preferences. Their preference for the "martial races," such as Sikhs, Muslims, and tribal groups, led them into a predicament, for relatively few of them competed for available positions. The other criteria they used are illustrated in the choice of Sinha as the first Indian member of the Viceroy's Executive Council. When Lord Morley, secretary of state for India, determined in 1908 to elevate an Indian to the Viceroy's Executive Council, several prominent men were suggested by the viceroy, Lord Minto. Sinha (later Lord Sinha) was belatedly put into the competition by Lord Minto. How did Minto justify his entry?

> Sinha stands high in public estimation as well as in his profession —and he and his family are socially in touch with European society. . . . In making a great change like this I think we should consider the line of least resistance as well as the ability of an individual. Moreover—please do not think me terribly narrow! but Sinha is comparatively white, whilst Mookerjee is as black as my hat! and opposition in the official world would not be regardless of mere shades of colour![16]

COMMUNAL CONFLICT AND COOPERATION

The Indian nationalist movement may be said to have emerged dialectically from the British organization of the Indian university system along western lines. These schools inculcated the educated class with one language in common—a foreign tongue—and familiarized them with nineteenth-century British political thought and its universalistic conceptions of man.

The educated class, which had multiplied fivefold between

1870 and 1892, was disproportionately drawn from sons of Hindu high-caste families from Bengal, Madras, and Bombay.[17] They largely composed the public from which the nationalist movement and revolutionary sects drew membership and leadership. Such a system induced expectations among rising young men which could not be met within that system. The upsurge of revolutionary movements after 1905 attracted members of the educated class who rejected any obligation to confine their political activity to the forms of petition and protest previously recognized as legitimate by the British. This movement, whose rhetorical fervor coincided with a series of assassinations and political crimes, provoked the British to curtail the freedom of press, speech, and association which had been permitted in India. That repression evoked sentiments of rejection among the loyal members of the Indian "political classes" and intensified the judgment of British hypocrisy held by members of those classes who did not proclaim their loyalty to the British raj. Between 1906 and 1916, class loyalties were split between the moderate constitutionalist and extremist nationalistic factions: the former pleaded for regulated advancement, hoping eventually to become a self-governing colony within the empire; the latter demanded self-rule, advocating direct action by nonviolent and violent means.

As Indian nationalism grew, it was countered by the development of communal consciousness which led to separate Hindu and Muslim organizations. Historians differ as to their interpretation of the causes of the rise of communal consciousness during this period. Some emphasize that the Hindu-Muslim split was a direct consequence of the British policy to divide and rule. Others see the Muslim response as an expression of the self-interest prompted by their awareness of disadvantages in free competition. Still others see their reaction as fundamentally a defensive reaction to the growth of orthodox Hindu consciousness and manipulated mass provocations. Regardless of the relative contribution of these causes, Muslim communal organization was encouraged by British officials and used to legitimate the British role as the arbiter between two "nations"—a prophecy that was, without design, self-fulfilling.

When Muslim organizations turned toward the British to be

their final arbiter, they were unwilling to cooperate politically with the Indian National Congress in common demands. When the leadership was able to make alliances, solidarity between the two communities was evident.

THE INDIAN NATIONAL CONGRESS

The Indian National Congress was first convened in 1885 by Allen Octavian Hume, a retired civil service officer: it was the first nationwide, noncommunal, and non-caste-based movement in India. Pattabhi Sitaramayya, a Congress historian, attributes its origin indirectly to the Britishers whose successful campaign against the Ilbert Bill two years previously had raised the consciousness of educated Indians.[18] The Congress, whose early years are characterized by some historians as examples of "political mendicancy,"[19] persisted in petitioning their rulers to pay more attention to Indian advice on the councils, to give equal chances to compete for the civil service, and similar reforms, constantly professing loyalty to British ideals and the crown.

Although delegates were drawn from the range of occupations held by the educated classes, it is estimated that of the nearly 14,000 delegates attending Congress conventions between 1892 and 1909, over 39 percent were lawyers. The percentage of Muslim delegates rose from 3 percent in 1885 to 18 percent in 1888, its highest point.[20]

The third president of Congress, Badruddin Tyabji, was a Muslim who attempted to persuade other Muslim leaders of the benefits of working within the Congress, which was then willing to give them assurance of a veto on all policies affecting communal interests. Nevertheless, Muslim associations rejected participation and reiterated their opposition to holding civil service examinations in India. Their attitude was expressed by Sir Syed Ahmed Khan's reply to Tyabji: "It is not obligatory on our part to run a race with persons with whom we have no chance of success."[21] Hindus of northern India also testified against holding local examinations before the Public Service Commission hearings of 1888.[22]

The Government of India began in 1888 to ignore Congress by refusing its officials permission to attend government meetings.[23]

Lord Curzon refused to grant audiences to its deputations, a policy which was abandoned by his successor in the viceroyalty, Lord Minto, in 1905.[24]

HINDU ELITES AND MASSES

Hindu revivalism in the 1890s was associated with the leadership of B. G. Tilak, who led the extremist faction within Congress which opposed any relationship to the social reformers and rejected emulation of the west. Earlier Hindu reform and restoration movements, such as the Brahmo Samaj (established in 1829) and the Arya Samaj (established in 1875), had tried to modernize Hinduism by ridding it of caste discrimination and certain contemporary mores which were religiously sanctioned, such as suttee, infanticide, and polygamy. The Brahmo Samaj attempted to reconstruct Hinduism on a monotheistic base; the Arya Samaj attempted to reinterpret the Vedas. Rejecting this approach, Tilak and his followers tried to defend the orthodox practice on the grounds that native custom rather than foreign innovation ought to be the norm. He enlarged the political public by organizing mass celebrations of neglected Hindu deities and provincial folk heroes.

The British policy in India from 1832 onward had been to respect native religions and remain neutral toward native and missionary schools alike. With the exception of earlier nineteenth-century legislation abolishing suttee (suicide of widows), *thagi* (ritual murder and robbery in the name of the goddess Kali), and infanticide, legislation against customs that were religiously sanctioned was avoided.

An earlier controversy over child marriage was reopened in 1890 by the death of an eleven-year-old bride from lacerations received during intercourse. The government proposed a new law in 1891 making the age of twelve a minimum for marriage; this proposal was supported by many Congress leaders, some Sanskrit scholars, and doctors. Tilak vigorously opposed its passage, first arguing for education rather than legislation and then denying that the girl's death was a foreseeable rather than a random event. Upon its passage, he charged the government with opening the gateway toward "committing open oppression" against the Hindu people.[25]

Tilak helped organize mass celebration of the Ganapati festival in 1893 and initiate the Shivaji festivals in 1896. The former was intended to replace a Muslim festival celebrated by both communities at that time of year. Communal riots regularly followed the Ganapati festivals: they were easily provoked by loud celebration outside mosques, which were interpreted as an insult to Allah.[26]

AN EPICAL ASSASSINATION

The plague of 1897 provoked much bitterness among Indians because of the rigid laws and autocratic administration of sanitary measures imposed on the people. Since the measures were also unsuccessful in arresting the spread of the disease, resentment was not abated by any visible benefits. A plague committee, headed by Mr. Rand, was appointed for Poona and vested with almost martial powers. Tilak became critical of British methods and wrote in his newspaper that "plague is more merciful to us than its human prototypes now reigning in the city."[27]

In 1897 Rand and an English lieutenant in his party were shot point-blank by a political follower of Tilak. Nine days previously, Tilak had made a speech (later published) discussing the morality of Shivaji's slaying of Afzhal Khan in 1659, which was interpreted as justifying political violence against foreigners. Translated from the original Marathi text, it read as follows:

> If thieves enter our house and we have not strength enough in our fists to drive them out, we should without hesitation lock them up and burn them alive. . . . Do not circumscribe your vision like a frog in a well; get out of the Penal Code, enter into the lofty atmosphere of the Shrimat Bhagavad Gita and then consider the actions of great men.[28]

Later that year, Tilak was indicted and convicted of sedition by the majority verdict of six Europeans on the jury. The three Indian members found him not guilty.

Tilak's conviction was protested by Congress and other leaders. Stanley Wolpert, in *Tilak and Gokhale,* reviews evidence which appeared after 1897 showing that Tilak did help the confessed murderer of Rand to elude the police, helped to mislead the police investigation, and may have had prior knowledge of the assassin's intent. However, none of this information was available to the jury; and Indians' perception of injustice was reinforced because a majority of the jury was from a political

class other than the defendant's whereas juries trying Europeans
were composed of a majority of Europeans by law. Tilak
emerged from jail a popular hero.

DECADE OF DIVISION: 1905–1915

National consciousness reached a new peak during Lord Curzon's viceroyalty as a consequence of the educated classes'
perception of educational and administrative reforms instituted
by the Government of India. That government's partition of
Bengal province in 1905, allegedly to rationalize the administration of a territory comprising 78.5 million people, brought much
agitation and criticism by Hindus who assessed the creation of a
predominantly Muslim province as an act of design. Curzon's
home secretary also conceived of it as a measure to "split up and
thereby weaken a solid body of opponents to our rule."[29] Bengal
was a center of anti-British agitation. Das draws on contemporary newspaper accounts describing responses of crowds to the
partition:

> There was a mass meeting "of all classes of Indians" at the Col-
> lege Square only a few hours after the news reached the city. The
> swadeshi vow was taken, but this time in an "altogether novel
> way." "A huge fire was lighted to which goods of British manu-
> facture were consigned. Even the on-lookers threw down into the
> fire the shirts . . . of English make which they had on their per-
> sons. While these British goods were burning, shouts of Bande
> Mataram rent the skies."[30]

The swadeshi vow (to use Indian goods only) was effective. A
survey by The Statesman revealed that sales of English cotton
goods to Bengal districts had declined from 77,200 rupees value
in September 1904 to 9,700 rupees in September 1905.[31] This
movement, as well as Japan's recent victory over Russia, increased the appeal of the extremist faction of the Indian National Congress. Tilak's role was opposed in Congress by
Gokhale, who was committed to advancement by constitutional
means alone, a strategy scorned by Tilak and his followers, who
noted that India did not have a constitution.[32]

The new viceroy, Lord Minto, was impressed by the necessity
of listening to the moderates in Congress, and he and the
secretary of state, Lord Morley, in turn impressed Gokhale with
the political usefulness of restraining extreme demands and

trusting to their good intentions. The formation of the Muslim League in 1906 (after protracted correspondence between Muslim leaders, Lord Minto's private secretary, and lesser officials) tempered the half-hearted desires of Lords Morley and Minto to conciliate the moderates.[33] Gokhale's role, which depended on both his persisting in hard bargaining and suppressing demands he considered premature, was made increasingly difficult by these officials' distrust of him during the period of Congress history when the moderate faction was folding.[34]

Although the partition was not supported unanimously by Muslims, a group of prestigious Muslim spokesmen formed a deputation to see Lord Minto in 1906.[35] This led to the creation of the Muslim League, whose stated purposes were:

> a) To promote among the Mussalmans of India feelings of loyalty to the British Government and to remove any misconceptions that may arise as to the intentions of Government with regard to any of its measures; b) to protect and advance the political rights and interests of Mussalmans of India and respectfully to represent their needs and aspirations to Government; c) to prevent the rising of Mussalmans of India of any feelings of hostility towards other communities without prejudice to the other objects of the League.[36]

Furthermore, it affirmed its judgment "that partition is sure to be beneficial" to the Muslim majority and that boycotting should be discouraged.

The government welcomed this mobilized group which might serve as a counterforce to the "Bengali Babus" who they believed falsely claimed to represent India. The Muslim League secured a permanent political base when separate electorates were recognized in the Morley-Minto reforms of 1908: Muslims were represented for the first time as a corporate community with their own rolls of electors and were granted a number of the total seats exceeding their proportion of the population.

Nevertheless, protest, boycott, and student demonstrations continued in Bengal. The temper of Congress had changed. The moderates and extremists, previously willing to concur in tactical compromises turning often upon ambiguous wording, were unable even to agree on the procedural questions and the 1907 Congress adjourned in disorder. Later, Congress's membership clause was rewritten to oust the extremists.

Meanwhile, the boycott movement continued. In fact, it was

coming to be valued as a measure to spur native industry in its
own right as well as a symbolic protest against the Bengal partition. The student protests evoked new school rules forbidding
participation in demonstrations, for the government threatened
to cut off funds, scholarships, and university affiliations if students did not cease such activity. These measures led to a boycott of schools and colleges and the establishment of counterin-
stitutions: there were twenty-four "National High Schools" in
East Bengal alone.[37] The Liberal secretary of state, Lord Morley,
foreseeing that such repressive measures would lead to greater
agitation, sanctioned the removal of the lieutenant governor of
Bengal, Sir Bampfylde Fuller, who had authorized them.[38]

The agitation also led the government to pass the Newspapers
(Incitement to Offense) Act terminating the license of any paper
inciting to murder, acts of violence, or any offense against the
Explosive Substances Act of 1908. This new act revived Indian
charges of repression similar to those aroused by the Vernacular
Press Act (or Gagging Act) passed under Lord Lytton's viceroyalty (1876–1880), which restrained Indian criticism of the government.

M. N. Das reveals there was continuous covert strife during
these years between the Liberal secretary of state, Lord Morley,
and the viceroy, Lord Minto, over the correct policy toward
antigovernment agitation as distinguished from revolutionary
violence and incitement. The viceroy desired a free hand, which
meant unrestricted control over the native publications—he dis-
dained the troublesome and time-taking guarantees of due process taken for granted in England.[39] This division helps explain
the vacillation and unique synthesis of repressive and reform
measures during their administration. This conflict over strategies of managing protest was reenacted in later administrations.

Unrest during these years was not confined to Bengal. Even in
the Punjab, which had always been positively contrasted to Bengal by British writers as representing the "real" India, where the
"martial classes" they favored predominated, unrest was reported among classes believed to be most loyal to British rule.[40]

PROTEST AND REPRESSION IN THE PUNJAB

The movements in the Punjab were divided by class and communal interests which often reinforced one another: the Muslims
tended to predominate in agriculture and the Hindus in money-

lending, commerce, and law. Both communal groups as well as the Sikhs were split by tactical disagreements and class differences, although militancy was originally associated with the Hindu extremists. Arya Samaj branches were widespread in the Punjab before 1905 and their leaders were influential in politics and law. Arya leaders persuaded the Punjabi Indian Association to send delegates to the Congress convention of 1904, which led to Punjabi politicians rejoining Congress.[41] Led by Lajpat Rai, they tended to align themselves with Tilak's faction.

Despite these factional differences, the Swadeshi movement gained many adherents in the Punjab. Norman Barrier believes that their enthusiasm was excited by the Japanese victory in the Russo-Japanese war, which reinforced their belief in self-help and indigenous development. Boycott of British goods was deemphasized, as was the Bengal partition, in order to secure Muslim support. Students there, too, joined in public demonstrations —it was estimated that "by October, 1905, as many as 10,000 Punjabis had participated in marches and mass meetings."[42]

Mass protest was not the rule in the Punjab. Local causes of unrest provoked different classes to organize against the British for distinctive reasons. Hindu money-lenders protested restrictions on land transfers disabling them from buying land directly from the peasants; the Land Alienation Act of 1900 aimed at strengthening the agriculturalists' position, as did British policy in the Punjab in general. Resistance was aroused among the tenant agriculturalists of the British model villages in the irrigated region along the Chenab Canal by the proposed passage of the Cape Colony Bill, legislation which increased the autocratic powers of local officials to regulate the upkeep of their tenants' domain. The dissatisfaction of the colonists was raised by the coincidental increase in water rates. The colonists organized, held mass meetings, published a newspaper, and appealed directly to the Government of India for relief. Only after the Punjab government passed the legislation and Ajit Singh, a Sikh agitator, began recommending direct action did the colonists withhold tax revenues in protest.[43]

Urban politics reflected both the tactics and the temper of the national division in Congress. When Lajpat Rai returned in 1905 from London, where he had journeyed as part of the Congress delegation, he turned away from efforts to conciliate both the Muslims and the British. His newspaper *Panjabee,* unlike the moderate *Tribune* (Lahore), had earlier refused to concede British good intentions in ruling India. It declared: "Exploit, Exploit, Exploit—that is the sum and substance of British rule in India."[44]

The *Panjabee* was prosecuted in April 1906 under a section of the Penal Code "which dealt with the offense of promoting enmity and hatred between classes." This indictment stemmed from what the British believed to be a false accusation the paper had published, charging British officials with having covered up a "deliberate murder" by two European officers. Racial hostility to the British was aroused by Ajit Singh, a popular figure able to appeal to all classes of the people, who advocated direct action, suggesting boycott and passive resistance to begin with.[45]

Urban riots during 1906 and 1907 were precipitated by two court trials. The first (after a judge upheld the *Panjabee* conviction) was started by a crowd led by Ajit Singh. No personal injuries were reported to the British, but looting did occur during the second one.[46] European fears were heightened by local attacks on them in plague-ridden districts: Barrier reports that "fear that British officers planted poison in wells or infected 'clean' villages led to assaults on European travellers and doctors."[47]

The first riot was condemned by many Indians in mass meetings.[48] Besides attacking the British, the *Panjabee* had attacked the Indian, Muslim, and Christian communities. Leadership among Hindus and Muslim alike was split. Influential leaders in both communities at times feared the rise of the extremists more than they did the British, even though they sometimes felt compelled to give the extremists public support when they were attacked.

The government of the Punjab responded to these threats by asking and receiving permission from the Government of India to deport Ajit Singh and Lajpat Rai under Regulation III of 1818. Lieutenant Governor Ibbetson requested power to prohibit public meetings and public speakers, suppress newspapers, and try individuals for conspiracy if they incited zamindars (agriculturalists) not to pay their government revenues. A weaker ordinance necessitating advance notice of public meetings was granted to him, the approval of which made the secretary of state, Lord Morley, very angry.[49] Although the viceroy's decision to deport Ajit Singh and Lajpat Rai had not been previously approved by Lord Morley, the secretary of state was pressed by Congress sympathizers on the floor of the House of Commons to answer for actions taken by the Government of India about which he had virtually no information.

Lord Morley suspected and Lord Minto became convinced, that the Government of India had been misinformed of the situation in the Punjab by Ibbetson. Ibbetson himself had been misled by credulous police agents there who transmitted deliberately planted but implausible rumors causing him to regard Ajit Singh and Lajpat Rai as coconspirators; actually, they were enemies. The viceroy, under direct threat from Lord Morley, retracted the deportations in November 1907. But the deportations served to squash opposition because of the lack of unity among opponents of the government.[50]

When political appointees found themselves threatened with loss of government jobs for belonging to groups suspected of inciting the "rebellion," these groups vied publicly with one another in demonstrating their loyalty to the government in order to protect their rights in the competition for positions.[51] This, in turn, led to an increase in communal tension.

Meanwhile, an independent investigation by the Government of India had convinced Lord Minto that the agriculturalists' objections to the Cape Colony Bill were both genuine and widespread. Torn between appearing to repudiate the "man on the spot" (Ibbetson), thus rendering the government liable to future agitation, and restoring the image of British favor for the agriculturalists, he vetoed the legislation.[52]

Lieutenant Governor Ibbetson's self-chosen successor, Sir Michael O'Dwyer, shared his assumptions—the axioms of empire described earlier—and regarded Ibbetson's repression as the decisive element in aborting a rebellion. Neither Ibbetson nor O'Dwyer understood the function that conciliation and accommodation played alongside of threat in preserving caste-class distance and communal rivalry among Indians. Barrier concludes that "the path from coercion in 1907 and its seeming vindication of swift, decisive action to quell disorder led directly to the bloodstained walls of Jallianwala Bagh."[53]

SEDITION AND MORE SEDITION IN BENGAL

By 1908, students were involved in other political strategies in Bengal besides picketing. Open terrorism and political assassinations plagued the government from that year on. While not all were successful, the targets were the highest rulers in the land: two viceroys escaped assassination narrowly.

Tilak was arrested for seditious editorials in his newspaper *Kesari.* These explained the inevitability of bombs being used in India and concluded that the youths involved in the recent murder of the Kennedy women (whose lives had been taken mistakenly instead of that of the intended victim, a district judge) were motivated "not for the sake of self-interest but owing to the exasperation produced by the autocratic exercise of power by the unrestrained and powerful white official class."[54] Tilak defended himself ably without counsel, declaring to the jury: "The point is whether I was within my rights and whether a subject of his Majesty in India can or cannot enjoy the same freedom which is enjoyed by British subjects at Home, and the Anglo- Indians out here."[55] He was convicted, as in the first trial, by a vote of seven Europeans against two Parsees after one hour's deliberation; subsequently, he was sentenced to six years' deportation which was never curtailed upon appeal.[56]

The Seditious Meeting Act of 1908 further restricted the rights of subjects but had little effect as a deterrent to terrorism. Officials believed they had traced these "outrages" to an anarchist movement led underground by Aurobindo Ghose.[57] Ghose was the English-educated son of a surgeon; notwithstanding a successful school career, he failed to pass the entry examination to the Indian Civil Service because he could not pass the horseback riding test. Ghose was the progenitor of the "New Thought" movement, which infused nationalism with a transcendental religiosity. The Mukherjees explain that he believed in both violence and nonviolence: "He never mixed up ordinary ethics with politics which has its own ethics—the ethics of the *Kshatriya* [warrior caste] not that of the *Brahmin,* and he was never tired of preaching the morality of the *Kshatriya* must govern our political thinking."[58]

The government did prosecute Ghose as editor of the *Bande Mataram,* a famed extremist newspaper. Ghose refused to take the oath and allowed the printer to take the conviction, although there was no doubt of his responsibility. Gloating on Ghose's acquittal, another Indian paper expressed the new spirit of assertiveness: "We shall make you drink *ghol* (whey) in as many ways as we can (to make one drink ghol is to harass one). At one time we shall deal you direct blows . . . and at others we shall kick you backwards and run away laughing merrily."[59] His brother, Barindra Ghose, started the *Yugantar* and later had his own school which taught "religion, politics and the manufacture of explosives."[60]

The youth brotherhoods were spawned from an eclectic ideological mix of the Bhagavad Gita, Mazzini, and Russian terrorism. The underground units with laboratories in townhouses, and their cohorts abroad who learned how to fabricate or smuggle explosives to their colleagues, are the prototypical elements of the revolutionary movement described later by Judge Rowlatt's committee (see Chapter 4).

Not satisfied with results under the act of 1908, the government instituted the Indian Press Act of 1910 which considerably expanded the scope of the prohibited acts by including, for example, criticism of executive officers and princes. R. R. Sethi concludes that this act muzzled the press completely. It was especially arbitrary because it was enforced by provincial officials rather than courts: "The Secretary of the Press Association of India (started in 1905 to protect the Press against arbitrary high-handedness of the Government) stated in 1919 that this Act had penalized over 350 presses, proscribed over 500 publications and required from 3300 newspapers deposits totaling over 40,000 pounds."[61]

The controversy generated by Lord Curzon's partition of Bengal abated only in 1911, when the king of England announced the annulment of that plan at the Delhi Durbar.

CONGRESS AND THE ENGLISH RADICALS

The Indian elite's resentment of the British for their castelike segregation and racial solidarity was tempered by the willingness of some dropouts from the governing class to identify with the educated classes' aspirations. These English men and women included Allen Octavian Hume (a founder of the Indian National Congress), Sir William Wedderburn, and Annie Besant (its presidents in 1906 and 1917 respectively).

Congress had maintained a lobby in London since 1886 and campaigned openly in the 1905 parliamentary elections. They solicited and received support from English Liberals, Radicals, and Labour and attracted some prominent politicians to their annual conventions. One of these was the prime minister, William Gladstone, who told the third Congress (1887) that

> I hold that the capital agent in determining finally the question whether our power in India is or is not to continue, will be the will of the 240 millions of people who inhabit India. The question who shall have supreme rule in India is, by the laws of right, an Indian question, and those laws of right are from day to day growing into laws of fact.[62]

Touring M.P.'s not only thwarted the bureaucracy's desire for a firm and free hand, they actively stirred up dissent, to the displeasure of the viceroy. Das relates that

> a typical example of how the English Radicals encouraged the Indian political movement was supplied by Keir Hardie who made a tour of India during the later part of 1907. He travelled through Eastern Bengal where he gave the anti-partition leaders much moral support. . . . To the Indian people he pointed out how the British policy aimed at dividing the Moslems from the Hindus to weaken their national movement. He advised the Mohammedans that they could make progress only by joining the Congress. He urged the agitators to carry on the agitation without violence. From Baroda, Keir Hardie sent the *Daily Mail* a wire saying that the people of India "were bound, gagged and at the mercy of the corruptest police in the world."[63]

These Englishmen enabled Indian liberals in Congress to see the more numerous and prototypical colonizers as "un-British" instead of seeing the Indian sympathizers as being deviant from their countrymen.

The Roots of the "Himalayan Miscalculation" during the Anti-Rowlatt Campaign of 1919

The idea came to me last night in a dream that we should call upon the country to observe a general *hartal*. Satyagraha is a process of self-purification, and ours is a sacred fight. . . . Let all the people of India, therefore, suspend their business on that day and observe the day as one of fasting and prayer.

—Gandhi

The anti-Rowlatt Bill campaign which led to the riot in Amritsar on 10 April 1919 and the massacre at Jallianwala Bagh on 13 April has been credited with igniting a new national consciousness in India. No longer was it possible to turn back to the political illusions held before that year. Since the campaign itself was originated by Gandhi to a greater extent than any later campaign authorized by Congress and was his first experiment with mass nonviolent action, it must also be appraised in terms of the criteria of nonviolence. Students of nonviolence, such as Joan Bondurant, have assessed it as a failure.[1]

Was it, as Gandhi put it shortly after the Ahmedabad riot, a "Himalayan miscalculation"[2] showing that the Indian masses were not ready for the campaign of active nonviolent resistance known as satyagraha? What elements of the situation account for the confrontations in Delhi, Ahmedabad, and Amritsar? Was it the Rowlatt Bills themselves that excited such indignation? Were the riots a response to a national grievance, to local causes, or to the way the British administration coped with protest? Were the riots expressly a sanction against the government or simply an expression of group solidarity? To understand how the Rowlatt Bills became such a powerful symbol, one must examine Indian expectations of the British after World War I.

INDIAN POLITICAL EXPECTATIONS AFTER WORLD WAR I

World War I evoked among Indians widespread identification with the British government, evidenced both by the "voluntary" recruitment of 1,215,000 soldiers and by the voluntary contributions of Indian princes and politicians. It also imposed much hardship. The British Government of India donated so much capital—£100 million, or a year's revenue—that Indian currency was threatened with inconvertibility in 1917. In addition, the cost of Indian troops fighting for the British in World War I was borne by India and constituted 20 to 30 percent of total government revenue.[3] Indian liberals affirmed their desire for a British victory. Gandhi actively recruited soldiers as he had during the Boer-Zulu War (1906), which was scarcely believed by him or anyone else to be a crusade for democracy, in order to demonstrate his loyalty.[4]

Indian soldiers were granted commissions in the Indian army during that war for the first time.

The Response To "Racialism" in the Empire

Expressions of discontent manifested during and after World War I also had their roots in movements arising abroad—which were themselves responses to the discrimination that Indian immigrants encountered in other parts of the empire—as well as in the national aspirations of the educated class.

The emigration of Sikh peasants from the Punjab to Canada after 1904 evoked hostility and physical aggression from white Canadians; unemployment aggravated the situation, leading to immigration curbs in 1908 which were designed to satisfy the popular demand to keep Canada white. Sikh immigration spilled over to California, where the Ghadr (Revolution) Party was founded in 1913; their newspaper proclaimed itself the "Enemy of the British Government." A shipload of illegal Sikh emigrants, barred from entry into Canada despite appeals in Canada and India, returned to the port of Calcutta on 29 September 1914. The passengers, irate at the cooperation of the Government of India with Canada and needing time to consummate business in Calcutta, refused orders to immediately board a train for their homes in the Punjab, where they were landless and jobless. The police fired after some "fracas," killing eighteen and wounding twenty-five persons. The others were rounded up and interned, although no weapons had been found on the boat.[5]

Ghadr members, volunteering in the United States, Canada, and Hong Kong and other ports in the Orient, returned by ship to India intent on pursuing terrorist activities, but they were detained upon arrival by a special ordinance passed to control the nearly 1,000 Ghadrites estimated to have returned by December 1914. Those who illegally entered the Punjab were disappointed to find their countrymen unsympathetic to their message. They then refined their strategy to rise up by subverting the army troops stationed there. However, the planned uprising in February 1915 was foiled by police infiltrators and the suspected troops were disarmed.[6]

Another Indian encountering racial discrimination in the dominions was Gandhi, who had invented the doctrine and methodology of satyagraha ("truth-force") while organizing the resettled Indian coolies of the Union of South Africa to resist that government's efforts to restrain their freedom of movement. Satyagraha ranges tactically from education and appeal to mass coercive claiming of rights and resistance to imposition of government claims. Within a broad movement, all tactics are integrated, if not by ideological consistency or belief on the part of all followers, at least by the forswearing of offensive violence and self-defense.

Satyagraha employed tactics that had been widely used before in India, such as boycott and the hartal. However, it had two singular characteristics, not attributable solely to Gandhi's charismatic force, which made it especially useful there. Firstly, it channeled mass discontent into more durable forms than did riots or spontaneous outbursts that might ventilate common resentment but could not alter the causes of the discontent. Secondly, it was based on a universalistic ethic which abhorred division between protester and antagonist (or any two humans); thus it created a solidarity among protesters that was not defined in terms of caste or religion.

Congress leaders were initially skeptical of Gandhi. During 1917 and 1918, however, he demonstrated the efficacy of satyagraha in India by organizing the Champaran indigo growers, the Ahmedabad textile workers, and the Kaira peasants in nonviolent campaigns.

The Muslim League and the Congress

In 1916, moderates and extremists were reunited in the Indian National Congress (INC), and Congress and the Muslim League had agreed on a plan for the self-government of India. The league's earlier opposition to self-government had faltered, and it affirmed it as a goal in 1913. The Lucknow reform pact concluded that year incorporated the principle of separate electorates, agreed on the ratio of representatives in different provinces, allowed a group veto on legislation affecting group interests, and provided for an assured majority of elected (rather than nominated) representatives on the councils.

By 1917, the secretary of state for India, Edwin Montagu, challenged by the newly unified coalition of moderate and extremist native politicians, announced the government's intention of progressively advancing Indian self-government. Although Montagu was a Liberal, he represented a bipartisan Unionist coalition cabinet claiming the support of the two major British parties at the time. The declaration affirmed that

> the policy of His Majesty's Government, with which the Government of India are in complete accord, is that of the increasing association of Indians in every branch of the administration and the gradual development of self-governing institutions with a view to the progressive realisation of responsible government in India as an integral part of the British Empire.[7]

Montagu toured India to gather support for such a plan from the governing class. Discouraged after a day of parleying with provincial governors, he wrote the following in his diary on 24 January 1918:

> I was then asked to give my views. I told them that I was more depressed than I could say by what they had said: that I did not seem to talk the same language as they did; . . . I heard them say, to my amazement, that it was a most disquieting sign that agitation was spreading to the villages. What was the unfortunate Indian politician in India to do? He was told he could not have self-government because there was no electorate, because only the educated wanted it, because the villagers had no political instincts; and then when he went out into the villages to try and

make an electorate, to try and create a political desire, he was told that he was agitating, and that the agitation must be put a stop to.[8]

Despite Montagu's discovery that the governing class had no desire to restructure political relationships, he persevered. The government's promise was elaborated in 1918 by a scheme to transfer certain departments in all provinces to ministries responsible to elected Indian legislatures while other ministries, including police and finance, were to be kept under the jurisdiction of the colonial governors of each province for an indefinite period.

The lack of accord among the imperial officers was not compensated for by the enthusiasm of the political leaders of the colonized natives. Congress leaders were split in 1918 as to which position to choose; their annual convention finally passed resolutions substantively criticizing the Montagu-Chelmsford proposals but assented to leave the departments of law, police, and justice under the authority of British governors for six years. Congress organized an Indian delegation to lobby for its proposals in London, and Montagu arranged another Indian delegation to support the official plan. That plan was passed by the House of Lords, through which it was managed by the recently elevated Lord Sinha, now under-secretary of state for India, on 23 December 1919. It is significant that during that same month, General Dyer's testimony on the Amritsar massacre (taken before the Hunter Committee) reached London; but no action was taken against him before March 1920, preventing his supporters from seizing the issue to discredit the reforms which the secretary of state had initiated.

Behind the Rowlatt Bills

During World War I, the Government of India had enacted new powers under the Defense of India Act (1915) designed to cope with the threat posed by the Ghadr movement. However, that act was also used to curb the influence of outspoken nationalists. The leaders of the pan-Islamic movement for protection of the Turkish caliphate were interned under the Act for the duration of the war for objecting to British policy in Egypt. (That movement was later to be led by Gandhi in a bid for Muslim support in 1919 when the peace terms were at issue.)

The government also interned Annie Besant, a British-born

leader of the Theosophical Society who identified with Indian aspirations (especially when her leadership of them was unquestioned), for speeches she made in 1917 before the Home Rule League, which she had organized. Her prosecution multiplied support for that organization and stirred Indians' admiration, which led to her being offered the Congress presidency in 1917. Tilak, who had formed his own India Home Rule League after Annie Besant's had been established, was similarly banned in 1918 from lecturing without permission of the district magistrate.

Even before this, at Lucknow in 1916, Congress had deplored the uses of the Defense of India Act and the Bengal Regulation III of 1818. Congress urged that "in application of the Defense of India Act. . . the same principle should be followed as under the Defense of the Realm Act of the United Kingdom" and noted that "the belief was honestly held that many young men with bright prospects in life had been ruined by the application of the Act."[9]

By 1918, the government held over 806 political prisoners in Bengal under these laws; a preliminary investigatory committee reported that "70 to 80 percent of them are inexperienced and young students."[10] A committee headed by Judge Rowlatt was appointed by the Government of India in December 1917 to investigate revolutionary conspiracies in India and recommend government policy to cope with them in the postwar world. The Congress, which convened that month, opposed the Rowlatt Committee's objective of "arming the Executive with additional powers to deal with alleged revolutionary conspiracy in Bengal."[11]

The report of the Rowlatt Committee relates the growth of a revolutionary press and schools and underground organizations to the commission of politically motivated burglaries ("dacoities"), assassinations, bombings, and sundry related crimes between 1898 and 1916. The burglaries, not patently political crimes and usually unsolved, were classified as political crimes because they were committed by *bhadralok*—members of the respectable classes—in order to obtain money for underground activities and could be recognized by common implements and techniques. Since Indians had been disarmed since the mutiny of 1857, guns were either homemade, stolen, or smuggled and their origins were easily traced.

The report shows that the majority of persons convicted of such crimes between 1907 and 1917 in Bengal were between sixteen and twenty-five years of age, came from two high castes (Brahmin and Kayasthas), and were predominately students, teachers, clerks, or "persons of no occupation."[12] These crimes were committed by groups organized independently of the later Ghadr conspiracy, which was German-assisted (although both Khushwant Singh and the Rowlatt Committee agree that no substantive aid was given).[13]

The Rowlatt Committee report disclaims belief in one centrally directed conspiracy but asserts that "all these plots have been directed towards one and the same objective, the overthrow by force of British rule in India. . . . All have been successfully encountered with the support of Indian loyalty."[14] Why, given that optimistic conclusion, were the British in need of new legislation? Although they had always been able to foil all attempts at armed revolt and had subverted plans to obtain German arms, they were unable to squash the underground movement. Most crimes were never solved, fewer were prosecuted, and even fewer defendants were convicted. The police, as the Rowlatt Committee described them, were generally illiterate, untrained in detection, and unequipped with modern communication devices. Not only could they not apprehend suspects, but government lawyers could seldom prepare a court case that would stand up. Confessions made before the police were inadmissible when brought into court, and substantiating witnesses were often unavailable because other witnesses had been murdered in the past.

To cope with the state's disabilities, the Rowlatt Committee recommended expediting judicial procedures to punish offenders by eliminating jury trials, legalizing trial without counsel, changing laws of evidence, and restricting appeals. The first bill introduced provisions amounting to house arrest of suspects and provided for additional powers to be invoked only if a general emergency was declared: these withdrew the right to trial, negated the necessity of a warrant before arrest, and provided for indefinite detention.

The committee provided a safeguard in an investigating authority composed of a judge and one nonofficial (Indian) who would review material on which orders were based. It also recommended guarantees for arrested persons which they apparently did not have before, such as provision of a written complaint of charges before trial. A second bill, which would have made possession of prohibited documents alone a crime, was withdrawn by the government.

Although the means proposed were both efficient and rational in terms of their goal of repressing political crime, the Congress was not persuaded that efficiency of means was the only issue involved. The Congress convention of 1918 professed its loyalty to the king, conveyed its congratulations on "the successful termination of the War"—and asked for the immediate repeal of repressive ordinances restricting political rights as a first step toward recognizing that India was "one of the progressive nations to whom the principle of self-determination should be applied."[15]

Despite widespread opposition to the Rowlatt Bills among both moderate and extremist Indians, the first bill passed on 18 March over the dissent of twenty-two out of twenty-three unofficial (native Indian) members of the Legislative Council serving the governor general of India. One Indian member (Bayya Narasimha Sarma) attempted to amend it, distinguishing between revolutionary activity and free speech by declaring that "the Revolutionary Movement means the movement directed to the overthrow by force of His Majesty's established Government in India." His proposal was brusquely rejected by Sir William Vincent, who replied that "to an ordinary man in the street the meaning of the word revolutionary was clear. . . . It could not be applied to any but a criminal movement."[16] Sarma resigned in protest. This must have confirmed to Indians that the British did not distinguish sedition or revolutionary activity from tolerable agitation if the end was the same—to replace British control with Indian rule.

Interpretations of Anti-Rowlatt Bill Sentiment

Some British historians and contemporary reporters have attributed the campaign against the Rowlatt Bills mainly to unscrupulous agitation. H. H. Dodwell, for example, writes that "a virulent campaign of misrepresentation was set on foot, and the wildest rumours were circulated as to the effects of the new laws."[17] Such misrepresentations included rumors that gatherings of more than four people would be arrested and parties to a marriage would need the government's permission.

Philip Woodruff, an observer of the governing class from his position in the Indian Civil Service, likewise does not concede that there were any substantive objections to the act but notes correctly that "the reaction was so bitter and so immediate because the Acts were a sign of mistrust—one sign of many, and of mistrust of a particular kind."[18]

Pattabhi Sitaramayya—the Congress historian—concurs with Woodruff that the "change of feeling" between British and Indian had occurred before the bills were drafted. Regarding Gandhi's campaign, he remarks that "most people did not understand why he should have chosen the petty and collateral issue of Rowlatt Bills for the inauguration of Satyagraha, although there was before India the mammoth issue of Self-Government."[19]

In Congress the extremists had become stronger, and earlier compromises over timing, which the moderate wing had previously won, were rejected. Contemplating the reaction to the government's later sanction against General Dyer, Edwin Montagu, secretary of state for India, wrote Lord Willingdon on 9 September 1920 that

> I personally do not believe that the Dyer incident was the cause of the great racial exacerbation which is now in existence and which has got to be lived through and down before we can get into a more hopeful atmosphere. . . . As soon as the Indians were told that we agreed with them and they were to become partners with us, it instilled into their minds an increased feeling of existing subordination and a realisation of everything by which this subordination was expressed. Similarly, when the Europeans were told that, after driving the Indians for so many years, that regime was to be over and they might find themselves forced to cooperation with the Indians, or even forced to allow Indians to rule India, their race consciousness sprang up afresh. . . . We ought to have let Indians run their own show from the beginning.[20]

Woodruff, looking back in melancholy, opines that

> Withdrawing then to a distance, so that India can be seen from far away, it is possible to say that in 1918 the system of the Guardians was still intact to the eye. The State was still ruled by trained rulers according to their own idea of what was good. But the system was to last no longer. It will appear to go on for another quarter-century, but it did really end in 1919.[21]

Woodruff recognizes that the turning point was the transfer of loyalties. But whose loyalty?

During the previous decade, the Indian political class had been split between loyalty to the emergent Indian nation, which dictated desperate and hopeless means, or loyalty to present British rulers, which dictated hopeless but acceptable means. Now, however, all agreed after the war on the imperative of realizing Indian self-government in the near future. Implicitly, the range of strategies was constricted and the right of the British to remain in India was conceded as long as they cooperated in transferring power to their successors. Honoring the British claim to loyal obedience was then conditional on the extent to which the British themselves honored their own declaration of 1917.

If that claim were honored, one test would be their willingness to let Indians define political crimes for themselves and decide on the means to cope with them. The Government of India failed to do this when they imposed the Rowlatt Act, passed in round-the-clock sessions over the persistent objections of Indian members of the Legislative Council in 1919. *The Stateman's* reaction indicates that spokesmen for the colonial class utterly failed to understand why Indians ought to object to that legislation; its editor repeatedly called the Indian opposition in the Imperial Legislative Council "ridiculous" and "unreasonable." Furthermore, Indian opposition was offered as evidence of their inability to govern themselves, as in *The Statesman's* following "demonstration":

> The behavior of the whole elected element in the Imperial Legislative Council in regard to the ROWLATT BILL. . . proves to demonstration that no reliance can be placed on the amenability to reason and necessity of Indians of the political class. . . . The SECRETARY OF STATE will be guilty of grave and deliberate injustice to those destined in the future to occupy the position of Viceroy or Governor in this country if he persists with his proposals as they stand at present.[22]

The Statesman's editorials of April 1919 persisted in holding the moderates responsible for the subsequent rioting because they failed to support the Government of India uncritically, which was asserted to be the duty of loyal citizens.

Gandhi, however, responded to other criteria of loyalty—the obligations of a midwife to the unborn Indian nation. Because satyagraha is based on a moral claim, the Rowlatt Act was an ideal target since it was a national issue transcending class, caste, language, and region. Undeniably, it was an opportune rallying ground for Gandhi to launch his first nationwide campaign: his opponents regarded it as opportunistic and incendiary.

PROTEST, DISORDER, AND RIOT

Gandhi had attempted to plead with the viceroy to withdraw the Rowlatt Bills to no avail; after it was clear that all Indian opposition was to be disregarded, he conceived of the way to involve masses nationwide in hartal before civil disobedience was initiated by selected volunteers. To begin with, he had been perplexed about how to violate the law, since it could not be breached automatically. He concluded that he would sell a book without an official press stamp. The masses, in his vision, were to play the Greek chorus, imparting ritual value to the events and shifting the focus to the Indians as a collectivity, rather than the British:

> The idea came to me last night in a dream that we should call upon the country to observe a general *hartal*. Satyagraha is a process of self-purification, and ours is a sacred fight, and it seems to me to be in the fitness of things that it should be commenced with an act of self-purification. Let all the people of India, therefore, suspend their business on that day and observe the day as one of fasting and prayer.[23]

On 24 February 1919, Gandhi began circulating his civil disobedience oath pledging signers to break laws selected by his newly formed committee, the Satyagraha Sabha, which would set limits and impose nonviolent discipline. The Sabha, formed in Bombay, was principally made up of members of Tilak's Home Rule League. However, Gandhi's call for hartal on 6 April (mistaken by some followers for 30 March) was publicized chiefly by the native press and mobilized by local branches of Congress, the Home Rule League, local organizations, and local leaders personally committed to Gandhi rather than the ill-coordinated Sabhas.

Gandhi's success in activating communities depended largely on his links with local leadership: where leadership was lacking or leaders were afraid of losing control over their followers, cooperation was lacking. Annie Besant feared civil disobedience and disassociated herself from the campaign early, as did many associates in Madras, but new supporters mobilized the masses in Madras.[24] Others, loyal to Tilak, did not mobilize their followers because they suspected that enhancing Gandhi's following would diminish Tilak's influence.[25] In Bombay, hartal was only partial: the police intervened to limit efforts of workers to dissuade others from working. A successful hartal was reported in Madras culminating in a "monster rally" at which the crowd was "very orderly." Annie Besant's influence there was evidently limited when she ceased resonating popular sentiment.

Disorders were the exception, rather than the rule. The fact that the concern of the Hunter Committee was the disorders arising in Delhi, Ahmedabad, Viramgam, and the Punjab has distorted judgment.

Hartals were observed in Bihar, Orissa, Madras, the Central Provinces, and Burma with no incidents of disorder reported. The Hunter Committee investigated disorders in three cities in Delhi and Bombay Presidencies out of more than fifty cities and towns outside the Punjab in which hartals were held. The committee estimated that at least one-third of all the hartals held in India protesting the Rowlatt Act on 30 March or 6 April 1919 were held in the Punjab. In the Punjab they investigated disorders occurring in three cities and towns out of the twenty-four in which hartals had been held in districts subsequently placed under martial law.

Hartals may be classified as to whether the observance—abstention from normal work activities—was complete or partial and whether such abstention was voluntary or enforced by threats of injury to noncooperating vendors. If a hartal was both complete and voluntary and only isolated threats were reported in a city, it may be regarded as a successful nonviolent hartal. Except where noted, the following evidence has been culled from the Hunter Report, which was used by the Punjab Subcommittee as documentation of these events.

What caused confrontations? Several patterns emerge. The first, illustrated by Delhi, was to become common in the civil disobedience campaign of 1931: the crowd attempts to coerce obedience to a hartal and the police compel conformity by dispersing the crowd, which provokes rock throwing and other attacks on the police, impelling them finally to fire.

The Hunter Committee reports that on 30 March 1919, crowds roamed the streets of Delhi attempting to persuade passengers of carriages to dismount and drivers to cease their daily business.

Disorders in the railway station followed the police response to the crowd's attempt to persuade the refreshment vendors at the station to close shop. One vendor refused because his contractual arrangement with the railways did not permit such a work stoppage. After two persons were arrested for assaulting the vendor, the crowds milling in the station expanded and confronted the police, pelting them with bricks and stones. This pattern was repeated later during the day, at which time the police, reinforced by infantry, opened fire. Eight men were killed. The limitation of firepower for defense despite two or three hours of confrontation between police and the crowd is illustrated by the following contemporary newspaper description of the last incident:

> The crowd maintained its threatening attitude in the Chandi Chowk and the Superintendant of Police on riding up, after hearing a couple of shots from the direction of the Town Hall, found about 15 British infantry and 15 policemen being heavily stoned. The mob surged over the railing into the Queen's Garden. It appeared inevitable that some of the police and infantry would soon be seriously injured and as the attacks of the mob continued, the order to fire on them was given. Two or three rounds per man were fired and three men were seen to fall, but others were probably hit. This ended the trouble and the rioters dispersed. . . . Though an armored car was sent from the Fort, the machine-gun in it was not fired.[26]

Gandhi denied the allegations against the crowds and accused the local government of overreacting even if the allegations were true, but he issued "a note of warning to all Satyagrahis" that such conduct was inconsistent with their pledge.

Hartal was continued and later repeated after the arrest of Gandhi on 10 April—only to be broken up by the police in a similar confrontation apparently provoked by them when on 17 April they sent, the Hunter Report tells us, "a number of police pickets down the street to inspire confidence in people who wanted to open their shops." This led to counteraction by "some of the more unruly members of the Delhi mob," which ultimately led the police to fire in self-defense, wounding about 18 people with buckshot, two of whom subsequently died.

The other pattern, that of an aggressive response to the detention of leadership, is most evident in the cities investigated in Bombay Presidency. Ahmedabad, Viramgam, and Nadiad are noted as large mill cities containing a high proportion of mill workers. Ahmedabad is of particular interest historically because Gandhi had organized a satyagraha there in 1917 to settle a wage dispute; the settlement made him a powerful force in that region and led to the founding of a nonviolent association to mediate labor disputes. This, too, was the site of his ashram or training center.

Ahmedabad had observed a successful nonviolent hartal on 6 April. On 9 April the Government of India decided to keep Gandhi from entering the Punjab to speak, fearing that riots would occur if they were forced to arrest him for committing civil disobedience symbolically. Because Gandhi would not assent to be barred from the Punjab, they arrested him to prevent his boarding a train to go there. News of his arrest swept Ahmedabad along with a rumor that Anasuya Sarabhai, a famed local disciple of Gandhi, had also been arrested.

Mills and shops closed down immediately on receipt of the news on 9 April. Crowds armed with lathis (iron-bound bamboo sticks) filled the streets, refusing to heed the orders of civil officials and sometimes jostling them. These milling crowds set fire to government buildings and banks, pelted the police with rocks, and pressed them into corners. The regular police were reinforced by 200 soldiers the first day and an additional 200 the next day, but they were at all times on the defensive. When crowds were temporarily dispersed or a section of the city was secured, they regrouped elsewhere. Generally, the military fired in self-defense only and inflicted few casualties. Despite the doubling of their force and the imposition of a martial law regulation authorizing them to fire on any gathering of over ten persons, order was never restored in Ahmedabad by the military. It took the return of Gandhi on 13 April, who according to the Hunter Report "upbraided them for their violence and exhorted them to resume their lawful occupation." Simultaneously, concessions were made to the nonviolent leadership by removing all restrictions imposed during the disorders.

Relative to the duration of crowd violence in Ahmedabad, far fewer lives were lost there than in Amritsar. Two British policemen and twenty-eight Indians were killed in Ahmedabad in three days as compared to at least twenty-three Indians and five British, including four civilians, in three hours in Amritsar on 10 April.

Viramgam was similar to Ahmedabad except that it had not held an organized hartal before Gandhi's arrest. The mill hands struck peacefully on 11 April but on 12 April they gathered to meet the train from Ahmedabad. They beat up the railway inspector and an Indian court officer and then set fire to the station, the rail siding cars, and the courthouse. At neighboring Nadiad, where the mill hands had been mobilized for the earlier hartal, no violence was reported—"perhaps owing to the teaching of one of Mr. Gandhi's followers, who came from Ahmedabad on the 11th April and exhorted the people to remain quiet" [HC:17].

Paradoxically, the charismatic attachment of the workers to Gandhi in Ahmedabad made secondary leadership there less effective. Gandhi's followers, the Satyagrahi, were actively involved in Ahmedabad in attempting to restrain the crowd so that the troops would not be forced to fire in self-defense, but little success is reported in that role. Peace was reached in Ahmedabad in effect by a negotiated truce and recognition of Gandhi's leadership as being indispensable: amnesty was conceded to all except those accused of murder.

If we were to rank the intensity of violence by the range of targets and the aggressiveness of the crowds, Ahmedabad would be ranked higher than Delhi. However, in neither case was there evidence to suggest that the expressed rage was anti-British or antiwhite (as distinct from antigovernment), as it was in Amritsar. One cannot account for the riot of 10 April in Amritsar, and the disproportionate number of protests in the Punjab, without considering how local grievances intensified the readiness of Punjabis to protest.

Protest in the Punjab

The Punjab, annexed by Great Britain in 1857, has been traditionally an area favored by English writers as representing the "real" India, as contrasted to the provinces which were corrupted by western education and the oppressive conditions of urban life in India. The Punjab is a center of Sikh worship; their holiest edifice, the Golden Temple, is in Amritsar. The Sikhs in 1919 were estimated to constitute 11 percent of the population of the Punjab, compared to 33 percent Hindu and 56 percent Muslim. The Sikhs, like the Muslims, had waged war against the

British during the previous century. Now they were considered among the most loyal of religious groups and counted among the martial groups and tribes contributing disproportionately to the Indian army during World War I. When returning Sikh emigrants were suspected of carrying the ideas of the Ghadr Party to the Punjab, the lieutenant governor, Sir Michael O'Dwyer, contained the influence of what seemed to him potentially infectious carriers of disloyalty by appointing local Sikh committees to supervise them, attesting to his belief in their loyalty. It is notable that in the disorder reports there is scarcely any mention of Sikh involvement in the protest movement against the Rowlatt Act, although frequent mention is made of Hindu and Muslim participation.

The following list indicates the size of cities, towns, and villages in the Punjab which were involved in disturbances in April 1919:

1. Cities: Amritsar (160,000) and Lahore (250,000)
2. Towns: Gujranwala (30,000), Gujrat (10,000–20,000), Kasur (24,000), Lyallpur (15,000), Wazirabad (10,000–15,000)
3. Villages (all under 10,000): Akalgarh, Chuhar Kara, Gojra, Hafizabad, Jalalpur, Jattan, Malawakal, Manianwala, Moman, Nawan Pind, Nizambad, Patti and Kem Karn, Ramnagar, Sangla Hill, Sheikupura, Tarn-Tarn

The Indian National Congress, in its report on the Punjab, later charged Sir Michael O'Dwyer with responsibility for provoking riots. Sir Sankaran Nair, a backer of the Government of India after Jallianwala Bagh, also held O'Dwyer responsible for the terrorism in the Punjab by virtue of his activities to stimulate recruiting during World War I. The latter charges were the basis of a libel suit against Sankaran Nair by O'Dwyer in 1924; an all-British jury found Sankaran Nair guilty. Official reports cited by the Indian National Congress Punjab Subcommittee (headed by Gandhi) show how O'Dwyer employed both incentives and systematic threats to raise the war loan and increase recruiting. The Punjab produced a higher ratio of recruits to population than any other province of India. By his own report, O'Dwyer had raised the quota enlisted from 1 man out of 150 in 1917 to 1 in 44 (or 1 out of every 14 of military age) in 1918 from Gujranwala.[27] Witnesses at the O'Dwyer-Nair trial testified that local officials resorted to torture, arbitrary arrest, and humiliation to obtain recruits. The jury evidently believed O'Dwyer's denial of knowledge and responsibility; but the Hunter Committee's testimony (vol. 6), which Datta has analyzed, presents some contradictory evidence, as do Home Department files.[28]

In 1919 O'Dwyer claimed that his intent was not to provoke but to prevent disorder, and the best means seemed to him to prevent any protest which might stimulate such disorder. He announced at a meeting of the Punjab Legislative Council on 7 April that

> the Government of this province is, and will remain, determined that the public order which was maintained so successfully during time of war shall not be disturbed during time of peace. . . . The British Government which has crushed foreign foes and quelled internal rebellion could afford to despise these agitators, but it has the duty of protecting the young and innocent whom they may incite to mischief and crime while themselves are standing aside.[29]

Local officials in the Punjab tried to inhibit protest quite directly. The District Report cites a number of instances where local officials forestalled hartals during April by calling in local leaders and warning them not to execute their alleged plans. They also were able to elicit statements against hartals from highly placed people in some towns.

In Amritsar the confrontation arose as a consequence of British response to crowds generated by the interning of Dr. Kitchlew and Dr. Satyapal, satyagraha leaders, on the morning of 10 April. The milling crowd, initially seeking news of their leaders and the opportunity to petition the district superintendent, was turned back from the bridges by pickets stationed there. Unable to maintain their position and pelted by stones, the pickets opened fire, killing twenty to thirty Indians. The mob then surged through the city, killing five Britishers and firing and looting banks and public buildings.

News of the first shooting quickly spread along the railway line of which Amritsar is the hub, inspiring more hartals and protest meetings, the killing of two Europeans at Kasur, and, frequently, sabotage of rail and telegraph lines. These events justified to the government the imposition of martial law on 15 April 1919. At this point it is worth noting how the type of pro-

test or disorder relates to previous organization of hartals and
police intervention after 10 April in the affected districts of the
Punjab.

In cities where the first hartal was organized before 10 April
1919, the following events were reported:

1. No crowd violence was reported in nine towns in Gur-
daspur District, in Moltan City, in seven towns in Jullundar District, in Lyallpur, Akalgarh, Ramnagar, and Sheikupura. That
is, there was no injury or attack issuing from crowds demonstrating: damage to railway or telegraph lines was reported in some
of these towns and villages but either the perpetrators were un-
known or not reliably identified or the damage was done by individuals or small self-selected groups.

2. Crowd violence without prior police intervention was reported only in Gujranwala (property damage).

3. Crowd violence after police intervention was reported in
Lahore (rock throwing) and Amritsar (killing).

If, however, the first hartal was organized after 10 April 1919,
we note the following:

1. Only Jalalpur and Jattan were without crowd violence.

2. Crowd violence without prior police intervention was reported in Nawan Pind, Gujrat, Sangla Hill, and Moman (property damage in all); in Gojra (attacks on Indian vendors); and in
Kasur (killing).

3. Crowd violence after police intervention was reported in
Wazirabad and Nizambad (rock throwing in both).

These data clearly show that after the shooting at Amritsar on
10 April there was less likelihood of aggressive crowd violence in
cities and towns where protests had been previously organized
for the anti-Rowlatt Bill campaign. Successful hartals without
later disorders were also reported in one or more towns in
another dozen districts in the Punjab. This implies that the
violence which erupted was not provoked by the nonviolent campaign against the Rowlatt Act—regardless of whether or not the
uneducated understood the meaning of that legislation—but was
an example of reactive rage to the detention of the leaders and
the shootings. The more "incendiary" pamphlets reprinted by
the Hunter Report have few references to the Rowlatt Act but do

reveal a passionate feeling of injustice and resentment against the indignities to which Indian people were believed to be subjected.

Nor is the possible relationship between the civil disobedience oath and the defiance of police authority relevant to the Punjab. Only 1,000 people had signed the oath throughout India by mid-March, 800 of whom were from Kaira and Bombay.[30] Furthermore, there is no evidence to suggest that the crowds throwing stones at the police were familiar with the oath.

The example of Lahore (population 250,000) is especially instructive as an exhibit of how the nonviolent organization of protest immunizes a community against spontaneous mass violence. Despite numerous police-crowd confrontations, the presence of many schools and colleges in Lahore, and the "incendiary" speeches reported by police agents, hartal was sustained by the people continuously from 10 to 17 April with no violence reported except for the stoning of the cavalry and the beating up of an Indian police agent caught in a public meeting. Hostility toward the government was expressed by people throwing filth into the streets when it was rumored that Lieutenant Governor O'Dwyer was to pass through Lahore. Pictures of the king and queen were reported to have been defaced or destroyed.

Even assuming there had been no physical injuries or attacks on persons at all, the spirit expressed in the foregoing acts is not consistent with Gandhi's concept of nonviolence. There is no reason to believe that Gandhi's message was understood by all the people who revered him at this time. One example of such misunderstanding is a poster reported to have been found in Lahore. It called on "Hindu, Muhammadan and Sikh brethren [to] enlist at once in the *Danda* Army, and fight with bravery against the English monkeys. . . . Fight on. . . . This is the command of Mahatma Gandhi" [HC:109].

The Role of the Police

Amritsar and Kasur, the two communities where deliberate and successful murderous attacks on British civilians occurred, also demonstrated the failure of the local Indian police to attempt to control the crowds. The police in Amritsar, when they were under Indian command, spent most of the afternoon hiding: those who fired at the crowd at the bridge were then commanded by British officials. Likewise, District Reports note that after the deputy superintendent of police left the station in Kasur, his men did nothing until his return. By contrast, the police in Lahore appear to have been active at all times.

This cannot be taken to imply that if the Indian police had performed their duties in Amritsar, there would have been no injuries. In Ahmedabad, armed Indian police were effectively trapped by a mob at one point, only to be rescued by the troops. The unarmed constables were simply stripped of their uniforms. Police fear of mob vengeance against them was realistic: in Viramgam, the Indian official who ordered the police to fire was pursued, murdered, and immolated by the mob that same day.

Who Riots?

Who riots? Answers to this question are difficult; however, both the Congress Report and the District Report tell us that those who organized the protest were not the ones who rioted. Lawyers were usually the largest single group among Congress organizers, while traders and merchants also were prominent. The rioters are often labeled "rabble" or "hooligans." Similarly, Datta refers to those who participated in the crimes of 10 April 1919 in Amritsar as "riff-raff . . . of low order."[31] The District Reports maintain these were urban rioters, although peasants visiting Amritsar might have indulged in looting. However, although Kasur was noted for "a very unruly element of the menial, leather-worker and butcher class" among the crowds [DC:20], Mark Naidis reports that of those convicted in Kasur and Lahore by the martial law commissions, nearly 70 percent were between twenty and thirty years old and over 50 percent of all convicted were literate.[32]

CONCLUSION

The Rowlatt Bills were correctly interpreted by the Indian educated or political class as a denial by the British bureaucracy of the Indian desire to decriminalize politics and, implicitly, of their capacity to govern themselves. The government's persistence in pushing the Act through despite the unanimity of Indian objections signaled their distrust of Indians and the Indians' objections signified to officials their disloyalty.

Gandhi's trust in the British was the ground that made him

seize upon the Rowlatt Act as a moral issue, and his sensitivity to opportunities for political mobilization brought him to realize that it could be a mass and national issue as well. What seemed to him opportune seemed to his opponents opportunistic. His very trust inhibited him from recognizing that the government would feel compelled to take countermeasures to prevent the confrontations and the loss of their authority that might occur if he were to be allowed to commit civil disobedience publicly. He did not realize that the Government of India's restraint and sometimes aid to protesters in previous satyagrahas was no precedent because protests in the provinces had never challenged the central government or apex of authority.

Despite this, the anti-Rowlatt Bill campaign was wholly successful in its instrumental aim: although the Rowlatt Act was not repealed, it was never enforced. It was largely successful in actualizing the commitment to nonviolence, but its failures demonstrate the contingencies on which the prevention of violence depend.

By relying on previous conventional wisdom that the way to avert crowd violence is to remove the "agitators" inspiring the crowd, the Government of India in fact made rioting more likely. Ralf Dahrendorf proposes that the better organized the parties to a conflict are, the less likely violence is.[33] Removing the leadership disorganizes one party and increases the likelihood of violent confrontation, since leadership can both inhibit and anticipate violence as well as form ties of mutual interest with the opposing class's leadership that crowds, lacking an executive center of control, cannot. The experience in the 1919 campaign confirms this. The maintenance of nonviolent discipline in a crowd depends on the administrative response and on the organization of the crowd. Both toleration of free speech and firm police control are needed. When the first-string leadership is removed, unless there is committed and recognized secondary leadership a more anarchic response becomes likely.

The Hunter Committee's testimony on the disorders revealed the perils of relying on firepower when there is a great disparity of numbers between police and subjects. Firing on crowds in such a circumstance is either ineffectual or likely to kill many, as in Amritsar. A violent police response—as in Amritsar—is likely to provoke mob violence in response. Such deaths are seen as a violation against the whole collectivity or nation, justifying reprisals. Only later did the British governing class understand their paradoxical dependence on Gandhi to restrain the movements he organized.

Mass demonstrations do provide opportunities for officials eager to repress a movement to incite crowd violence in order to justify terror, just as they provide opportunities for demonstrators to provoke police violence by violating laws or administrative limits to demonstrate how violent the authorities can be. There is, however, no evidence that the crowd violence issuing from the joining of Gandhi's and the Government of India's strategy in 1919 was anticipated or sought by either.

Lieutenant Governor O'Dwyer's responsibility for provoking the riot in Amritsar by exiling the leaders was a consequence of his belief in the imperial axiom that early repression is the best mode of preventing disorder. That ideology did not admit the likelihood or legitimacy of conflict between the governing class and the subjects—all opposition was shallow or spurious, conjured up by "agitators" who preyed on the ignorant masses. Contrary to his conclusion that the nonviolent movement was responsible for the disorders, examination of the distribution and type of disorders reported after 10 April in the Punjab shows that crowd violence was less likely where nonviolent protest had been organized before 10 April 1919. By trying to eliminate conflict, O'Dwyer inflamed the masses he thought he was protecting from agitation.

CHAPTER 5
Assessing the Hypothesis

In Chapter 1, Durkheim's theory on the function of crime and punishment was used to develop a theory of crime and punishment which illuminates our observations on the course of Indian political history between 1857 and the massacre at Jallianwala Bagh on 13 April 1919.

This chapter explains how the critical propositions asserted there were tested. These are the following:

1. If persons are not defined within the universe of obligation, then offenses against them are not violations of the common conscience (proposition 8).

2. Offenses against persons outside the universe of obligation will not be socially recognized and labeled as crime (proposition 13).

3. Assuming judges to be representative of their class of origin, the ability of judges to identify with the victim of an offense depends on the victim's inclusion within the judge's universe of obligation (proposition 14). Since the judges in an imperial order are from the governing class, if the victims are of the subject class and the perpetrators of crimes against them are of the

governing class, the judges are more likely to identify with the perpetrators than with the victims. If the perpetrators are of the subject class and the victims of the governing class, the judges are more likely to identify with the victims.

Each proposition specifies then a stage or locus of judgment. Proposition 8 explains how people evaluating offenses referring to the common conscience as a standard recognize violations. Proposition 13 predicts how offenses will be accounted for within an organization or by a society: if not accounted for as crime, they will be either accounted for in some other way or not recognized. Proposition 14 explains the different judgments of crimes by the governing class and crimes against the governing class. This is illustrated by the Government of India's response to the events of 10 April and 13 April 1919. The accounting for the Jallianwala Bagh massacre by the governing class (proposition 13) is demonstrated by examining the Government of India's own accounting for the disorders and its recommendations. The validity of proposition 8 is tested by comparing judgments of members of the British Parliament during the Dyer debate of 1920, showing that those members who defined Indians within the universe of obligation were more likely to condemn Dyer than those who did not.

Both the riot at Amritsar on 10 April that killed five Britishers and the shooting at Jallianwala Bagh on 13 April that killed 379 Indians by official count were instances of collective violence that could have been labeled and sanctioned as crimes. Of the 298 Indians accused of participation in the Amritsar disorders, 218 were convicted and 51 initially sentenced to death [DC:8]. But the killing of 379 Indians was charged to law and order. Initially it was approved by General Dyer's superior and the lieutenant governor of the Punjab. Eleven months later, after the Hunter Committee's investigation and upon its recommendation, Dyer was removed from employment by the commander in chief of the Indian Army. Critics later charged that the Government of India had condoned Dyer's action by not submitting the charge to a court-martial and thus had absolved him of responsibility. It was clearly a noncriminal sanction, and the lightest one that could have been taken against him, as the secretary of state for war, Winston Churchill, told the House of Commons in July 1920.

How was it that the massacre was approved and, even when subjected to the scrutiny of the Hunter Committee, not labeled a crime when it could be clearly demonstrated that it violated all regulations regarding firing on civilian populations, regulations known to Britishers as the minimum-force principle? Later this principle and historic precedents guiding officers will be specified in the discussion of the Hunter Committee's criteria. To show that the shooting was not categorized as crime, we shall examine the social accounting of the massacre and similar acts of terror during martial law from the time they were committed until the parliamentary debate on the Dyer case in July 1920.

On 19 September 1919, the Legislative Council of the Government of India passed a Bill of Indemnity exonerating all officers from claims for actions taken under martial law in the Punjab; moreover, it held a preliminary inquiry regarding General Dyer's case, in which he was defended by the adjutant general, Sir Havelock Hudson. A month later, the council appointed an investigatory committee headed by Lord Hunter, a Scottish jurist. That committee was composed of five Englishmen, including its chairman, and four Indians—all had served the empire in an official capacity. The Indian National Congress's own investigating committee of four lawyers, headed by Gandhi, later undertook an independent investigation when the Hunter Committee refused to release Indian witnesses from prison so that they might be heard.

Lord Hunter's committee produced the "Report of the Committee Appointed by the Government of India to Investigate the Disturbances in the Punjab," hereafter referred to as the Hunter Report (Cmd. 681); the government of the Punjab submitted "District Accounts Submitted by the Government of the Punjab," hereafter referred to as the District Report (Cmd. 534); and the Indian National Congress's Punjab Subcommittee produced the Congress Report. These reports established official definitions of the situation for different political audiences.

In Chapter 6 these reports are systematically compared to demonstrate how the social interpretation of violence is related to the political class of the investigators. The ideologies behind these reports are inferred in terms of defenses of the past order and intentions toward the future order of class relations in India. The ideological functions of strategies of evaluation in these reports emerge in response to the following problems:

1. What facts are admitted in delineating the scope of the report? That depends on the purview of the report dictated by the organization authorizing it, the selection of witness, and rules of evidence.

2. How is the situation defined? How are similar acts by actors from different classes classified? What assumptions are taken for granted regarding the motives of representatives of the governing class and the subject class by the report writers?

3. What normative criteria are deemed relevant to evaluate the situation? These include laws, organizational rules, precedents, and values. Values are revealed by statements of goals, states to be avoided, assertions of preference, and axiomatic presuppositions.

4. How are characteristic modes of reasoning and nonrational defenses used to integrate or segregate "facts" and values?

5. How does the agenda of future relationships between the parties influence the committee's report? How is guilt assigned or distributed? What claims are demanded from the other party? What vouchers of good faith are offered to be redeemed by one's own party? What sanctions would affirm that such claims or vouchers have been accepted?

Evaluation split the Hunter Committee along the national axis. While there was consensus (concurred in by the Congress Report) on the detailed events of April 1919, there was disagreement, if not dissensus, as to what they meant and what ought to be done. The majority concluded that General Dyer had a "mistaken conception of his duty" and exonerated all other accused officers; the minority condemned Dyer's actions categorically as "un-British," as it did the other officers' acts. The Indian National Congress demanded removal of all the officers guilty of collective punishment (See Chapter 6) as well as Sir Michael O'Dwyer, the retired lieutenant governor of the Punjab, whom they held responsible for the repressive policy before and during martial law.

After General Dyer was removed from office, he requested the Army Council to review the subsequent demand by his commander in chief for his resignation. The secretary of state for war, Winston Churchill, acting on behalf of the Cabinet, wanted the Army Council to confirm the government's decision, but the council insisted upon granting Dyer, now represented by counsel, a hearing. They concluded by concurring with the government's action and removing him from command.

The Dyer debate in Parliament in July 1920 was initiated by separate motions in each House. Commons rejected the motion to cut the salary of the secretary of state for India—a symbolic renunciation of government policy. But the Lords passed Viscount Finlay's motion—"that this House deplores the conduct of the case of General Dyer as unjust to that officer, and as establishing a precedent dangerous to the preservation of order in face of rebellion."

The debate in Commons was in fact initiated by two resolutions to cut the salary of the secretary of state for India; these motions were substantively identical but opposed in intent. The first motion was offered by representatives of the Labour Party to voice objections to the government for not having made adequate restitution to the Indian people by simply dismissing Dyer. The second motion was put forth by conservative opponents of the Cabinet who wanted to repudiate the sanction against Dyer. Separate votes were taken on each motion; left-wing critics who voted against the government on the first motion (yes on Div. 195) usually voted no on the second (Div. 196), backing the government against an attack from the right. All comparisons in this book are based on the vote on the second motion (Div. 196), which corresponds in political significance to the Lords' motion.

The debate on the government's sanction against Dyer in Parliament enables one to test proposition 8 (from Chapter 1) directly: If persons are not defined within the universe of obligation, then offenses against them are not violations of the common conscience.

Insofar as the votes were consistent with the intent of the makers of the motions in both Houses, this was a test case: those who condoned Dyer's action should vote to sanction the government; those who condemned Dyer's action should vote against sanctioning the government. However, only the speakers on the motion have left us a record of their motives, values, and rationales. If proposition 8 is correct, speakers defining Indians within the universe of moral obligation voted against the motion condemning the sanction against Dyer and those not defining them in that universe voted for the motion. Conversely, speakers voting against the motion should be more likely to exhibit signs of moral inclusiveness than those voting for the motion. (The converse has been stated probabilistically because not all speakers made explicit their assumptions regarding moral obligations.)

In an attempt to disprove the hypothesis, an alternative explanation for the speakers' willingness to approve or tolerate collective violence was explored and its implications tested.

A COUNTERHYPOTHESIS

Collective violence is a response to perceived threat to significant values; the most significant value in a hierarchical power structure is the retention of authority. The magnitude of violence depends on the means at the disposal of the threatened class and the extent of threat perceived. If legal sanctions are unavailable or regarded as inadequate, violence will be legitimated as a collective act of self-defense.

If readiness to condone violence is related to the perception of threat, one would expect that speakers who believed that British rule was seriously threatened were more willing to tolerate the massacre than speakers who did not. This leads to two hypotheses:

1. Speakers appraising events in Amritsar before the massacre as evidence of rebellion, conspiracy, or international revolution are more likely to assert that Dyer is innocent, or that his guilt is impossible to assess, or that he committed an error at worst, and vote for the motion than those believing what took place in Amritsar was a riot in response to British repression.

2. The speakers' evaluation of the minimum-force rule depends on their political definition of the situation. Those affirming that the situation was a rebellion, conspiracy, or revolution are more likely to postulate a counterrule or loose interpretation

of the rule or else acknowledge it with indifference, converting it into a normative alternative.

DEBATE ANALYSIS

The debates consist of the testimony of thirty-three speakers in both Houses, thirty-one of whom have votes recorded on the motion. To establish the plausibility of the key hypothesis, speakers voting for the motion to repudiate the government policy (in Lords, Lord Finlay's motion; in Commons, Div. 196) are compared to those voting against.

Two types of content analysis were devised to test the hypotheses. First, all speeches, themes, and assertions were evaluated by coding them on an original schedule which incorporated specific options to test both hypotheses. Second, the formal logic of all arguments on both sides was analyzed, starting with the assumptions of the speakers. Thus the reader can judge for herself or himself what each method yields and can assess whether quantification and search for specific themes yields useful knowledge or lends reliability to the logical analysis. Both analyses are quantitative and each depends on the other, since they were undertaken simultaneously.

Each speech was coded for the presence or absence of significant factual assertions, axioms related to assessment of values (universalism, justice, trust, authority), as well as appraisal of the minimum-force rule and judgment on the correctness of General Dyer's shooting and the fairness of the sanction. (See Appendix A for the original coding schedule.)

Reliability was established by independent coding of five randomly selected speeches in each House. Items on which the intercoder agreement was less than .8 were discarded from further analysis. Appendix A describes some of the difficulties encountered and possible reasons for lack of agreement on certain items and classes of items.

To do a systematic analysis of every argument concluding with a judgment on General Dyer and/or support or opposition to the motion, all rhetorical assertions and implicit propositions were converted to the best-fitting logical form in order to lead (without error) to their conclusions. Finally, all arguments of each camp were aggregated to establish "trees of judgment" illustrating how the axioms terminating in condonation of Dyer by proponents of the motion differ from the axioms leading to his condemnation by opponents of the motion.

HYPOTHETICAL EXPECTATIONS

First, the assumption behind comparison of both groups—that the vote on the motions was a direct function of tolerance for the firing at Jallianwala Bagh—was tested. It was expected and shown that the speaker's vote on the motion was positively related to his judgment of the gravity of General Dyer's offence.

Second, the key hypothesis was tested. If correct, speakers defining Indians within an inclusive universe of moral obligation should vote against the motion: those not defining the universe of obligation inclusively should not vote against the motion but for it. One would expect speakers voting for the motion to negate the sanction to be more likely characterized by moral exclusiveness and speakers voting against the motion to be more characterized by inclusiveness. (Item IV.I. on the Code Sheet in Appendix A taps exclusive and inclusive assumptions.) One of the speakers' options showing inclusiveness was to deny that European or white lives are more valuable than those of Asiatics or nonwhites; another was to assert that justice demands the same rule be applied to nonwhites as to whites.

Sentiment is tapped by identification and empathy indexes. The identification index is the relative number of positive references to Indians as an audience or constituency of the speakers which ought to be taken into account minus the negative references. The empathy index consists of the number of the following citations of Indian victimization which are mentioned by the speaker: the Crawling Order made dwellers on that street crawl; the shooting killed 379 Indians; the crowd was innocent or helpless. An inverse of the empathy index was produced by counting the denials of the first two facts and third judgment.

If moral inclusiveness is a function of the ability to take the role of the other and empathize with people who are unlike one in some significant respect, positive scores on these measures ought to be related to a vote against the motion, and negative scores to a positive vote for the motion.

Other relations of theoretical interest stem from the model of a two-class order based on ethnic stratification. If legitimacy is a function of solidarity, illegitimacy results from lack of solidarity. If the end of retaining India is taken to be a given, a state of illegitimacy perceived by the subject class strategically demands that the governing class use coercion more extensively than would be required in a political relationship conceded to be legitimate by the subject class. How conscious are members of the governing class of these implications? Are speakers who take retention of authority as an end and also recognize little solidarity between British and Indian more ready to use force? Do they recognize that the empire depends on the use of force? Is there a discernible set of propositions integrating axioms, ends, judgments on the rule, and specific judgments on Dyer and the motion? Does another set unite critics of the motion? How do these sets correspond to political ideologies of imperial rule?

Such hypothetical chains of axioms, ends, and judgments are illustrated in Figures 1 and 2. The dashes indicate the linkage predicted from the original hypothesis and the arrows indicate other expectations; these are also consistent with the counter hypothesis.

Insofar as values avowed or values to be avoided are not logically related to the speaker's conclusions regarding either the guilt of General Dyer or government sanctions, one may expect that defense mechanisms come into play. Such mechanisms include denial, projection, and displacement. Denial is indicated by rejecting the factuality of significant findings established by the Hunter Committee. Projection is revealed when the speaker reverses the role of the actors at Jallianwala Bagh in his argument, casting General Dyer as innocent and the crowd as guilty. Displacement is exhibited by the diversion of argument toward the government's responsibility or the secretary of state for India's motives rather than arguing substantively on the justification of the shooting. Unfortunately, not all these mechanisms could be tested, either because of the unreliability of items on the schedule or because too few speakers made allegations on the subject.

Results of the logical analysis, starting with the speakers' assumptions, are presented in Chapter 7; results of the content analysis are presented in Chapter 8.

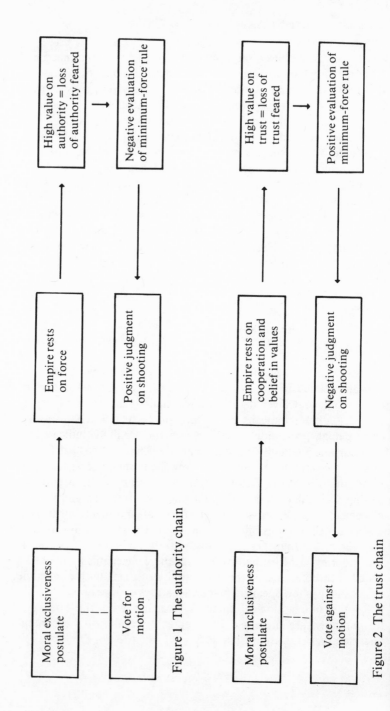

Figure 1 The authority chain

Figure 2 The trust chain

CHAPTER 6
The Public Accounting

Gen. Dyer explained . . . "The wounded only had to apply for help. . . . I was ready to help them if they applied."

—Hunter Report

The news of General Dyer's action on 13 April 1919 was promptly conveyed to his military superior, General Beynon, and to the lieutenant governor of the Punjab, Sir Michael O'Dwyer, by April 15. Dyer's action was approved by General Beynon and later by Lieutenant Governor O'Dwyer, from whom Beynon requested the approval Dyer sought. O'Dwyer sent an abbreviated message to the viceroy at Delhi, and this message was wired verbatim to London immediately. The India Office (London) then changed the wording slightly and announced to the public on 18 April 1919 that "at Amritsar April 13th the mob defied the proclamation forbidding public meetings. Fire ensued and 200 casualties occurred."[1]

During the latter part of April 1919, General Dyer traveled to Sikh villages in the Punjab with some officers in order to conciliate their leaders and allay hostility stemming from rumors. Stories had been circulated earlier that month that the Golden Temple had been bombarded and that Sikh women were searched at the Amritsar railway station. These rumors provoked Sikh participation in the disorders of April 1919. Dyer's mission

was apparently successful. He was honored with the sacred symbols of the Sikh community at the Golden Temple.[2] Khushwant
Singh says this led to a schism among the Sikhs, marked by formation of a new group opposed to the pro-British priestly elite.[3]

General Dyer served in May 1919 as head of a special Sikh
brigade, which he had recruited, in the Afghan War and was
commended in June 1919 by the commander in chief for his per-
formance. After returning to his original brigade, he was given
command of the 5th Brigade, which his biographer Ian Colvin
says "suggested to him that he enjoyed the confidence as well as
the gratitude of the commander-in-chief."[4] Dyer submitted his
first written report since his initial one on the shooting in Amritsar in response to a request by the commander in chief on 25
August 1919.

OPENING THE ACCOUNT AT THE TOP

Meanwhile, Secretary of State for India Montagu pressed the
Government of India for an inquiry into the case of the
disorders, first recommending such an inquiry in his budget
speech of 22 May 1919. Montagu's initial impressions based on
that ambiguous wire from Delhi were clarified by two conversations with the recently retired lieutenant governor of the Punjab,
Sir Michael O'Dwyer, in London in June.

What could be done? If he had unilaterally condemned Dyer
on O'Dwyer's second-hand report that Dyer fired without warning and without being threatened, or even demanded a court-
martial for him, he would become the butt of attack by the
whole imperial class in India and Britain and risk rejection of the
proposed Government of India Act incorporating reforms at the
hands of their allies in Parliament. And he would be censured
for prejudging the issue without the accused being heard if he attempted to have Dyer quietly removed from command. On the
other hand, he was pressed by the Indian delegation in London
whose support he also needed for the reforms he had spent three
years in developing from the government's 1917 promise to
legislation. To avoid both risks and develop a joint resolution,
what better method was there than to appoint a committee composed of official Britishers and Indians (loyal to the government,
of course)? He wired the viceroy on 18 July that he was making
"a statement in Parliament to the effect that you are going to

appoint a committee and have asked me to select a chairman. . . . It would sooth the Indian delegation here.''[5]

Although the government of India's officers dreaded reexamining those events, the viceroy yielded to Montagu's insistence. The government first had considered Dyer's action during the 19 September 1919 meeting of the Imperial Legislative Council, at which time an indemnity bill was passed exonerating officers from suit for damages for actions performed under martial law. However, it was made clear that the Indemnity Bill did not prevent any action being taken against Dyer later. The members of the Hunter Committee (excepting only its chairman, Lord Hunter, who was selected by Montagu) were appointed by the viceroy on 14 October 1919 after further discussion with Montagu.

The Hunter Report was preceded by a compendium of District Reports which were submitted officially to the Government of India on 11 October 1919 by the government of the Punjab. These reports enable one to compare the results of provincial officials' self-reports with that of the Hunter Committee in order to see how self-investigation differs from the scrutiny of those up above in the hierarchy.

The Hunter Committee sat for forty-six days from 29 October 1919 hearing testimony in Delhi, Ahmedabad, Bombay, and Lahore. Dyer testified before the committee on 19 November 1919 at Lahore: his testimony was soon published in Indian and later in British newspapers.

The committee's majority censured General Dyer in their final report on 8 March 1920 for "a mistaken conception of his duty," but their report satisfied no party. In rendering judgment, the committee had split on national lines. Both the British majority and the Indian minority appended separate conclusions to the Hunter Report—hence references to the Hunter Report will be to the body of data gathered and references to the Majority and Minority Reports will be to their judgments on that data.

Confronted with the committee's findings, every member of the Viceroy's Executive Council, including the military, recommended Dyer's dismissal or that stronger action ought to be taken against him. Vincent, the Home member, rejected trial by court-martial because of the "adverse effect on army discipline." How were they to explain their action? The Government of India on 11 May 1920 restrained Montagu from issuing the following sentence in his original press release: "His Majesty's Government repudiates emphatically the doctrine of frightfulness upon which Dyer based his action."[6] They feared its implication that Dyer's act represented "frightfulness" and foresaw that it would become "a catchword to influence widespread ill-feeling."[7]

Finally, the Government of India and the secretary of state for India agreed on a draft, which Montagu issued on 26 May, stating that "the principle which has consistently governed the policy of His Majesty's Government in directing the Methods to be employed when military action in support of the civil authority is required may be broadly stated as using the minimum force necessary. . . . Brig.-Gen. Dyer's action was in complete violation of this principle."[8]

Dyer, however, had become a hero to the imperial class of Britishers in India; he had no reason to accept government condemnation and a sudden decline in his status with resignation. After the Hunter Committee had been appointed, Dyer was elevated from command of a brigade to command of a division; only on 14 February 1920 was this new role formally confirmed as an acting command post only. In March 1920, the commander in chief of the Indian Army twice summoned Dyer, then on sick leave, to report to Delhi. Upon his arrival on 22 March, Dyer was informed by Sir Havelock Hudson, the adjutant general, that the commander in chief was removing him from command and he would be asked to resign his commission because of the Hunter Committee's censure. Dyer refused to resign. Instead he requested the Army Council in London to review his case, which they did, confirming the government's action in July 1920. Departing from his command post in April, the general was greeted at the train station by "a great guard of honour of all the non-commissioned officers at the railway station itself. This demonstation had been arranged by the men and NCO's upon their own initiative without any authority from their own officers. . . . He left Jullundur with the cheers of his comrades ringing in his ears."[9]

APPOINTMENT OF COMMITTEES: PERSONNEL AND PURVIEW

The Hunter Committee and Indian National Congress Punjab Subcommittee reports offer us an opportunity, perhaps unique in the history of reports on violence, to compare accounts of the victims and the executors of violence. Each began, appropriately enough, with judges of different political backgrounds and commitments. Besides Lord Hunter, a Scottish jurist, the committee was composed of three British officials of the Government of India and one unofficial Britisher plus three Indian lawyers practicing before government courts. Datta reveals that the Government of India favorably considered appointing Tej Bahadur Sapru, an Indian Liberal of independent spirit who was highly erudite and respected, but was vetoed by the government of the Punjab. Many of the British regarded one or more of the Indian members as biased while Congress politicians regarded them as weak. However, this did not prevent members of the Punjab Subcommittee from passing them leads enabling them to pose searching questions in examining witnesses.

The Hunter Committee was restricted in scope to examining the causes, sequence, responsibility, and propriety of actions taken to suppress the disorders in Delhi, Bombay, and the Punjab. Most of the committee's witnesses were British military or civil officers in India. Its outlined procedure for voluntary witnesses required that they first file a preliminary statement of the facts "which they desired to prove and an outline of the points or contentions which they were prepared to substantiate" signed by a legal practitioner, along with a list of additional witnesses needed and a synopsis of the evidence they would cite. All testimony was public except that of Sir Michael O'Dwyer and a few key officials: that secret testimony was recently found by Datta in the hitherto undisclosed vols. 6 and 7.[10] When requested by the All-India Congress to release temporarily the principal imprisoned Punjab leaders for questioning, the committee categorically refused. Consequently, the Punjab Subcommittee of the Congress refused to cooperate with the Hunter Committee. However, it did rely on the Hunter Committee testimony (which it reprinted in the Congress Report) to corroborate its own conclusions regarding General Dyer, Lieutenant Colonel Carberry, and Colonel Johnson, among others.

Local Congress committees did testify before the Hunter Committee at Delhi and Ahmedabad (events of which were not covered in the Congress Report). The Punjab Subcommittee offered to bring in new testimony on 30 December 1919 and requested the reopening of testimony in order to put the Indian political prisoners released by the king's Christmas pardon on record, some of whom also appealed independently to testify. Lord Hunter justified his refusal in the report, remarking that "the request to reopen the inquiry was in the circumstances quite unreasonable because the Committee had already sat at Lahore for six weeks. . . . Lord Hunter regrets that he is unable to accept the suggestion of your committee" [HC: v].

The Punjab Subcommittee of the Indian National Congress, headed by Gandhi, was appointed on 14 November 1919 to compile its own independent analysis of the necessity of and execution of martial law in the Punjab. The five appointed members, aided by a hired firm of English lawyers, interviewed and cross-examined 1,700 witnesses, most of whom were victims or witnesses either of the massacre or of martial law administration.

If there was a difference between the scruples of the investigators, the Punjab Subcommittee was the more demanding in refusing to accept charges without corroborating testimony. No charges were accepted without naming the officers involved, nor could they be submitted anonymously: names of all witnesses were published along with their testimony, making those persons potentially liable to legal action by the officers named. Some charges (such as the "ill-treatment of women") were ruled out because of lack of independent corroboration or because the witness himself had participated in a criminal act, such as extortion. The Hunter Committee made vital inferences on the basis of testimony of police undercover agents (such as CID inspectors) whose accounts sometimes contradicted independent Indian testimony on record.

Neither committee sought access to Indian street leaders active in rioting or attempted to assess their characteristics objectively. The Hunter Report takes as an a priori assumption the innocence or righteousness of the executors of law and order while the Congress Report presumes the innocence of the victims. But victims could have little to gain beyond an enhanced sense of moral rectitude whereas executors could conceivably be indicted criminally or punished bureaucratically for "excesses" exposed before the Hunter Committee. Therefore, virtually all the Hunter Committee's witnesses must be considered interested witnesses with crucial roles in creating or suppressing the disorders they described.

WHOSE VIOLENCE AND WHOSE VICTIMS?

To the British, violence was a metaphor. The word is used in both the Hunter Report and the District Report to characterize political language, denoting the temper of speeches of Indian leaders before the disorders. This temper seems to be measured on a fever thermometer, ranging from reasonable to violent, which is consistent with the contagion metaphor employed as in this Hunter Report description: "The towns had their own problems, but political activity by and among the educated classes there had possibilities of immediate danger if it infected the rural population with antipathy to the Government or disbelief in its power" [HC:58]. Fire imagery symbolizing the process of agitation appears continually in the District Reports: speeches and ballads are inflammatory or incendiary, rebellion is scathing, raging, fiery.

The active verb and noun is "outrage." The District Report repeatedly tells of "outrages," including everything from upsetting the furniture in the town hall to the murder of British civilians. The Hunter Report includes several maps locating outrages, but only British victims of Indian outrages are considered. There is no marker of any sort at the site of the Jallianwala Bagh in Amritsar where General Dyer fired, killing 379 Indians, by government estimate.

The Congress Report freely refers to mob violence as well as the massacre at Jallianwala Bagh, although the former is sometimes referred to as "excesses" attributed to provocation by the O'Dwyer administration. Pictures reiterate the theme of victimization—there are ones of an eleven-year-old child convicted of "waging war against the King-Emperor," limbless victims of bombing and firing, and other stark illustrations of the statistics.

DEFINING THE SITUATION

The central question occupying the Hunter Committee was the justification of martial law in the Punjab, for which they referred to the Bengal Regulation of 1804 and classic law texts. The Majority Report frankly asserts this was not a procedural question but a logical prerequisite for the type of judgment at which they arrived:

> If, on the other hand, it was necessary and right to resort to mar-
> tial law, the conduct of the Government is justified in principle
> and intention; any error which could be shown to exist is an error
> of method. . . . Though not without a real importance, as we
> have already shown, a mistake in method is of less importance; it
> would mean at most that a special Ordinance was necessary and
> should have been passed. [HC: 22]

Rebellion was assumed by *The Manual of Military Law* to be
synonymous with insurrection, signified by armed attack on
government buildings or personnel.[11] Yet, in Amritsar on 10
April, no offices of government (except for three postal substa-
tions, which were looted) had been attacked, and no soldiers,
police, or civil officials had been injured except an off-duty
sergeant (Rowlands), evidently a chance victim of the mob. What
was the Hunter Committee's answer to the question whether
there was open rebellion?

> It is a question of fact, and, on the information submitted to us,
> we think the answer should be given in the affirmative. . . . On
> 10th April at Amritsar the mobs had burned Government build-
> ings because they were Government buildings. . . . The first few
> minutes . . . they murdered all Europeans on which they could
> lay their hands. . . . They were not even Government officials.
> But the Raj is a British Raj; they were in some sense its represen-
> tatives or symbols, and for this they were murdered. The railway
> and the telegraphs were attacked partly as Government institu-
> tions and partly to paralyse the Government by preventing news,
> by derailing troops, and otherwise immobilising the forces. [HC:
> 66]

Justification for such an interpretation was confirmed by citing
Annie Besant, former Congress president, who had broken with
Gandhi during the anti–Rowlatt Bill campaign. She wrote in a
letter to *The Times* on 21 December 1919 that "the cutting of
telegraph wires, the derailment of troop trains, the burning of
railway stations, the attack on banks, the setting free of jail
birds, are not the action of Satyagrahis nor even of casual
rioters, but of revolutionaries" [HC: 66–67].

The minority refused to accept Annie Besant's belated authority since she had no knowledge of the immediate facts (having
been in Madras), and they rejected belief in the existence of a
rebellion. They implied that the committee's use of Besant as an
authority was opportunistic:

We do not know whether those who have invoked the authority of this dictum of Mrs. Besant will be prepared to accept her judgement on the Punjab disturbances, pronounced by her on the 21st of December, 1919 to the following effect:— "I have been shocked to read the evidence given by the military witnesses before the Hunter Committee. Nothing more than is recorded out of their own mouths was done by the Germans in Belgium." [HC: 106]

Partisans of Dyer, especially Sir Michael O'Dwyer, later attacked the committee for not also finding a conspiracy.[12] Establishing a conspiracy was essential to justify Dyer's action and to maintain their ideology of imperial rule. Colonel O'Brien's testimony illustrates the source of this belief. The committee member questions O'Brien as to how he knew the disorders were organized:

Q. So, according to that, the organization that you refer to was in the Punjab, outside Gujranwala?
A. I didn't say that. I say that it was certainly outside Gujranwala.
Q. Was it outside the Punjab or inside?
A. That I cannot tell you.
Q. You cannot say where the organization was?
A. No. I have no information.
Q. You do not know whether there was any organization at all?
A. No.
Q. And then why do you say here "it was organized . . ." when you never knew whether there was an organization at all or not?
A. As I said, it was only my assumption. I don't think the Gujranwala people would have started it of their own accord, therefore I assumed that it must have come from outside. [HC: 93]

The conspiracy theory and the outside-agitator theory are, indeed, functionally equivalent; both explain how disorders can erupt while maintaining belief that the natives are either too happy or too impotent to protest.

District Reports refer to incidents of disorder and damage as organized crimes, proving it by citing cases of the leaders having been convicted of such crimes or participation in criminal conspiracies by the martial law commissions created by the Punjab government. Since the logic is circular, it is self-confirming.

The Punjab Subcommittee denied that there was any rebellion or conspiracy to overthrow the government, interpreting the mob activity as a response to government misjudgment in firing on the crowd in Amritsar on 10 April. Their report switches from interpreting the events in terms of their participants' motives to the objective perspective ("mob violence"), dwelling on consequences. Whether or not there were leaders emerging among such Indian crowds articulating the objectives of the crowd is not studied; nor is the possibility that the crowd provoked the British firing on 10 April considered. Similarly, the responsibility for convening the illegal meeting at the Jallianwala Bagh on 13 April is not assessed, despite contemporary belief that its Indian organizer was an agent of Dyer working within Congress.[13]

When Indians did not live up to Gandhi's nonviolent norm, he dismissed them as an anonymous collective actor—"the mob"— just as the British did.

THE SCALES OF JUDGMENT

The District Report consistently assesses the action of General Dyer and other officers in terms of their effects on restoring belief in the government power, reestablishing *authority* on a firmer base. Regarding the firing at Jallianwala Bagh, it says: "He did not order the crowd to disperse, but proceeded to take action to disperse it at once by fire . . . the number of casualties were not counted" [DC: 5]. Its immediate effect, it goes on to say, was to prevent an uprising. A testimonial from two (presumably British) long-time residents of India is then presented: "The people realized the Goverment was in earnest and that it was determined to protect them even against their own will" [DC: 6].

The Hunter Report explicitly accepts several ends and corresponding legal duties and restrictions as factors to be taken into account. The duty to preserve human life is reconciled with the others by what is referred to as the minimum-force principle. The Majority Report compares each instance or sequence of firing in terms of the gravity of threat and appropriateness of response, approving of all cases except that of General Dyer. What are the guidelines of the minimum-force principle?

These rules, precedents, and interpretations are spelled out in

The Manual of Military Law (1914), a document Dyer used in his defense before the Army Council and in his role as deputy assistant adjutant general for instruction in military law during World War I. The manual (chap. 13) tells how to evaluate signs and classify types of disorders, specifying the legitimate ends in view in using force in each type of situation, the procedural rules to be followed, the criteria that justify exceptions to these rules, and the potential liability of the officers. The chapter is replete with examples from English history.

Civil occasions when force may be used are classed as cases of unlawful assembly, riot, or insurrection. Insurrection is distinguished from riot in that the object of violent attack is a public symbol rather than private property. However, these categories may at times be stages in the life history of a crowd:

> An unlawful assembly is an assembly which may reasonably be apprehended to cause danger to the public peace, through the action of the persons constituting the assembly. As soon as an act of violence is perpetrated it becomes a riot; while if the act of violence be one of a public nature, and with the intention of carrying into effect any general political purpose, it becomes an insurrection or rebellion and not a riot.[14]

This passage clearly implies that seditious speech alone does not convert an unlawful assembly into an insurrection. Unlawful assembly, like riot, constitutes a misdemeanor, but the possible sentence is longer for cases of riot. Insurrection, however, is an act of treason which may lead to capital punishment.

Dispersion of an unlawful assembly by force is justifiable only if that assembly is verging on riot, but if

> there is no immediate apprehension of violence, it can scarcely be justifiable to attempt to disperse it by force, or wise, as a rule, to display force. . . . If resort be had to force, the principle is that so much force only is to be used as is sufficient to effect the object in view, namely, the dispersion of the assembly; and if injury results to any person from the use of that force, the question to be tried is whether the means used were or were not more violent than the occasion required.[15]

In case of riot, the prescribed procedure is to read an injunction from the Riot Act (1732), ordering people to desist and disperse, and wait one hour before applying any force; however, if the mob has committed or seems about to commit a felony, officers need not wait that hour or even wait to read the Riot Act. But even then, the manual warns,

> deadly weapons ought not to be employed against the rioters, unless they are armed, or are in a position to inflict grievous injury on the persons endeavouring to disperse them, or are committing, or on the point of committing, some felonious outrage, which can only be stopped by armed force.[16]

Only armed insurrection

> would justify the use of any degree of force necessary effectually to meet and cope with the insurrection.[17]

Most important, armed men are responsible under the law as are all citizens. They may be indicted and tried for murder and manslaughter, as may any citizen who may lawfully fire during a riot. It is affirmed that

> the primary duty of preserving public order rests with the civil power. An officer, therefore, in all cases where it is practicable, should place himself under the orders of a magistrate. . . . Still, the law of England is that a man obeys an illegal order at his own risk, and circumstances might arise which would justify the officer in firing or not firing, notwithstanding the magistrate might give orders to the contrary.[18]

By these criteria, Dyer's firing not only violated but contradicted the minimum-force principle. The end in view—creating a "widespread effect"—was outside the law. Although the means were consistent with Dyer's end in view, they were not consistent with any legitimate end sanctioned by the law and thus could justify a criminal indictment or court-martial. The only possible definition of the situation which would justify that extent of force would be a case of armed insurrection. But the assembly at Jallianwala Bagh was only an unlawful assembly of unarmed men who posed no threat even of riot.

THE NORMALIZING OF SLAUGHTER

Thus, the one incident which could neither be ignored nor justified by the majority was General Dyer's shooting. Yet Dyer's action had been approved by all his military superiors and by Sir Michael O'Dwyer, who had stated publicly: "Speaking with perhaps a more intimate knowledge of the then situation than anyone else, I have no hesitation in saying that Gen. Dyer's action that day was the decisive factor in crushing the rebellion, the seriousness of which is only now being generally realized" [HC: 30–31].

General Dyer was "open to criticism," the majority said, on two counts: "[First] that he started firing without giving the people who had assembled a chance to disperse, and [second] that he continued firing for a substantial period of time after the crowd had commenced to disperse" [HC: 29]. Both are procedural norms. The first charge is partially neutralized by the majority by speculating on what would have happened if Dyer had adhered to procedure. They assert that since it would be irrational to believe the crowd would have dispersed even if Dyer had ordered them to do so, he would have had to fire anyway.

The second charge was still judged within a bureaucratic frame of reference by "normalizing" his action as a deviation from the rules, or improvisation, based on the purported organizational goals rather than organizational rules. The majority accepted his intention at face value, citing his self-report of 25 August that he wanted to produce "a wide moral effect," but concluded that

> in our view this was unfortunately a mistaken conception of his duty. If necessary a crowd that has assembled contrary to a proclamation issued to prevent or terminate disorder may have to be fired upon; but continued firing upon that crowd cannot be justified because of the effect such firing may have upon other people in other places. The employment of excessive measures is as likely as not to produce the opposite result to that desired. [HC: 30–32]

First, intent has been displaced upon an approved value—duty—in the pursuit of which an honorable man has erred. He had committed an error not only by violating procedural norms but because such a violation, if pursued universally, would not necessarily reinforce obedience to authority. The end in view could not be upheld as a standard for assessing deviant behavior, the majority said, because consequences may be the opposite of those consciously anticipated. Furthermore, Sir Michael's assessment was challenged "in view of the fact that it is not proved that a conspiracy to overthrow British power had been formed prior to the outbreaks" [HC: 31]. No question of legal culpability was raised, nor was the nature of the "moral effect" which the general intended probed.

The Minority Report rejected this displacement of General Dyer's clear intent and condemned him categorically, but not without suggesting that it also worked better in the long run to play by the rules:

> It is pleaded that Gen. Dyer honestly believed that what he was doing was right. This cannot avail him, if he was clearly wrong in his notions of what was right and what was wrong; and the plea of military necessity is the plea that has always been advanced in justification of the Prussian atrocities. Gen. Dyer thought that he had crushed the rebellion, and Sir Michael O'Dwyer was of the same view. There was no rebellion which required to be crushed. We feel that Gen. Dyer, by adopting an inhuman and un-British method of dealing with subjects of His Majesty, the King-Emperor, has done great disservice to the interest of British rule in India. [HC: 115]

The judgment of the Congress Report was equally categorical:

> No provocation whatever was given to the Military Authorities and nothing, either in Amritsar or outside it, justified the massacre. It was a calculated act of inhumanity, and if the British rule in India is to be purged of this inexcusable wrong, Gen. Dyer must be immediately relieved of his command and brought to justice. [INC: I, 58]

STRATEGIES OF DEFENSE

Appeals to racial fears are explicit in the District Report and implicit in the Hunter Report. Posters, such as one in Lyallpur where there was a rumor that Sikh women had been ravished by British officers at Amritsar, are cited out of context without noting there were no reports of attacks or threats against European women there. These must have reinforced the false rumor that Miss Sherwood, attacked at Amritsar on 10 April, had been raped.

Conjecture on Indian intentions is freely offered. When the Hunter Report examines the disorders preceding shootings and martial law, the aggressive intent of the mob is often established by a single remark overheard by an Indian police agent whose evidence is accepted regardless of other Indian reports to the contrary. When officers' actions taken against crowds are examined, the intention of the officers is not discussed.

By ignoring the officers' motives, the Hunter Committee obscured the relationship between incidents in different towns and similarities from which one might abstract a pattern. Relevant norms, such as the gratuitousness of injuries inflicted and the traditional rights expected by Indians, were either overlooked or considered as an afterthought.

Several strategies are employed to clear away as many charges against officers as possible. One strategy is to neutralize the onus of the charge by denying its verifiability and then withholding judgment. This is cloaked in abstracted rationality, so unlike everyday British empiricism. The Hunter Report observes that

> Gen. Dyer's action in not attending to or making provision for the wounded at Jallianwala Bagh has been made the subject of criticism. . . . On being questioned as to whether he had taken any measures for the relief of the wounded, Gen. Dyer explained that the hospitals were open and the medical officers were there. "The wounded only had to apply for help. But they did not do this because they themselves would be in custody for being in the assembly. I was ready to help them if they applied." . . . It has not been proved to us that any wounded people were in fact exposed to unnecessary suffering for want of medical treatment. [HC: 31]

Another strategy is to mitigate the onus by showing that the act conformed to bureaucratic norms: "Major Carberry was carrying out orders." Once it was established that an actor was playing an assigned role and that role was legitimated by martial law, many cases could be eliminated from judgment if they fell within limits of procedural norms, as did all firings on crowds except at Jallianwala Bagh. Errors in method are treated as tactical misjudgment or a poor selection from options equally legitimate. Such errors may be judged "injudicious" or "unwise." This was how the rituals of abasement imposed on Indians, such as the crawling, salaaming, and saluting orders, were reviewed. Regarding General Dyer's Crawling Order:

> Above all, from an administrative point of view in subjecting the Indian population to an act of humiliation, it has continued to be a cause of bitterness and racial ill-feeling long after it was recalled. [HC: 83]

Regarding Colonel Johnson's orders of compulsory marches for students:

> Measures of a disciplinary character were no doubt called for, but we think the orders to which we have referred were unnecessarily severe. It would have been more prudent, in our opinion, if the military authorities had consulted the college authorities as to the orders to be passed. [HC: 83–84]

Judgment is sometimes deferred regarding individual acts but is made against the procedure previously sanctioned as lawful—reform is called for to limit floggings. But another type of deferred judgment exonerates military procedures by reference to their immediate necessity and future utility; the fact that innocent persons will be killed or injured is taken as a foreseeable but unavoidable consequence. Unlike flogging, the utility of the airplane could not be denied in future warfare:

> We are not prepared to lay down as a charter for rioters that when they succeed in preventing the ordinary resources of Government from being utilised to suppress them, they are to be exempt from having to reckon with such resources as remain. In acting as they did, Major Carberry and his fellow officers carried out the instructions which had been given to them, and it does not appear to us that blame can be imputed to any of them. . . . It is difficult to feel certain that it was necessary to fire with the machine-gun upon the parties at Dhulla and the Khalsa High School in order to disperse these parties effectively; but we are not prepared to impute blame for the officers' decision, taken in the air and at the moment. [HC: 49]

This last defense was to resound in the House of Lords among General Dyer's supporters in July 1920. If the means were to be justified by the ends in the air, why not among the rifles? Was not the survival of the British Empire at stake?

The Congress Report judges these and similar acts by reference to the substantive guilt or innocence of their victims as well as the nature and consequences of the punishment meted out. Judgments are categorical and curt—"trials were . . . more farcical than elsewhere," "wanton and unjustified," "inhuman"—and often implicit, the evidence itself being employed to speak to what its authors conceived to be mutually understood universal values. Since the theory of rebellion was rejected by Congress, the instrumental utility of martial law is not assessed.

The minority, having rejected the rebellion framework, also rejected the majority's evaluations of the officers' acts as lapses from administrative standards. Instead, they focused on intent and consequences, as in the following review of Colonel Johnson's orders against students: "We are of opinion that these orders on their merits were unjustifiable and were conceived in a spirit of some vindictiveness, and were eminently calculated to leave behind considerable feelings of bitterness in the minds of the young generation" [HC: 121].

Similarly to the Congress Report, the minority often simply presents evidence verbatim to establish collective punishment ("all students punished because two failed to salaam"), arbitrary or representative punishment ("six boys flogged at Kasur because they happened to be biggest"), economic sanctions ("reprisals on property of absentees and their relations"). Regarding military attacks on anonymous targets (such as random aerial bombing and machine-gunning from a train) the minority is less categorical, relegating blame for the pilot's action to Sir Michael O'Dwyer's orders.

INTERPRETING THE CAUSES

Agreement exists between the Congress Report and Hunter Report that the specific cause of the disorders of 10 April 1919 was the detention of Gandhi and the leaders in Amritsar, Kitchlew and Satyapal. They also agree on widespread opposition to the Rowlatt Bills among both "moderate" and "extreme" Indian politicians, although the Hunter Committee tends to dwell on the agitational character of the opposition. Both likewise agree that there was restiveness caused by expectation of greater self-government, conceived to be India's due as a repayment of her loyalty and contributions to the war effort. However, the implications of the Hunter Committee's observation are diminished by their citing the greatest number of possible causes—frustration of the educated classes caused by the Defense of India Act, the concern stirred by the pan-Islamic movement over the dismemberment of the Turkish caliph's suzerainty, high prices caused by the failure of the monsoon, and the nature of the "martial classes" of the Punjab who had contributed more than their share of the recruits demanded of the Punjab. (The District

Report replies indirectly to charges of coercion and terrorism in recruiting by citing the receptivity and relative number of recruits produced by each town and comparing their resistance to the extent of protest during the anti–Rowlatt Bill campaign.[19])

The District Report cites similar causes, including a decline in prices for piece goods obtained by the Marwari traders and in grain prices adversely affecting the wholesale merchants. But the report concentrates on other causes said to be peculiar to Amritsar. The growth of Congress activities and the recently hotly contested municipal elections are political causes adduced to account for the agitation in Amritsar, besides the more general Khilifat agitation. Unrest is ascribed to the urban classes exclusively; when the "agriculturalists" are observed to riot in Amritsar, it is explained that visiting villagers took advantage of the breakdown of law in order to loot, rather than being inspired by political reasons.

The reader who is unacquainted with the reoccurrence of natural and social disasters in India may be overwhelmed with the number of causes, any combination of which might justify protest. The well-to-do are upset by falling profits, the poor by high prices and plague deaths, the Muslims by the Turkish question, the educated by the slowness of reforms. Both the Hunter Report and the District Report name so many causes of unrest that no one cause or party may be arraigned for responsibility for the disorders.

The Congress Report does not hesitate to attribute design to events: the root of all the disorders was provocation by Sir Michael, originally motivated by hostility to the "educated classes," an often repeated theme. O'Dwyer was held responsible for rural unrest by virtue of the suffering imposed in rural areas during his recruiting. Recruiting and raising the war loan were provincially coordinated and employed local tax collectors. For the war loan they assessed the financial capability of potential donors, stimulated rivalries between towns, and reciprocated with chairs and certificates for the donors. It was made clear that government positions, paid or honorific, depended on cooperation. Recruiting quotas were established by the government and pledged to work along the lines of "voluntarism" for each district, tax zone, and village. Local tax assessors designated voluntary recruits, whose families might then voluntarily indemnify the government for their services by a subscription to the war loan.[20]

Congress's assertion that O'Dwyer had provoked the disorders by his enmity to the "educated class" is traced back to a speech he had made in 1917 reprimanding the Indian members of the Imperial Legislative Council for initiating suggestions for reforms. He regarded himself as solely responsible for the Punjab and rejected suggestions to install an executive council there. His vigorous prosecution of newspapers in the Punjab between 1914 and 1918 and his public disdain for Indian politicians—whom he characterized in Legislative Council debate (employing Burke's simile) as "grasshoppers under a fern who make the field ring with their importunate cries"[21]—demonstrated his determination to enforce his will.

He warned leaders publicly that they would be held responsible for agitation against the Rowlatt Act. Local British officials in the Punjab persuaded Indian leaders in some towns not to hold protest hartals in April, we learn from the District Reports. But in Amritsar this was not possible, and O'Dwyer ordered the internment of Dr. Kitchlew and Dr. Satyapal, leading to the riot of 10 April.

The Congress concludes that O'Dwyer, having united all classes against him, invited violence by his unwillingness to tolerate opposition:

> He must have known that this could only end in exasperating a people, who had already been incensed against his rule. We feel tempted to say that he invited violence from the people, so that he could crush them. The evidence in the appendix shows that he subjected the Punjabis to the gravest provocation, under which they momentarily lost self-control. [INC: I, 33]

The minority of the Hunter Committee made no effort at counterexplanation after having discarded the rebellion theory for lack of substantive evidence. They cited comparisons to previous revolutionary movements in India, India's past loyalty to Britain during the war, the notable absence of anti-European sentiment during the hartals, and the implausibility of barefooted men without arms beginning to wage war against the British Empire by first seizing the deputy commissioner's bungalow in Amritsar. On several occasions the minority imply that Sir Michael's theory was composed to justify martial law which was never needed. The opening of "War Diaries" (of which Sir Michael denied knowledge before the committee) simultaneously in Amritsar and Lahore on 10 April and later in other towns in the Punjab was considered significant. There is substantive agreement as to the chain of events preceding and following martial law between the Minority and Congress Reports. The minority confirms that "the Punjab Government under Sir Michael O'Dwyer had for various reasons come to be regarded by the educated and politically minded classes as opposed to their aspirations" [HC: 92].

DISTRIBUTION OF RESPONSIBILITY

Linking the evidence agreed on by both the Hunter Report and the Congress Report, one finds mutual recognition that the Rowlatt Bills did provoke a concerted negative Indian response, one whose intensity was heightened by Gandhi's campaign. His leadership evoked mass protest which evoked repression which provoked disorders of varying seriousness which spread within a few days to towns and villages around Amritsar (see Chapter 4). The anti-British rage revealed by the mob's choice of targets in Amritsar led General Dyer to "punish" that city by firing on the thousands gathered at the Jallianwala Bagh on 13 April, a motive freely admitted by Dyer once he had secured widespread public recognition of his deed. That firing and Dyer's Crawling Order became emblems to Indians of the short-lived and often sadistic reign of terror imposed on the Punjab during martial law between April and June 1919. Where along this cycle of provocation and reprisal does each party fix the blame?

The majority of the Hunter Committee ascribed responsibility to Gandhi's Satyagraha movement for the preaching of civil disobedience. The majority reasoned that if disobedience is not civil, it will result in disorder; and if it is civil and widespread, the Government will be overthrown without force. It is not just the means, but the end itself, which is unacceptable:

> We believe Mr. Gandhi is honestly opposed to the employment of force or violence in the prosecution of his aims. But the general teaching of the doctrine of civil disobedience to laws to masses of uneducated men must inevitably lead to breach of the peace and disorder. Apart from the use of force, civil disobedience to laws, if extensively preached and practised, would mean the paralysis of

> Government. As we said in the *Waqt:* "If the entire country re-
> sorts to passive resistance, where is the Government that will
> withstand it? There can be no need for wielding the sword, be-
> cause the *Satyagrahi* does not offer physical resistance." [HC: 63]

The Punjab government had decided this movement was an illegal conspiracy, although the Government of India had not.
Another conclusion, that the government was equally responsible
for initiating violence by its repressive response to pacific protest, was drawn on the floor of the House of Lords by Lord
Sinha, the Indian undersecretary of state for India, in July 1920.

The minority concurred with the majority's condemnation of
Gandhi's Satyagraha movement but attributed equal emphasis to
Sir Michael O'Dwyer's administration as being responsible for
the underlying unrest in the Punjab. Since it did not credit the
existence of a rebellion, it held the officers as well as O'Dwyer
responsible for their actions under martial law.

The Congress Report places the blame on the administration
of Sir Michael O'Dwyer for provoking the disorders and on him
and the viceroy for imposing martial law and standing behind
General Dyer and other accused officers. The concept of provocation does not mean, however, that the mob is less culpable.
A Congress historian tells how Gandhi especially insisted on
this.[22] The report stated:

> Whilst, therefore, we deplore the deportation order and the fir-
> ing, and consider both as unjustifiable, and the absence of any
> ambulance arrangement as inhuman, nothing can be held to justi-
> fy the wanton destruction by the mob of innocent lives and pro-
> perty. [INC: I, 50]

The Punjab Subcommittee was torn between explaining the
crowds' responses as a symptom or reaction to an immediate
provocation and displacing the responsibility for the crowds'
behavior. In the latter case, the subcommittee implied the
crowds' behavior was not politically intelligible in its own right—
assuming the primitive notions of crowd behavior current in this
period—but only a symptom of the real contest between the British administration and the Indian educated classes. Thus, it
stated:

> The foregoing chapter makes it sufficiently clear that the people
> of the Punjab were subjected to a variety of pin-pricks by the
> local administration, and that, by its studied contempt for them,

it had made it well-nigh impossible for the natural leaders of the people—the educated classes—to control the populace. [INC: I, 24]

While O'Dwyer and others feared the educated classes would agitate the otherwise readily repressible rural and urban uneducated classes, the foregoing passages imply a belief that only the educated could repress those classes and that if the educated classes did not receive the deference which was owed to them, it was not their fault but that of the British.

The majority-minority split in the Hunter Committee preceded their conclusions. General Dyer responded contemptuously toward the Indian committee members but deferentially toward the British, constantly looking in their direction. Datta reports that there also were "unpleasant incidents" between British and Indian members, such as the following exchange described by one of the latter, C. V. Setalwad:

> During one of the discussions I had with Lord Hunter, he lost his temper and said, "You people (myself and my Indian colleagues) want to drive the British out of the country." This naturally annoyed me and I said: "It is perfectly legitimate for Indians to be free of foreign rule and Independence can be accomplished by mutual understanding and goodwill. The driving out process will only become necessary if the British are represented in this country by people as short-sighted and intolerant as yourself." After this, though under the same roof, we, the Indian members, ceased to talk to Lord Hunter.[23]

Also, members of the Punjab subcommittee gathering material at this time were leaking information to two of the Indian members of the Hunter Committee, which made them more hostile to O'Dwyer's administration and more skillful and critical at examining Dyer and other officers. The criticism by some members of Parliament that Dyer had been cross-examined by skilled lawyers without benefit of counsel was insightful. Dyer had indeed been skillfully cross-examined; however, even had he not been so examined, the committee would have been able to draw the same conclusion on the basis of his statement of 25 August 1919.

Thus, the response of the goverment's selected "moderates" did not differ from that of the nationalists—not only because the overwhelming weight of evidence supported an indictment of both Dyer and the military occupation of the Punjab, but also because their daily experiences of being treated as subordinates made it clear they were in essentially the same position as all their other countrymen.

WHY DISORDER COMMISSIONS FAIL

The focus of each report reflects the political class perspective of its authors. The District Report is a recitation of the injuries received by the British alone and judges all military means used against their subjects as legitimate. The Hunter Report, written for a government which had co-opted Indians into its highest councils, considers injuries inflicted by that government's staff, but they are regarded as deviations from duty or mistakes in method and weighed in terms of bureaucratic norms rather than in terms of human consequences or, in legal terms, as crimes. Not even the massacre perpetrated at Jallianwala Bagh was labeled a crime. Varied logical defenses are used to avoid perceiving any common pattern rather than integrating facts and values in appraisal. The Congress Report and the Minority Report focus on injuries sustained by the Indians but do not exonerate Indians participating in previous mob violence as they simultaneously appeal to the conscience of the English public.

It is evident that violence reports serve functions besides fact-finding. Each, in this case, projected blame on the other party and exonerated its own constituency. The Hunter Committee majority's definition of the situation as an instance of rebellion was used to authorize and legitimate the imposition of martial law, thus mitigating the stigma that would be attached, if viewed in a civil context, to such acts as bombing civilians and forcing Indians to crawl, bow, or touch their toes. The District Report finding that the disorders were produced by the criminal activities of convicted criminals exonerated the O'Dwyer administration from blame. The Congress Report indictment of the O'Dwyer administration served to reject accusations against the Satyagraha movement and the local leadership in Amritsar.

The assertion (later much elaborated) that there was a conspiracy behind the alleged rebellion served to confirm the government of the Punjab's dictum that what was wrong with the Punjab was not its governors; finding widespread popular discontent, such as the Congress Report claimed existed, would tend to bring its governors into disrepute.

Demonstrating that such beliefs serve a function in the psychic economy of a colonial class does not negate or confirm the truth of the explanation. There are such things as conspiracies; but there is no evidence in the Hunter Report to prove there was one in the Punjab in 1919 that would account for these disorders. The alternative explanation—that they were spontaneous collective outbursts of rage by Indians to a perceived collective attack on them—would account for the murders, property damage, and sabotage of communications.

Some definitions of the situation open up and others foreclose new relationships between parties in conflict. The District Report charge that the disorders were examples of crime and their instigators were criminals is a definition of the situation foreclosing new relationships. Crimes in every society are those acts which cannot be tolerated.

While rebellion and revolution are definitions which would preclude a colonial class from negotiating, their implications in other settings depend on the dominant ideology. Rebellion, to many Americans, is a justification for disorders rather than a category legitimating the repression of them. Revolution, one could expect, would be a justification for disorders among Soviet satellites and counterrevolution would be the definition of the situation chosen by the governing elite and their foreign overlords which would legitimate repressing those disorders.

Congress and the Minority Report's denial that there was a rebellion and their claims enabling the British to disavow the acts imposed by the military might be considered a bid to renegotiate a new relationship with their British rulers. However, this was made politically too expensive by their attack against the O'Dwyer regime. O'Dwyer's combination of autocracy, paternalism, and repression was typical of the imperial class's preoccupation in the later nineteenth century with the insecurity of British rule. Such insecurity and a need for reprisal was again evoked by the attack on a British woman at Amritsar. These fears enabled the British official and military class who administered Indian rule to justify their previous policy, accepting O'Dwyer's explanation that the disorders were a product of tolerating rather than repressing agitation.

Apart from this question, the Congress Report concurs with the assumptions of the Hunter Report regarding the necessity of maintaining British rule. Nowhere does the Congress Report deny the legitimacy of British rule nor the necessity of maintaining order; it explicitly recognizes the justification for shooting into unruly crowds but questions its necessity in Amritsar on 10 April. Its judgment of means and ends is in terms of universal values allegedly held by the British. The Minority Report's imputation of violation of those values as un-British itself implies some transcendent national image to which Britons ought to conform regardless of personal character.

In demanding judgment, both the Congress and the Indian members of the Hunter Committee were only asking for payment in coin—and token payment at that—to ratify the trust which was the basis for the Cambridge-educated barristers' accepting national subordination. Both co-optation into the new legislature and other chambers and the nonviolent appeal to the conscience of the British preached by Gandhi presumed trust in the professed aims and underlying conscience of the British raj. If temporary subordination were to be internalized as legitimate, the Indians had to and evidently did regard themselves as having the rights of Englishmen. No violation, symbolic or physical, of their persons which reduced them to inferiors could be accepted. Collective punishment naturally led to an imputation of racial or group inferiority or expendability; this stigma could only be forgiven by the Indians by categorical counterjudgment of these punishments and their executors on the part of their governors.

There is sufficient evidence that these demands were correctly understood by the Government of India and the Cabinet. Yet the interests and ideology of the imperial bureaucracy were hardly attuned to the post–World War I demands from the top for a newer ideology of "liberal and progressive" imperialism. The unarticulated and nonverbal creed of General Dyer and Colonel Johnson seemed to be that the Indians owed them loyalty; the revenge of the mob in Amritsar proved to them that Indians were not to be trusted. They had always been latent enemies; now they could be treated as such.

Ultimately, the social structure of empire rested on the everyday performances of this network of the military, Indian mercenaries, police informers, and Anglo-Indian civil servants integrated in a bureaucratic chain. To discover a pattern of responsibility going up that chain might undermine the loyalty of its servants and provoke political attacks against the government by supporters in the pro-imperialist public and elite in England. To discover more than individual liability would have meant asking the Government of India to indict itself, which it was manifestly incapable of doing.

CHAPTER 7

The Reasoning Why: Analysis of the Parliamentary Debates

I am going to submit to this House this question, on which I would suggest with all respect they should vote: Is your theory of domination or rule in India the ascendancy of one race over another, of domination and subordination—or is your theory that of partnership?

—Edwin Montagu

Is there a Member of this House who believes that we govern India with the approval of those governed by us? . . . If we do not hold India by moral suasion then we must hold it by force. . . . This has an undoubted bearing on the case of General Dyer.

—Brigadier General Surtees

Debates were held in both Houses of Parliament in July 1920 on the sanction the Government of India had taken against Brig. Gen. Reginald E. Dyer for ordering the Amritsar massacre of 13 April 1919.[1] These debates were the first oportunity for a politically responsible body in Great Britain to express its toleration or condemnation of General Dyer's action. The Government of India, responding to censure of its investigating committee (Hunter Committee), had removed Dyer from his post and put him on unemployment pay, but Dyer had refused their request to resign, appealing their judgment to the Army Council.

The debates afford us an opportunity to determine what distinguishes Dyer's outspoken partisans from his opponents. I have hypothesized that Dyer's opponents will be distinguished from his supporters by their readiness to define Indians within the universe of moral obligation and will attempt to demonstrate this in this chapter by a formal analysis of the argumentation of the debate (treating the speeches in both Houses as one debate), starting from the speakers' own assumptions. But before this is undertaken, one might ask how Reginald Dyer first appeared in public eyes, and what was the political significance of the division in Parliament in terms of party, class, and regional interests.

PUBLIC OPINION IN GREAT BRITAIN

The British public in London was first informed of the nature of the firing in Jallianwala Bagh by reports in December 1919 of General Dyer's testimony before the Hunter Committee. *The Nation* remarked on 20 December 1919 that

> the mails arriving from India at the end of last week brought the first news to reach this country of a massacre near Amritsar, in the Punjab, which occurred a full eight months ago, on April 13th. . . . Mr. Montagu (Foreign Secretary) who sympathizes with the "profound disturbance" which this belated disclosure has caused in public opinion, admitted on question time on Tuesday, that he learned the details of this affair like the rest of us, for the first time from the Press the other day.

The shocked responses were cabled back to India by Reuters. The *Daily News* headlined it "Frightfulness," the *Daily Herald* entitled its lead article "Imperial Atrocities," and *The Times* of London said in smaller print that it was a massacre; the *Morning Post* alone defended Dyer. Bitter resentment over the British press reaction was noted in the British-Indian press in India by *The Times of India* (Bombay) at year's end.

The Times (London) published a letter on 30 December 1919 from Sir Michael O'Dwyer, who had retired in May 1919 as lieutenant governor of the Punjab, stating that he had told Montagu all the details of the shooting in two interviews in June 1919. By 17 June 1920 *The Times of India* reported that the British-Indian press was unanimous in denouncing Montagu's "mendacity" (in denying prior knowledge of Amritsar) and calling for his resignation.

The questionable belated knowledge of Montagu and the turnabout denied by the Government of India prepared the ground for a public counterattack by Sir Michael O'Dwyer, whose regime in the Punjab had been charged explicitly with responsibility for the Amritsar massacre by the Indian National Congress and implicitly by the Minority Report. While defending General Dyer before the Hunter Committee, O'Dwyer had carefully disassociated himself from responsibility for the Crawling Order and other acts under martial law, arguing that he had requested civilian control over the military but had been denied such by the Government of India. Later, he was to open a broad attack vilifying Montagu as the political source of civilian control over the Government of India's bureaucracy by the Foreign Office.[2]

DYER'S TESTIMONY IN ENGLAND

The Army Council resisted pressure from Secretary of State for War Churchill, Montagu, and Bonar Law (leader of the House of Commons) to confirm the censure without delay, and it agreed to hear Dyer's case on 9 June 1920.

After hiring a solicitor to defend him, Dyer changed his story and style completely. Writing to his commander in chief in August 1919, Dyer had stated that his intent was to produce "a sufficient moral effect, from a military point of view, not only on those who were present, but more especially throughout the Punjab." Testifying before the Hunter Committee, he disclaimed fear of being rushed by the crowd or being unable to disperse them with less force and admitted, responding to a question whether his idea was to strike terror, that "I was going to punish them." Did the committee understand whether he was referring to the crowd at Jallianwala Bagh on 13 April or to the mob that killed five Britishers in Amritsar on 10 April? Did Dyer understand? While the question had been ignored by the Hunter Committee, Dyer would now spell out his belief that the mob was one and indivisible, a continuous and reemergent entity. Dyer had been frank and consistent, even bragging of his motive in November 1919 before the Hunter Committee, and unwilling to take up any leads exonerating his action from legal culpability. But in June 1920 he presented a systematic and sophisticated defense before the Army Council—a defense made to fit the regulations for the use of firepower against civilians laid down in *The Manual of Military Law*. He maintained that the assembly of men gathered at the Jallianwala Bagh on 13 April 1919 was not an unlawful assembly but a case of rebellion—the only class of action that would justify firing as much as necessary to quell it. Dyer argued that he had sought to achieve a legitimate objective in dispersing that assembly. He concluded that he had secured that objective as the rebellion ceased after that day and that he had used the minimum force necessary to achieve that effect. His testimony, released by the government and published in full by several London and British-Indian newspapers after the Commons debate, depicts a climactic confrontation:

> Here it is sufficient to say that I knew that the final crisis had come, and that the assembly was primarily of the same mobs which had murdered and looted and burnt three days previously, and shown their truculence and contempt of the troops during the intervening days, that it was a deliberate challenge to the Government forces, and that if it were not dispersed, and dispersed effectively, with sufficient impression upon the designs of the rebels and their followers we should be overwhelmed during the night or the next day by a combination of the city gangs and of the still more formidable multitude from the villages.[3]

Dyer rejected the Hunter Committee's interpretation of his duty in that situation. He abstracted their presupposition deprecatingly:

> The principle in the only sense in which it is relevant to or supports the criticism of my action comes to this—that my sole right was to secure the purely mechanical effect of causing the crowd to move off from the place where it was and go resolved into its individual elements to some other place or places. What it might do wherever it or its elements went was no concern of mine. The fact that it might go off full of derision and contempt of my force to burn and loot elsewhere, or to surround and overwhelm my troops as they moved out of the city, was not to influence my action at all.[4]

PARLIAMENT'S EVALUATION: A HUNG JURY

Churchill announced to the House of Commons on 7 July 1920 the Army Council's unanimous reaffirmation of the decision of the commander in chief of the Indian Army to remove General Dyer from his employment and inform him that he would not be offered further employment in India. It was, he told them, the lightest sanction available. Dyer could have been stripped of rank and status or tried on criminal charges.

Sir Edward Carson, the prominent Unionist member from Ulster outside the governing coalition, brought up a motion on the floor of Commons on 8 July 1920 to reduce the salary of the secretary of state for India, Edwin Montagu, by £100 to express disapproval of the conduct of the Dyer case and his censure. A similarly worded resolution was brought up by Ben Spoor, floor whip for the Labour Party, in order to condemn all responsible for the Government of India's policy. His colleague J. R. Clynes stated that "we shall go into the Lobby, not for the purpose of reducing the salary of the Secretary of State for India, but as a protest against the action of the Government in taking no steps to remove those conditions of repression which provoked these instances of disorder and commotion and led to the unhappy Amritsar affair" [PDC:1804]. Their demand expressed a resolution unanimously passed at a recent Labour Party conference, whose sentiments, Spoor claimed, "much more correctly express what I believe to be the general feeling of the public in this country than the exhibition we have had here this afternoon" [PDC:1738].

By mutual agreement, a vote on Spoor's resolution was taken first; it failed by 247 to 37. When the second vote was taken, 34 of the left-wing opposition voted against the motion (Div. 196), helping to defeat it by 230 negative votes to 129 affirmatives. The vote was a test vote for the Cabinet.

The debate in Commons showed the interaction of ideology, party interests, and regional interests on imperial policy. Both parties of the left, Liberals and Labour, repudiated terrorism as a means of control, but the Unionists or Conservatives were divided on the uses of force for several reasons. Sir Edward Carson, mover of the motion in the House, and his supporters were not principled reactionaries like Sir William Joynson-Hicks (another motion advocate) but were generally hostile to the government because they represented Ulster and distrusted the government's fidelity to their interests in arranging a settlement in strife-torn Ireland. Their espousal of a hard line in India was not merely a tactical move to embarrass the government but was understood by contemporary observers to symbolize the policy they would like to see imposed on Ireland, where they feared Home Rule would ultimately mean the submission of the northern counties to a Catholic majority. *The Statesman's* London correspondent commented on 10 August 1920 that

> so far as Sir Edward Carson is responsible for those disciplinary movements the cause is doubtless to be found in the position in Ireland. . . . Instead of with a sword in one hand and an olive branch in the other the Government, in their [the Carsonites] opinion, ought to confront the recalcitrant population with swords in both hands. . . . They have shown it on such questions

as the Dyer affair and again in divisions of a more general
character, none of them of any special interest to Ulster.

Carson's opposition to rebellions and conspiracies was selective:
in 1914 he had encouraged gun-running and paramilitary training
in Ulster.

Although a majority of the coalition Unionists voting in Commons did vote against the motion, almost all the motion supporters were coalition Unionists. The motion received disproportionate support from Ulster members. Had not all the Labour
and Liberal members almost uniformly voted against the motion
(on Div. 196) the government would have been defeated. No
M.P.'s in the dominant coalition besides Cabinet members spoke
up in Commons against the motion except for Lt. Gen. Sir
Aylmer Hunter-Weston (Unionist) and Thomas Jewell Bennett
(Liberal). It was noted at the time that members with military officer's titles constituted a large part (55 members, or 43 percent
of 129 ayes) of motion supporters. However, 56 percent of the
military titled members whose vote is recorded voted against the
motion. All but one of the orators in Commons who held or had
held high Cabinet rank, including one past prime minister
(Herbert Asquith) and future prime minister (Winston Churchill)
of England, voted against the motion.

The Commons debate was marked by acrimony, for many
coalition Unionists reacted with indignation to Secretary of State
Montagu's charge of "frightfulness." His judgment, deleted by
the Government of India's press release, was vented spontaneously in the House in a tautly reasoned and hardly hyperbolic
j'accuse against the assumptions of the imperial class. Bonar
Law and Winston Churchill acted swiftly to bring members into
line to support the government, but the unpublished debate on
Edwin Montagu threatened to supplant the public debate on
Reginald Dyer.

The charge against Montagu by former Punjab Lt. Gov. Sir
Michael O'Dwyer—of hypocrisy and dissembling—was revived by
his speech. Montagu was already a marginal man among the imperial bureaucracy as a Jew, Liberal, and reformer: now he was
portrayed by his enemies as practically a foreign agent. To be
sure, even British radicals like Colonel Wedgewood regarded
Jews as members of a different race than the British, more akin
to the Indians, but they did not conceive of race as racists did.[5]

Montagu believed this himself, seeing this as an asset enabling him to associate with Indians more freely than could his colleagues.[6] But now his status as an outsider and the fact that he had concealed his own cognizance of the massacre—probably to avoid charges that the Dyer censure was biased by his own prejudgment as well as to conciliate both Indian politicians and the imperial class—enabled Dyer's partisans to deflect the charges against Dyer by projecting blame for Indian unrest onto Montagu. But these incidents did not stand alone—they could be fitted into the charges holding "international Jewry" responsible for communism, revolution, and war then propagated by publication of the fraudulent *Protocols of the Elders of Zion,* first published in London in February 1920 by His Majesty's Printers, Eyre & Spottiswoode, Ltd.[7] To make sure its readers saw the relation, the *Morning Post,* which later raised a public fund of over £26,000 for Dyer as "The Saviour of India", reprinted *The Protocols* in their columns that August. The *Morning Post* noted editorially that "in Palestine, ruled like India by a Jew, both Christian and Mohamedan are accusing the British Government of broken faith. . . . The course of events, in fact, is following the Bolshevik indications of the Bolshevik purpose with very remarkable accuracy."[8]

The anti-Semitic nature of the hostility to Montagu was suppressed on the floor. But Thomas Jewell Bennett, a member of Commons and a Liberal like Montagu who urged defeat of the motion, wrote in a letter to *The Times* on 12 July 1920 that the debate was "charged with personal antipathy towards Montagu— not free, as I am well warranted in saying, from the racial prejudice which worked mischief in France during the anti-Dreyfus controversy."

An advocate of the motion in the House, Ronald McNeill, denied Bennett's interpretation the next day in *The Times.* It is scarcely remarkable that men assuming an exclusive universe of obligation would expect betrayal from one not of their own kind, especially when there was a thriving new international propaganda movement explaining that all social turbulence was directed by a Jewish conspiracy. Ergo, look for the Jew. Neither is it a likely coincidence that a British novel published in 1920 compressed the stereotype of the radical M.P.'s who had betrayed the British governing class in India for the preceding

twenty years with the archetypical image of the Jew as the per-
fidious stranger. Allen Greenberger describes Casserley's villain
of the *Elephant God* as follows:

> Although the M.P. bears an "historic Highland name" he actual-
> ly is a foreign Jew who has become a Scot and he "hated the
> country of his adoption, as only these gentry do, and was ready
> to believe any lie against it and eager to do all in his power to in-
> jure it." "The Hebrew Highlander" describes himself as "a
> Pacifist and a socialist" and says that he does not "hold with
> soldiers or with keeping coloured races enslaved." . . . Macgregor
> is perfectly willing to see the anti-British forces move into the
> open, even with the support of the tribes beyond the Frontier, but
> he does warn them not to "kill the white women and children—at
> least not openly. They might not like it in England, although per-
> sonally, I don't care if you massacre every damned Britisher in
> the country."[9]

When one recalls that Lt. Gov. Sir Michael O'Dwyer had explained the Punjab "rebellion" as a product of foreign conspiracy which was originally planned to coincide with the third
Afghan War in May 1919, it becomes clear that we are confronted with a caricature of Edwin Montagu cloaked in this fic-
titious garb.

Scarcely two weeks after the Commons debate, on 20 July
1920, the House of Lords was to vindicate General Dyer by passing the motion (129 to 86) "that this house deplores the conduct
of the case of Gen. Dyer as unjust to that officer and as
establishing a dangerous precedent to the preservation of order
in face of rebellion." *The Times of India* (Bombay), noting the
good health of some nearly centenarian Tories, explained that
"the defeat of the Government was a foregone conclusion for
the friends of Gen. Dyer organized their forces with great vigour
and many unfamiliar faces from the backwoods were to be seen
on the crimson benches."[10]

The Lords, unlike Commons, was distinguished by the
speakers' deferential recognition of one another's authority.
Their deference was not ceremonial only: the Lords speakers in
the Dyer debate were a jury of the highest rank drawn from the
imperial governing class. Reviewing the careers of the sixteen
speakers, one finds that of the nine men who had served in India, five had been governors of the provinces, one had been
viceroy, and two became secretary of state for India. The one Indian, then undersecretary of state for India, Lord Sinha, was the

first Indian to ascend to the Viceroy's Executive Council and to a governor's chair, later in 1920. Other speakers included one present and two past lord chancellors and two secretaries of state for the colonies, one of whom had also served as secretary of state for India. Many speeches were enriched by the speaker's observations on his experiences in India. Apart from the archbishop of Canterbury, only two orators had not served in India or held a Cabinet post. Clearly, these sixteen speakers did not claim to represent a cross section of Lords. They spoke as experts as well as political men and advocates. They were men used to making public decisions, men who had a duty, they believed, to form opinions and persuade others.

Among the nine orators in Lords who had served in India, three voted to support Viscount Finlay's motion, five voted against it, and one abstained. Two of those who voted for it reasoned distinctively from the majority of its supporters in both Houses. All the present or past Cabinet members, except for Viscount Finlay (lord chancellor 1916-1919), voted against the motion. Apart from the archbishop of Canterbury (who voted no), the two remaining speakers without either Indian experience or high Cabinet rank voted for the motion. Thus, only six of the sixteen speakers in Lords voted for the motion, although it was passed by a three to two vote in Lords. The Lords demonstrated their sympathies to the British governing class in India by drawing sufficient peers away from their estates to form a majority. The army and the Indian Civil Service saw the sanction against Dyer as an attack on their prerogatives, since sons of peers were more likely to enter these organizations than were sons of the middle and working classes. The elite of that class who made imperial policy evidently did not accurately represent such a proimperialist public.

Notwithstanding Lord Sinha's and other peers' declaration that passage of Viscount Finlay's motion would be interpreted in India as condoning General Dyer's action, the Dyer debate in Lords was a call to the colors for principled reactionaries to stand up and articulate first principles. It drew new recruits— such as Lord Sumner, whose first speech (offered in the debate) was punctuated by many "Hear, hears"—to join the veterans of lost causes. These veterans included the Marquess of Salisbury, remembered for his hopeless battle to revive the powers of the House of Lords, and Lord Ampthill, who opposed passage of the Government of India Bill implementing the Montagu-Chelmsford reforms in December 1919.

ARRIVING AT JUDGMENT

Where do the two camps fundamentally diverge in respect to rendering judgment? To answer this question, I analyzed all arguments of each speaker that concluded in a judgment of Dyer's action, support or opposition to the motion, or support or opposition to the policy which the motion is interpreted to reject. Implicit premises were explicated to fit them into the best logical form according to the methods recommended by Irving Copi.[11] Sets of arguments were then divided by their makers' vote (both houses added together) on the motion into pro-Dyer and anti-Dyer camps. The arguments of each camp were aggregated and then reanalyzed to see how common were the initial premises and where the arguments deviated. The "trees" of judgment emerging from these syntheses are presented in the following paragraphs. Unlike some other tree models, the intersections do not necessarily indicate alternative assertions among which a speaker selects one line of argument; sometimes they represent divergent and often complementary arguments, one or more of which is pursued by each speaker.

The Equal Justice Tree

Most opponents of the motion—that is, the anti-Dyer camp—began with one or more assumptions on the equality of all lives, the equality of obligation to all people, or the single standard of justice which implies that any rule advocated must be consistently applied to all cases (see Figure 3). Lord Curzon expressed it bluntly:

> We cannot have—here I both agree and disagree with Lord Sumner—one rule for the treatment of our fellow-subjects in India and another rule for the treatment of our fellow-subjects here. . . . I suppose every one of you has read the account of the Jallianwala Bagh. . . . Extracting from all these presentations the real core of truth, is there anyone in your Lordships' House who can read that tale without sentiments of horror, and even of shame? If we condone this error we endorse the principles upon which Gen. Dyer acted, which have been defended here as sound principles. I agree with Lord Meston that we shall deal a blow at our reputation in India, we shall lower our own standards of

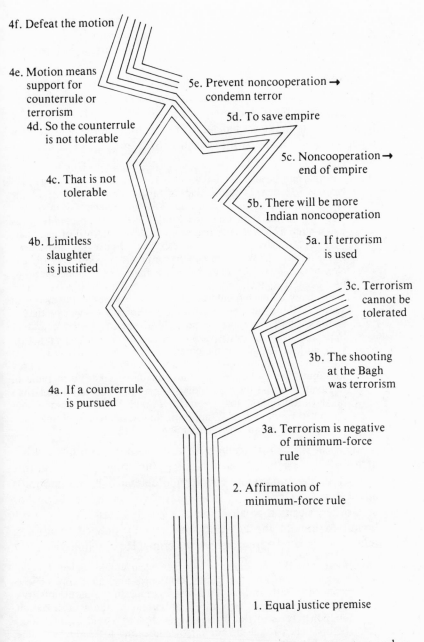

4f. Defeat the motion

4e. Motion means
    support for
    counterrule or
    terrorism

5e. Prevent noncooperation →
    condemn terror

4d. So the counterrule
    is not tolerable

5d. To save empire

4c. That is not
    tolerable

5c. Noncooperation →
    end of empire

5b. There will be more
    Indian noncooperation

4b. Limitless
    slaughter
    is justified

5a. If terrorism
    is used

3c. Terrorism
    cannot be
    tolerated

3b. The shooting
    at the Bagh
    was terrorism

4a. If a counterrule
    is pursued

3a. Terrorism is negative
    of minimum-force
    rule

2. Affirmation of
    minimum-force rule

1. Equal justice premise

Figure 3 The equal justice tree (width of branches represents number
of speakers employing this argument)

justice and humanity, we shall debase the currency of our national honour. [PDL:366]

Another rhetorical method of dramatizing this principle was to extend Dyer's justification by analogy and thus make explicit how unacceptable the consequences would be if it were to be followed. The analogy that later drew Lord Sumner's disdainful repudiation was made by the Marquess of Crewe:

> Here are 300 or 400 people who were shot at sight because a meeting had been proclaimed. Well for "India" read "Ireland." No one will deny, I think, that so far as the maintenance of the law is concerned, the South and West of Ireland are in a considerably worse state than the Punjab ever was; probably in as bad a state as it was ever feared it could be, in April of last year. Yet, for "Amritsar" read "Limerick" or "Ennis," or some town in the South and West and conceive a precise repetition of the circumstances there. You may be sure that, after public meetings had been forbidden and a crowd collected to hear a speech, a great many of them would be of the same species as the men who committed the outrages at Amritsar. But who will say that it would be wise, or right, or possible to open fire on a crowd of that kind listening to a speech, and to go on shooting until they were all killed? And yet the parallel seems to me fairly exact; and unless we are to admit—which I am sure no one here is prepared to admit—that although it is unfortunate to take life in India in this way, yet the lives of Indian rioters are less important than those of European rioters, you must take the Irish parallel and see what would be said supposing indiscriminate shooting took place in the same way in an Irish town. [PDL:263]

All speakers in this camp with a consecutive argument either affirmed the necessity of upholding the minimum force rule directly or denounced the counterrule defended by the motion's advocates. Lt. Gen. Sir Aylmer Hunter-Weston declared that law and order meant that all soldiers, as well as all citizens, were bound to uphold the law and were equally obliged to use the minimum force to repress disorder or crime. He concluded that

> these are the principles which are clearly laid down for our guidance, and are continually drummed into all Army officers from their earliest days. To allow anything in the nature of Prussian "frightfulness" is entirely abhorrent to the British nation, and, therefore, to the British Army, for, as I said in this House before, when I had the honour of addressing it for the first time, in the dark days of War, the army and the nation are one. [PDC:1746]

Using force to create a "wide impression," to inspire awe, or to make people submissive out of fear is known as "frightfulness," "Prussianism," intimidation, or terrorism. Dyer's action at Jallianwala Bagh is an instance of this policy. Frightfulness, the opposite of the minimum-force policy, is evaluated not only as inhuman but *un-British,* and half the speakers in this camp condemned it on these grounds. Churchill, for example, proclaimed that

> we cannot admit this doctrine in any form. Frightfulness is not a remedy known to the British pharmacopoeia. [PDC:1728]

The intrepid Colonel Wedgwood avowed that

> it is more important to save the national honour than to save any particular item in the nation. I would rather, for the interests of our country, that English men and women had been shot down at Jallianwala by Indians than that Indians had been shot down by Englishmen. . . . The principal charge I make against Dyer is not that he shot down Indians, but that he placed on English history the gravest blot since in days gone by we burned Joan of Arc at the stake. [PDC:1788]

Mr. Young made an astute analysis of why terrorism cannot be considered an extension of punishment and how it is antithetical to law, if not to order:

> The principle of the minimum force applied to immediate circumstances is the charter of protection of the lives, liberty, and safety of the civilian population from unduly violent action. . . . Once remove that, and the authorities are set at liberty to take what action they please for intimidation, and it must be the characteristic that action for intimidation will be indiscriminate. Punishment is then set free in its relation to crime. . . . Intimidation is as well served by action against the innocent as the guilty. What appears to me as the last and strongest argument against an extension of the rule is this. . . . The only way to prevent the would-be wrongdoers from committing crime is to convince them . . . that crime, and crime only, is immediately followed by punishment. [PDC:1786]

Two different but complementary lines of argument stem from categorizing the shooting as an instance of terrorism. The Marquess of Crewe, employing the first line, repudiated the argument that certain means may be justified because of one side's inferiority with conventional means by generalizing the doctrine to illustrate how it might be used to rationalize the use of unacceptable means. Denying that such consequences are tolerable, he then denied the doctrine of using any means necessary:

It is surely a most dangerous argument to use, that because your force is a small one you may legitimately employ methods which a larger force would not think of employing. Poison gas would disperse a much larger crowd very quickly with a much smaller number of men, but nobody suggests that it should be adopted as a means of dealing with unlawful gatherings, however forcibly, by Proclamation or otherwise, you have announced your intention to punish them. [PDL:261]

The second line of argument asserts that terrorism will provoke further disorders or noncooperation on the part of the Indians, which will lead to the decline of the empire. Montagu opened the debate in the House of Commons, compressing this and several previous arguments together, in a speech audibly interrupted by angry grumblings:

The whole point of my observations is directed to this one question: that there is one theory upon which I think Gen. Dyer acted, the theory of terrorism, and the theory of subordination. There is another theory, that of partnership, and I am trying to justify the theory endorsed by this House in passing the Indian reforms last year. . . . I am going to submit to this House this question, on which I would suggest with all respect they should vote: Is your theory of domination or rule in India the ascendancy of one race over another, of domination and subordination—(HON. MEMBERS: "NO!")—or is your theory that of partnership? If you are applying domination as your theory, then it follows that you must use the sword with increasing severity—(HON. MEMBERS: "No!")—until you are driven out of the country by the united opinion of the civilised world. *(Interruption.)* (An HON. MEMBER: "Bolshevism!") If your theory is justice and partnership, then you will condemn a soldier, however gallant . . . who says that there was no question of undue severity, and that he was teaching a moral lesson to the whole Punjab. [PDC:1710]

The forecast that terrorism implied the death toll of the empire was reiterated by Spoor and Clynes (Labour spokesmen) and Bennett and Colonel Wedgwood. Ben Spoor prophesied that:

India may be governed by consent; India will never again be governed by force. . . . The only logical course, if we are to expect consistency at all, is to be found in the pursuance of the liberal spirit which is supposed to inspire the reforms of last year, and which we are told this afternoon aims at leading the people of India into liberty. If this last course is followed, it obviously involves the condemnation of all those who have been responsible for this reactionary policy. We of the Labour party, and I speak for all my colleagues, stand for the last course. . . . It involves the recall of the Head of the Indian Government, the trial of Sir

Michael O'Dwyer, Gen. Dyer and the others implicated, a trial in his Majesty's Courts of Justice. [PDC:1741-2]

Ben Spoor criticized the secretary of state for India, Edwin Montagu, for not having made adequate restitution to the Indian people when he simply removed Dyer from his post.

Lord Sinha, representing Montagu, had the formidable mission to convince the Lords of the need to reaffirm the Cabinet's imperialist policy rather than Dyer's, to defend the Government of India's role in the case, to represent the sentiments of his countrymen—and yet to distinguish his position, and that of the moderates, from the "extremists" and Gandhi. Unlike Montagu, who was referred to resentfully and derisively by his opponents, Lord Sinha was complimented by his peers for his moderation and tact. He concluded with even-handed admonitions to both parties:

> *Satyagraha,* passive resistance, civil disobedience, or by whatever name it has been called, has been, to some extent at any rate, if not to a great extent, responsible for the spirit of lawlessness which resulted in these disorders. I ask my fellow-countrymen to lay well that lesson to their hearts. I ask them to dissociate themselves from a similar pernicious movement started by Mr. Gandhi —a movement which he calls by another name, that of non-cooperation. It can only lead to the same disastrous results as the *Satyagraha,* or the civil disobedience movement, produced in April of last year. . . . If the Government of India is only allowed to pursue the wise course it is now pursuing, I have no doubt that soon there will not be a single Indian, either Hindu or Mussulman, who will subscribe to, or act upon, that doctrine.
>
> But if there is that lesson to be learned by my countrymen, there is also another to be learned by the Government. . . . Do not interfere too hastily or too violently, with an agitation of this nature. . . . Ruthless methods of repression and coercion result in disorder as much as passive resistance, and direct action, or civil disobedience. [PDL:251]

That "pernicious movement" of noncooperation, disputed in July but advocated by an unexpected majority in December 1920, had been propagated by the organization of which Lord Sinha was president in 1916, the Indian National Congress.

While all the doctrinaire anti-imperialists from both the Liberal and the Labour Party end up in the government camp opposing the motion, the majority of spokesmen against the motion were not anti-imperialists. Several of these men, like the ex-viceroy, Curzon, and Winston Churchill, conceived of themselves as representing a higher image of imperialism. Churchill proudly boasted that

> governments who have seized upon power by violence and by usurpation have often resorted to terrorism in their desperate efforts to keep what they have stolen, but the august and venerable structure of the British Empire, where lawful authority descends from hand to hand and generation after generation, does not need such aid. Such ideas are absolutely foreign to the British way of doing things. [PDC:1729]

To such men as these, the Crawling Order was as dreadful as the massacre at the Bagh, as it was to Gandhi.[12] Lord Carmichael, former governor of Bengal, was unable to make up his mind as to whether Dyer's action was justified; he claimed that if he voted, he would vote against the motion to express his disapproval of the Crawling Order.[13] Such speakers derided Dyer's later rationalization that it was intended to make Indians show reverence for the site at which Miss Sherwood was attacked by proceeding as they would in a temple.

The Authority Tree

Most of the motion's supporters—that is, the pro-Dyer camp—began with the premise that they must save India: by saving it they meant saving it for British rule, an objective not always made explicit.[14] A few expressed some presuppositions about the nature of that rule or axioms about authority in general. (See Figure 4.)

Lord Ampthill maintained that saving India from rebellion was not only in the interest of Britain but of India:

> The noble viscount has further invited the opinion of this House as to whether the course of action adopted by His Majesty's Government did, or did not, constitute a dangerous precedent; in other words, whether it was in the best interests of India, for no country has a higher interest than that of the preservation of law and order. [PDL:288]

Authority was proclaimed to be indivisible and nonnegotiable by Lord Sumner:

> No Government can tolerate a challenge to its authority; and, sooner or later, a Government which lets itself be challenged must come to an end. [PDL:338]

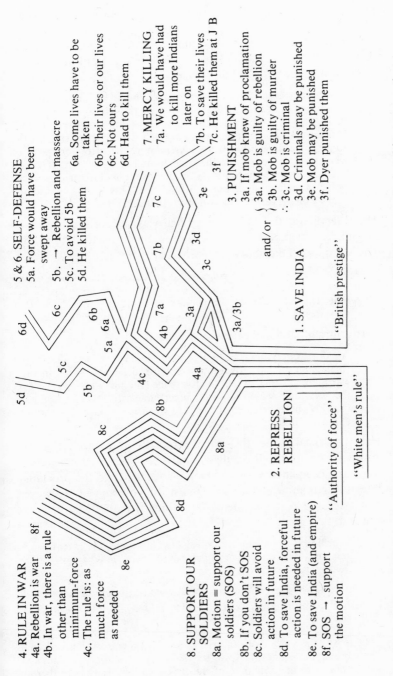

4. RULE IN WAR
4a. Rebellion is war
4b. In war, there is a rule other than minimum-force
4c. The rule is: as much force as needed

8. SUPPORT OUR SOLDIERS
8a. Motion = support our soldiers (SOS)
8b. If you don't SOS
8c. Soldiers will avoid action in future
8d. To save India, forceful action is needed in future
8e. To save India (and empire)
8f. SOS → support the motion

"Authority of force"

"White men's rule"

2. REPRESS REBELLION

1. SAVE INDIA

"British prestige"

3. PUNISHMENT
3a. If mob knew of proclamation
3a. Mob is guilty of rebellion   and/or
3b. Mob is guilty of murder
∴ 3c. Mob is criminal
3d. Criminals may be punished
3e. Mob may be punished
3f. Dyer punished them

5 & 6. SELF-DEFENSE
5a. Force would have been swept away
5b. → Rebellion and massacre
5c. To avoid 5b
5d. He killed them
6a. Some lives have to be taken
6b. Their lives or our lives
6c. Not ours
6d. Had to kill them

7. MERCY KILLING
7a. We would have had to kill more Indians later on
7b. To save their lives
7c. He killed them at J B

Figure 4   The authority tree (width of branches represents number of speakers employing this argument)

While a few speakers in this camp generalized that force is the basis for all rule, Brigadier General Surtees was frank to say why force must be the basis of Indian rule:

> We cannot, even if we wish, surrender India. We are irrevocably committed to it. Is there a Member of this House who believes that we govern India with the approval of those governed by us? It is an undisputed fact, and one which has some bearing on the Amritsar incident, that if a *plebiscite* were taken to-morrow as to who should govern India the result would be against us. If we do not hold India by moral suasion then we must hold it by force— possibly thinly veiled, but still by force. This has an undoubted bearing on the case of General Dyer. [PDC:1777]

The assembly at the Jallianwala Bagh was categorized by ten of the thirteen members of this camp as an instance of rebellion. The Marquess of Salisbury explained that

> if these men who were collected at Jallianwala Bagh knew of the Proclamation, they were guilty of rebellion. I do not mean to say that they all deserved the penalty of death. . . . But I say that they are not to be looked upon as innocent persons. [PDL:272]

Lord Ampthill declared categorically that

> Anyone who knows anything about India is aware that every single man of that crowd knew of the Proclamation and, in fact, was there in order to defy it. Everyone had had warning, and further warning was not only superfluous, but would, unquestionably, have defeated the object which it was Gen. Dyer's duty to pursue. [PDL:297]

Half the speakers in this camp explicitly recognized that the crowd was willfully disobedient, and knew of the proclamation. Rebellion is equated with knowing disobedience to the proclamation rather than armed attack against the government. However, it merits grave punishment, according to the Marquess of Salisbury:

> Rebellion is the greatest crime against the state. . . . It is the most heinous thing which a subject can do, and it is, in its nature, treason. [PDL:272]

Rebellion is not the only crime the crowd gathered at Jallianwala Bagh had committed. Viscount Finlay added another assumption (3b):

> It was the same mob, in effect, Gen. Dyer says, which had committed the crime of April 10. They knew of the Proclamation. They were there in spite of the Proclamation. They were there in

spite of the Proclamation in order to show that they were stronger than the Government, and to defy the order of the Government. [PDL:232]

Lord Ampthill presumed also that it was the same mob:

> But does any one doubt that if General Dyer had done less, that this vast defiant mob of rebels would have dispersed to perhaps ten different places in order to resume the work of murder, pillage and arson, which they had commenced on the previous days. [PDL:297]

If they had committed such crimes, they were criminals who deserved to be punished. Refuting the equal justice argument of the anti-Dyer camp, Lord Sumner said that he, too, believed in one rule for all people, regardless of race or nationality. Any mob which murders Englishmen will, in return, receive the same treatment as the gathering in Jallianwala Bagh. But,

> I decline to discuss the hypothesis that in any country—in Limerick, in Glasgow, or anywhere else, in the state of civilisation and with the long political experience that our populations have enjoyed—it is possible that such a case should arise as that which arose at Amritsar. Therefore, my answer leaves out of account the cities that have been named, because I refuse to consider that such cases can arise there. But if it should arise, in any part of the Empire where such things are possible, that in the course of one afternoon bank managers should be clubbed to death and burnt in a pile with their bank books, a lady beaten and left for dead, a guard hammered to death, a sergeant with his brains beaten out, a lady doctor searched for all over the hospital where she ministered; if it were possible that thousands of rebels should assemble and set fire to Government buildings and property and at the same time endeavour to isolate the locality from help, then the answer is, that the same rule should apply there as applied at Jallianwallah Bagh. According to the measure of the necessity of the case would be the force that would be employed. [PDL:338]

Viscount Finlay reaffirmed that these were not innocent people; therefore, they were people who might rightfully be punished:

> Let me not be misunderstood. No man is more averse from what is called frightfulness than I am. The essence of frightfulness, of which we have had of late years some conspicuous examples on the continent of Europe, is that innocent people are treated severely and harshly with a view of producing an effect elsewhere. In defense of such conduct I never should utter a word, but the question here is a totally different one. [PDL:225]

General Dyer, then, punished a crowd of criminals who had not been apprehended previously. However, this limb (3) of the authority tree is complementary to a thicker bough which classifies the gathering as an instance of rebellion. Assuming this to be the case, what is the counterrule that should be followed?

Rebellion is a state of war; the extent of force one may use is without limit in war.

Sir William Joynson-Hicks avowed that

> if there was a real rebellion, as I submit there was, and as the Commissioners found there was, then General Dyer's action was justified. It was a rebellion which might have led to almost anything; in fact, it was open rebellion.
>
> It is not a question in these circumstances as to how far General Dyer should have gone, because he was at war with a section of the people of India, and a section of the people of India were at war with General Dyer. [PDC:1759]

Colonel James also implied, in a string of metaphors as telling as his conclusion, that there is no legitimate limit:

> They say that it was brutal and horrible to kill so many people. There are three ideas which occur to me. You cannot put out a fire in a warehouse, which has caught well alight, with a teacup. Equally, as has been said, if your house catches fire, it is no use telling the fireman, after he has put your fire out, that he has used too much water to do it. You cannot kill a tiger gently; I defy you to do it. Lastly, supposing a burglar came into your house, and you had a life-preserver, and hit him on the head with the intention of stunning him, it is impossible to say what force you would use. [PDC:1753]

Finally, Lord Sumner (known in his undergraduate days for his radical views) proclaimed this provocative conclusion:

> And it is the foundation of the whole of this case that Gen. Dyer was right in firing; that he was right in taking human life; that the occasion had arisen—the most painful of any in civil administration—when, in order to maintain civil order, and the authority of the Government, opponents, even unarmed opponents, had to be killed. . . . According to the view which the Government has taken of it, it was the number of lives taken at Jallianwallah Bagh that was by far the main part of what was done by Gen. Dyer which is deserving of criticism and censure. It becomes a question then of numbers. No one can possibly tell how many persons it would have been proper, lawful and necessary to kill. [PDL:327]

Lord Sumner was willing to concede that the crowd was unarmed; some in his camp denied this, however, dwelling on the
injuries which can be inflicted with bamboo clubs.

From accepting the counterrule of limitless force—or, stated
positively, as much force as is necessary to suppress rebellion—
two branches diverge. One (limb 7) asserts that if the rebellion
had not been squashed by sufficent force at Amritsar, more Indian lives would eventually have had to be taken. About half the
speakers in the pro-Dyer camp affirmed this position. Lord Sumner, as usual, extended it to its extremity:

> If worse happened than did happen—I am not going to prophesy
> or paint a black picture—who would have suffered more than the
> Indian population themselves? It was in mercy to them, in order
> that they might not die, that it became the duty of General Dyer
> to use force and put to death those who were challenging the
> authority of the Government, who were rebels, only not in arms.
> [PDL:338]

The Marquess of Salisbury declared that the motion which
condoned that policy was a lesson for the benefit of Indian people, just as Lord Sumner had shown that it was a mercy killing:

> The people of India are entering upon a great experiment; and
> surely the lesson which, above all others, you must teach them is
> that there is nothing in self-government which authorises dis-
> order. . . . Those who are interested in this experiment in India
> ought to be the first to wish to inculcate the same lesson in the
> people of India. They should say, "We are going to entrust you
> with great liberty, but that does not mean the licensing of dis-
> order. On the contrary, we will show you that the worst thing you
> can do is to defy the authority of the Government." [PDL:374]

Another line (terminating in limb 5d) asserts that if General
Dyer had not fired without warning, his force would have been
swept away by the weight of the crowd and rebellion and massacre (of the British population) would have occurred. Viscount
Finlay, the mover of the motion, proposed a variation of this approach (limb 6): it was a case of English lives or those of Indians. However, any invidious racial evaluation was concealed by
characterizing the party deserving of being saved as innocent and
those who must be killed as guilty:

> If he had hesitated, the rebellion would have acquired irresistable
> momentum. Your Lordships will recollect that there were many
> women and children who had taken refuge in the so-called fort,

who, if the mob had triumphed, would have been at their mercy. I shall not picture what their fate might have been. If life is to be taken—and it is a hateful necessity—I would rather that the lives taken were those of the members of a criminal mob than of law-abiding citizens who have been loyal to the Crown and to the Empire.[PDL:230]

Both Brigadier General Surtees and Mr. Palmer similarly implied that further horrifying consequences would have occurred if Dyer had not fired as he did. Surtees attempted to place the firing in historical perspective:

> Many Members of this House, if they do not remember, as I do, are still cognisant of the facts of the Jamaica Rebellion in 1865, which rebellion was put down properly and most strongly by Governor Eyre. Governor Eyre was persecuted by John Bright and John Stuart Mills [sic] in the same way as General Dyer is being persecuted by certain individuals, and on that occasion Sir John Pakington, speaking in Debate in this House said:
> "He acted in full pursuance of the belief that the handful of Europeans who inhabited that island was not safe from attack by the 400,000 half-civilised and infuriated negroes."
> I think something similar to that was in General Dyer's mind. [PDC:1776]

Palmer then reminded his colleagues what else might have happened to their innocent women and children:

> In a city of the Punjab frightened [European] women had taken refuge in one of the rallying points, as they were called, waiting eagerly for the arrival of the troops, and whilst there notices were issued by the natives stating that there were 80 women and children waiting to be ravaged. In fact, no girls' school was sacred. [PDC:1781]

The majority of the original nine men who asserted that the gathering at Jallianwala Bagh was an instance of rebellion agreed that the motion was a censure of the government's censure of Dyer. Although the government had chosen the lightest sanction available—removing Dyer from his position rather than stripping him of rank, forcing his resignation, or holding a court-martial—its condemnation of the policy by which he had justified his action was explicit in the press releases on the case. Furthermore, the censure had been confirmed by the commander in chief of the Indian Army, the Government of India, the Foreign Office, the Cabinet, and the War Council. Why did the motion's advocates believe it to be imperative to negate that censure?

Sir Edward Carson, former first lord of the admiralty, recalled his experiences in service and avowed that

> you must back your men, and it is not such a distinction, as I have already shown, that is the origin of this matter as to this error of judgment, that will ever give confidence to those faithful and patriotic citizens who have been the men who have won for you and kept your great Empire beyond the seas. [PDC:1715]

The consequences believed to follow from not supporting "the man on the spot" were the real issue, according to the Marquess of Salisbury:

> Do not let us think too much of Gen. Dyer. I know that he did some things of which many of your Lordships do not approve. I agree. . . . But what is the broad question. The issue your Lordships are going to try to-night is whether, when officers do their very best in positions of great difficulty (and positions in which, if they had not done their duty, the most formidable consequences would have ensued) they are to be supported by the Government or not. That is the real issue. If your Lordships do not support this Motion you will strike a great blow at the confidence of the whole body of officers throughout your Empire. [PDL:375]

THE AUTHORITY OF FORCE AND THE
FORCE OF AUTHORITY

Lord Sumner said that if the empire was to be preserved, "it is by the prestige of the British name, by the authority of force, which is in reserve but rarely used, that dangers like this are to be met" [PDL:339]. Brigadier General Surtees reminded his colleagues that British rule was the rule of one or a few white men over thousands of natives of other races: they could easily be overwhelmed by them, "but for one thing. That one thing is British prestige. Once you destroy that British prestige, then the Empire will collapse like a house of cards" [PDC:1775].

Both Sumner and Surtees concurred in foreseeing that the awe which made force unnecessary was vanishing. They predicted that the empire would increasingly have to rely on the military to repress rather than impress the colonials. Lord Sumner contemplated "with alarm the prospect, in the years to come, that it will be increasingly often the duty of military men to deal with sudden outbreaks, or sudden appearances of rebellion, which do not bear the character of an armed revolt but which must be

repressed at once, and therefore sternly and unhesitatingly"
[PDL:339].

If the empire must depend increasingly on the military, it was
essential that the military be ready to act "unhesitatingly."
Surtees begged his colleagues

> to consider carefully the effect of this Debate, not only in India,
> but among the civilised and uncivilised peoples among whom we
> rule. . . . An indiscreet speech or a careless vote may cause a fatal
> explosion. This House, unlike the Hunter Commission, cannot
> confine itself to local issues, but must concern itself with the
> probable effect of its speeches on the multitude of races which are
> swayed by various influences. [PDC:1775]

It would deter trouble if the natives realized this. A vote against
the motion would relay the wrong message.

CHAPTER 8
Testing the Hypothesis
Through Content Analysis

This chapter is devoted to an exposition of findings based on content analysis. Since the speakers' logic was analyzed in the preceding Chapter in their own words, examples will be omitted from this chapter to avoid repetition. All code references are to the Code Sheet in Appendix A.

In Chapter 5, it was assumed that the vote on the motion was a judgment on the firing at Jallianwala Bagh. That judgment was first rated on a 1 to 5 scale—from "Dyer innocent and firing correct" to "firing was a crime" (IV.G)—for all speakers expressing an explicit judgment; later the fourth and fifth steps were aggregated because only one speaker was ranked on the fifth step.

The assumption was correct. Among speakers making an explicit judgment of the firing, a positive or neutral evaluation is always associated with a vote for the motion and a strong negative judgment with a vote against. Those who called the shooting an "error" of judgment, concurring with the Hunter Committee's majority evaluation, were more likely to vote for than against the motion.

Not surprisingly, half of the motion's opponents called the

shooting (or all the collective punishments inflicted against Indians) an instance of "terrorism," "frightfulness," "intimidation," or "Prussianism" while almost the same proportion (5 of
13) of its supporters denied that the shooting was a case of terrorism. (The remainder in both camps refrained from labeling it;
no man affirmed the opposite view to that expressed by the majority of his camp.) Half the motion's opponents judged the
shooting and the Crawling Order in the context of martial law,
but all the motion's advocates save one restricted their judgment
to the massacre. The shooting at Jallianwala Bagh was not the
only issue to the motion's opponents, but it was the sole issue on
which its supporters chose to defend Dyer.

THE TOLERATION OF COLLECTIVE VIOLENCE

The judgment on upholding the sanction against General Dyer
enables us to test the proposition that sanctioning of offenses as
crimes depends on inclusion of the victim in the judge's universe
of obligation. It was hypothesized in Chapter 5 that speakers
defining Indians within the universe of moral obligation would
vote against the motion condemning the Dyer sanction and those
not defining them within that universe would vote for the motion. Conversely, speakers voting against the motion would be
more likely to show signs of moral inclusiveness than those
voting for the motion.

Moral inclusiveness or exclusiveness is denoted on the level of
normative beliefs, cognitive appraisal,[1] and sentiment. Belief, in
cases where relevant assertions are made, is expressed by the
speaker's own assertion of premises regarding the equal value of
all lives and equal justice due all people. Speakers' assertions on
this matter could be divided into instances of affirmations,
denials, or denunciations of "racialism" with scarcely any exception. An additional assertion—the equal justice premise of one
rule for all cases—was coded separately but given the same
logical value for analysis as the denunciation of racialism. These
assertions, their logical values as indices of moral inclusiveness
(+) or exclusiveness (−), and their item numbers on the Code
Sheet (see IV.I) in Appendix A are shown in Table 5.

Analysis showed that 11 of the 12 men asserting morally inclusive postulates voted against the motion, as was hypothesized.
However, over a third of the speakers voting against the motion

Table 5 Codes of Assertions Related to Moral Inclusiveness

Assertion	Logical value	Code Sheet item
No assertion made	0	X
Assertion some (or our) lives are more important than others (or theirs)	−1	0
Denial of charge of "racialism" or resentment at charge expressed	0	1
Denunciation of belief (attributed to others) that Indian (or native) lives are less important or affirmation of equal value of all lives	+1	2
Affirmation that equal justice is due Indians or due all people or all British subjects in all places regardless of race	+1	Y

and over half of those voting for the motion expressed no postulates on this theme. Since only one speaker, Viscount Finlay, the mover of the motion, asserted a preference for protecting English lives before those of Indians (implying an exclusive postulate), one cannot conclude that supporters of the motion are more likely to hold exclusive postulates from this evidence alone but it does show they were extremely unlikely to hold inclusive ones.

The finding that all four speakers who denied "racialism" being present in the debate voted for the motion is certainly thought-provoking, if inconclusive in its implication. Such a denial is not a logical equivalent of an inclusive or exclusive postulate, but denial may serve as a psychological defense against admitting rejected but covertly held private prejudices into public rhetoric. Such sentiments may be those of the speaker who wants to make his arguments seem more respectable, or they may be prejudices rejected by the speaker but present among spokesmen in the same camp. Thus, denial may be either a tactic based on hypocrisy or an assertion that one rejects the implications of code words commonly employed in political rhetoric.

Moral inclusiveness was presumed to be demonstrable by belief, consistency in appraisal, and positive empathy with Indians as victims, as well as by identification with Indians as a community whose views ought to be considered in arriving at a decision. Unfortunately, it was impossible to measure the presence or absence of a double standard between judgment on Dyer and judgment on the crowd at Jallianwala Bagh because some of the original items coded were later eliminated from the analysis due to low intercoder agreement.[2]

Sentiment was measured by indices of identification and empathy. To obtain a measure of positive identification, the number of paragraphs containing negative general references to Indians was subtracted from the number containing positive reference to them as either an audience or a constituency within the empire which ought to be taken into account. Since references to particular Indians, such as Gandhi, or judgments on the rioters of 10 April 1919 and the crowd at Jallianwala Bagh on 13 April 1919 were not counted as general references, this is only a crude index of the intensity of positive and negative characterization of Indians.

To make figures comparable, the net number of paragraphs with positive identifications (subtracting paragraphs with negative from those with positive identifications) in each speech was converted into a ratio of the total number of paragraphs and the ratio was then classed into below average, average (median), and high classes. Most speakers scarcely referred to Indians at all as an audience. Corresponding to expectations, tabulation showed that proportionately more of the motion's opponents (six out of eighteen) fell into the high-identification category than of the motion's supporters (two out of thirteen). Three of the motion's supporters (and none of its opponents) were in the below-average category because they showed more negative than positive identification with Indians.

Supporters of the motion employ more testimonials both from English men and women resident in India and from native Indians supporting Dyer's action than opponents employ to support their argument. However, the supporters cite two and a half times as many testimonials from Englishmen as from Indians. Most testimonials from Indians are from "loyal" natives, naturally, or refer to the Sikh initiation rites offered to Dyer which are imputed to signify that community's approval of him.

The presence of empathy was measured by an affirmation of one or more key items. The negation of empathy was indicated by a denial of one or more of them or by affirmation of the contrary. These items are listed in Table 6.

The great majority of speakers (8 of 10) who empathized at all with the Indians voted against the motion. All those with negative indices of identification voted for the motion. The opponents were much more likely to show sympathy for the Indians than were the motion's supporters. The majority of the motion's supporters made assertions which would refute the existence of grounds for sympathy by denying that any Indians were victims or minimizing the number of victims. No men who voted against the motion or abstained made any such assertions.

To assess the hypothesis, the positive and negative indices of moral inclusiveness demonstrated by postulates, identification rank, and empathy index were aggregated to produce a "moral inclusiveness score" of $+3$ to -3 (exclusiveness). The hypothesis that speakers voting for the motion were more likely to be characterized by exclusiveness and speakers against the motion by inclusiveness was confirmed. The absence of any positive (inclusive) or negative (exclusive) indice for a speaker adds up to a zero score, as does the same number of positive and negative indices. Few speakers were characterized by contradictory indices.

Looking at the twenty-five speakers with a positive or negative score for whom a prediction of the vote could be made in Table

Table 6   Codes of Indices of Empathy

Positive indices of empathy	Code Sheet Item	Negative indices of empathy
The Crawling Order made people crawl. (Affirm)	III.D. 8	The Crawling Order did not make people crawl. (Affirm)
At least 379 Indians were killed by the firing at Jallianwala Bagh. (Affirm)	III.D. 13	Fewer than 379 Indians were killed by the firing at Jallianwalla Bagh. (Affirm)
The crowd at Jallianwala Bagh was innocent of wrongdoing and/or helpless victims. (Affirm)	III.E.	The crowd (each, all, or every member of it) was guilty. . .(Affirm)

Table 7   Moral Inclusiveness-Exclusiveness Score of Each
           Speaker by Vote

Score	Voted yes	Voted no	No vote recorded
Inclusive			
+3		Bennett Wedgwood	
+2	Lamington	Birkenhead Buckmaster Churchill Crewe Curzon Montagu Sinha Spoor	Carmichael
+1	James	Canterbury Clynes Harris Meston	Asquith
Neutral			
0	Davidson Midleton Palmer Sumner	Hunter-Weston Law Milner Young	
Exclusive			
−1	Ampthill Carson Joynson-Hicks Salisbury Surtees		
−2	Gwynne Finlay		
−3			

7, we find the vote of twenty-one is what we would predict from their moral inclusiveness score. At most, the score "mispredicts" two of twenty-five votes, or 8 percent. Herbert Asquith's speech, strongly urging his colleagues to defeat the motion, indicated that he intended to vote against the motion, so it seems probable that he was not a deliberate abstainer but was not on the floor when the vote was taken (11 P.M.). Lord Carmichael, who did abstain deliberately, indicated that if he voted he would vote against the motion (see Chapter 7, note 15). Lord Lamington, one of those mispredicted, protested during and after the vote that he did not vote to express approval of Dyer's action.[3]

As might be expected by chance, the speakers for whom no prediction could be made (zero score) evenly split on the vote.

ASSESSING THE COUNTERHYPOTHESIS

It was previously proposed that if readiness to condone violence is explained by the perception of threat, one would expect that speakers who believed British rule was fundamentally threatened would be more tolerant of the shooting than would speakers who did not so believe. Two predictions were extracted from this.

The first prediction was that speakers appraising events in Amritsar before the massacre as evidence of rebellion, conspiracy, or revolution would be more likely to assert that General Dyer was innocent, that his guilt was impossible to assess, or that he committed an error and to vote for the motion, than those believing that what occurred in Amritsar was a riot or response to British repression would be to exonerate Dyer and vote for the motion. Since the vote on the motion corresponds almost perfectly to the judgment on the gravity of Dyer's action, and the vote is available for all members whereas an explicit judgment is lacking for some, this hypothesis was tested against the vote on the motion.

The expected relationship was confirmed. Ten of fifteen speakers who called it a rebellion voted for the motion, but the contrary relationship is even stronger. Among speakers defining the situation as a riot or civil disorder or in another category (usually a denial of rebellion without an explicit assertion of riot), all but one voted against the motion. However, one-third of those calling it a rebellion also voted against the motion. How do they differ from their colleagues who defined the situation as a rebellion and voted for the motion? Two of the five speakers defining the context to be either rebellion, insurrection, conspiracy, or revolution who voted against the motion asserted a morally inclusive postulate. This relationship is suggestive but weak.

The second prediction was that a speaker's evaluation of the minimum-force rule is a function of his political definition of the situation. Those who affirmed that the situation was a rebellion, conspiracy, insurrection, or revolution were more likely to postulate a counterrule or loose interpretation of the rule than speakers who called it a riot, civil disorder, or other civil disturbance.

Analysis shows that a speaker's support for the minimum-force principle is associated with his definition of the situation. All those calling it a riot, response to repression, or other category who made any assessment of the relevance of the minimum-force rule held it to be appropriate, while of the ten speakers calling it a rebellion, four affirmed the rule. Those four were all opponents of the motion, while the six denying the relevance of the minimum-force rule or affirming a counterrule supported the motion. Looking at it another way, one sees that in every case of denial of the minimum-force rule, the speaker claimed there was a rebellion (or worse) while those who did not deny the rule tended to vary in their definitions. We infer then that all cases in which one affirms the counterrule are cases one must call rebellion, but all cases called rebellion are not cases in which the counterrule is affirmed. Therefore: Affirmation of the counterrule determines the definition of the situation as rebellion and entails support of the motion. Thus, it is their willingness to use more force than the conventional norm which logically predicates that these men must define the situation as rebellion and not vice versa. What determines the speaker's willingness to use force?

Two chains of ideological consistency were explicated in Chapter 5. These are recapitulated in Table 8 with reference to the code items by which they were indexed on the Code Sheet.

Difficulty in assessing these links arises from the fact that not all speakers made assertions about each theme. This produces two problems. We cannot make "predictions" about the vote of speakers who did not assert their assumptions. It also reduces the number of cases for analysis. Hence, cross tabulation may produce clear and logically explicable but unconvincing results, because too few cases fall into the subclasses of both categories from which to draw conclusions.

Since zero scores on both the authority index (the sum of affirmations of four statements expressing fears of loss of authority in the empire in different ways) and the trust index (the sum of affirmations of two statements expressing fears of loss of

Table 8 Two Chains of Ideological Consistency

Universalism Value Postulate

IV.I.0: Some lives are more important than others.	IV.I.2/Y: Affirm equal value of native lives *or* equal justice due to them.

Axioms of Empire

IV.B.1: Empire finally rests on force.	IV.2/3/4 *or* combination: IV.B.2: Empire depends on cooperation and/or partnership. IV.B.3: Confidence in British fair play/ equal justice. IV.B.4: The only justification for empire is . . . justice.

Feared Loss of Values

Authority Index (sum of following items affirm): IV.E.1: Dyer saved India. IV.E.3: If he had not fired, rebellion (and massacre) would have occurred. IV.E.4: If he had not fired, subject peoples would be more apt to rebel in future. I.E.5: If sanction against Dyer is upheld, officers will be less apt to do their duty (when faced with rebellion demanding firm action).	Trust Index (sum of following items affirm): IV.E.2: Indian people distrust us (as result of the firing). IV.E.6: If sanction against Dyer is not upheld, Indians and other native peoples will lose faith in British justice.

Evaluation of Minimum-Force Rule

IV.A.1: Counterrule (most effective means and/or any means necessary) asserted. *Or* IV.A.2: Rule's application depends on political context; it ought not to be followed under all circumstances. *Or* IV.A.3: Rule acknowledged with indifference and not related to values or consequences.	IV.A.5: Rule taken as an imperative. *Or* IV.A.4: Rule accepted as correct but caveats made as to possibility of employing it reliably.

Judgment | ### Judgment

IV.G.1: Action at Jallianwala Bagh correct; Dyer innocent. *Or* IV.G.2: Correctness . . . impossible to assess.	IV.G.4: Firing . . . a "grave" error, "massacre," etc. *Or* IV.G.5: Firing was a crime.

Vote Yes on Motion	Vote No on Motion

---

trust) could be attributed to such omissions, this would invalidate assuming the index to be ordinal and making predictions
on that basis. To guard against such a logical leap, scores on
both the authority index and the trust index have been
dichotomized between those with a positive score (expressing
some feared loss) and those with a zero score (not expressing any
feared loss).

LINKS IN THE CHAIN

What is the relation between inclusiveness postulates and axioms
of empire? The actual link confirms that hypothesized: virtually
all the men (eight of nine) who asserted a justice postulate and
talked about the foundation of the empire claimed it was based
on cooperation or partnership and/or a belief in equal justice or
fair play for all British subjects. Conversely, eight of nine men
who asserted such a consensual conception of the empire and indicated assumptions about inclusiveness also claimed their belief
in racial equality and/or one rule for all fellow-subjects. Those
not asserting inclusive postulates who also assert axioms of empire divide equally in both camps, but the speakers' axioms are
not stated in half the cases.

What is the relationship between speakers' axioms of empire
and the losses they fear of prized values? The findings correspond to those predicted. If the speaker held that the empire was
based on force, in four of five cases his fears were those of loss
of authority. If the speaker said that the empire was based on
some common belief or standard rather than force, he was not
likely (two of thirteen cases) to express fear over loss of authority.

Any speaker who expressed fears of loss of trust on the part
of Indians stated (if he also asserted an axiom of empire) that
the empire was based on some consensual grounds rather than
being maintained fundamentally by force. However, only about
half those asserting such an axiom expressed any fear of loss of
trust. This may be so because authority was more central to the
debates and many categorical affirmations and denials were
made about it in order to evaluate the necessity of Dyer's conduct.

What is the relationship between expressed fears of loss of
authority or trust and the evaluation of the minimum-force rule?

To answer this question, the evaluation of the minimum-force rule was dichotomized as in Table 7: speakers were divided between those affirming that it ought to be followed (positive) and those who either affirmed a counterrule or denied that the minimum-force rule was imperative in all situations (negative).

Table 9 shows that the evaluation of the rule corresponds perfectly to speakers' expression of feared loss of authority: if the speaker expressed such fears and made a categorical statement about the rule, he asserted that it need not be followed on all occasions, that it was not relevant, or that a counterrule authorizing unlimited force was the rule to be followed. If he did not express any fears of loss of authority and expressed an evaluation of the rule, he supported it. Conversely, all speakers who negated the minimum-force rule also expressed fears of loss of authority in India in the past, present, or future.

All speakers who feared loss of trust affirmed the minimum-force rule, as was predicted. However, the converse is not true; fewer than half affirming the rule expressed fear of loss of trust of Indians.

How well does the evaluation of the minimum-force rule alone explain the speakers' judgment of the gravity of the shooting? Among the sixteen cases in which speakers expressed an explicit judgment on both the rule and the shooting, the relationship was almost perfect (rank-order correlation = .99); the degree of ap-

Table 9   Fears Expressed of Loss of Authority/Trust by Speakers Related to Their Evaluation of the Minimum-Force Rule

Loss feared by speakers	Evaluation of rule by speaker (number)			Total speakers expressing fear
	None	Affirmed	Denied	
Authority				
No fear expressed	11	11	0	22
Some fear expressed	5	0	6	11
Trust				
No fear expressed	10	7	6	23
Some fear expressed	6	4	0	10
Total speakers				
Evaluating rule	16	11	6	33

proval of the shooting can be explained by the degree of approval of the rule. It has been previously shown that a vote for the motion is positively related to support for the shooting.

How well does feared loss of authority or trust account for the vote directly? One can predict for almost two out of three speakers how they will vote from the fears they express; however, the converse is true of the authority index but not of the trust index. The great majority of speakers voting for the motion expressed fears of loss of authority whereas the speakers voting no did not express any such fears, and only half expressed fear of loss of trust.

THE ROLE OF DEFENSE MECHANISMS

Originally it was hypothesized that various psychological stratagems would be exhibited by speakers whose vote was inconsistent with the normative postulates they expressed. However, this chapter has shown an unexpectedly high degree of logical consistency between a speaker's assumptions and his conclusion, as has the analysis of the argumentation in Chapter 7.

Both because there are too few "deviant" speakers to analyze and because several coded categories were discarded owing to low agreement between coders (see Appendix A), analyses of some defense mechanisms, such as segregation and displacement, have been omitted.[4]

Denial was examined by whether supporters and opponents of the motion denied certain facts. These have been selected from all the facts which could be asserted or denied because they were critical to the Hunter Committee's conclusion and made explicit in their report, which was available to members of Parliament. These facts, regarding the shooting at Jallianwala Bagh, are the following:

III.D.1. Dyer ordered fire on the crowd without any warning.
III.D.2. Dyer did not cease firing when people began to leave.
III.D.6. The crowd at Jallianwala Bagh was unarmed.
III.D.7. Dyer subsequently stated (August 1919) that his intent was not just to disperse the crowd.
III.D.13. Dyer's firing at Jallianwala Bagh was found to have killed 379 Indians. (Ambiguous statements about the number were counted as affirmative if they were equal to or greater than

379, as denials if they were definitely less than that number, and as "other" if the quantity was vague, e.g., "several hundred.")

Few of the motion's supporters denied these relevant facts; however, more of the motion's opponents affirmed them than did its supporters.

Projection is indicated by the reversal of roles: of those speakers who claimed that the shooting was correct and Dyer was a victim improperly accused, how many said the crowd was collectively guilty or each man was guilty of rebellion (or murder)? Six supporters of the motion judged the firing to be correct: four of those regarded Dyer as a victim and the three of the four who made any judgment on the crowd said categorically that they were all guilty. Projection is prevalent among a minority of supporters, but these are among the most intense and convincing supporters: they are Lord Finlay, Lord Sumner, and Sir William Joynson-Hicks.

Not surprisingly, analysis shows that only supporters of the motion characterized the crowd categorically as guilty; if they characterized the crowd at all, all but one called it guilty, admitting of no qualification. Opponents of the motion, on the other hand, were more likely to admit that some members of the crowd may have participated in previous mob action or knew of the proclamation than to insist that everyone at the Jallianwala Bagh was innocent. The two camps' characterization of the crowd does not correspond to a mirror image of good and evil, passive and rebellious: only the motion's supporters are distinguished by such stereotypic black and white perceptions.

OTHER CHARACTERISTICS OF SPEAKERS

Originally, it appeared that the speakers against the motion offered more logical arguments than did its supporters. Count was kept of the number of invalid conclusions reached for all speakers after attempting to explicate the implicit premises or find an alternative form to validate the conclusion. After this was done for all speakers, there was no substantive difference between the proportion of logical errors found in both camps. However, the supporters of the motion offered more arguments than did its opponents: an initial count showed the thirteen supporters offered forty-five arguments (an average of over three each) as compared to the nineteen opponents (including Asquith, a nonvoter) who offered a total of forty arguments, or slightly over two each.

These arguments do not include the rhetorical appeals for support. Many rhetorical appeals, such as the due process or fair-trial theme, seem on first reading to be significant themes in the debate but actually played almost no part in the speakers' substantive judgment of the correctness of the shooting and their votes on the motion in the great majority of cases. If all such rhetorical appeals had been coded, proportionately more of the supporters' arguments probably would have been classified as informal fallacies of logic. These include Lord Ampthill's declaration that everyone who knows India knows that every member of the crowd at Jallianwala Bagh was aware of the proclamation, an example of an *argumentum ad populum*. This was taken as an empirical premise in one of the arguments leading to an exoneration of Dyer's action, but its truth value was not assessed although it could be easily disproved. Other rhetorical appeals for a vote for the motion which would be classifiable as informal fallacies include the argument that Dyer was innocent of any wrongdoing because he was not convicted by a court of law, which is rather an irrelevant argument since he was neither accused nor tried. The attacks against Montagu were *ad hominem* arguments contextually, logically irrelevant to proving Dyer's innocence.

Did the attack against Secretary of State Montagu project the onus of charges against the bureaucracy and displace their hostility toward Indians? Although Indians are not a reference group, supporters of the motion, rather than appealing to prejudice, were apt to make a point of disclaiming prejudice. Even Brigadier General Surtees, who explained why more force had to be used in India than elsewhere at the earliest signs of disorder, referred to the people of India as "enlightened." Mr. Gwynne purposely opened his speech by disavowing any prejudices:

> The hon. Gentleman who has just sat down [Col. Wedgwood] has suggested that this is really a controversy between Indians and Europeans, but I venture to say that it is nothing of the kind. There are in India a great majority of citizens who are loyal and patriotic, but there are also a minority who are disloyal and unpatriotic, which is the same as in this country. It is, I think, un-

fortunate to suggest that because some of us feel that Gen. Dyer
has not received justice that we should be stamped as taking the
part of the Anglo-Indians against the Indians. There are a great
many Anglo-Indians and Indians who are fully alive to the fact
that although Gen. Dyer had to perform a very unpleasant duty,
he really did save an appalling situation. [PDC:1793]

Only seven months earlier, the Government of India Bill incorporating the Montagu-Chelmsford reforms had passed both
Houses of Parliament.[5] Even so staunch an opponent of it as
Lord Ampthill disclaimed any belief in racial superiority and asserted then that it was the Hindu caste system, which "is ab-
solutely opposed to the democratic doctrine of the equality of all
men before the law,"[6] that prevented democracy in India, not
British resistance to granting Indians any rights which were their
due. With this in mind and putting oneself in their place in the
post–World War I epoch which was opened by promises of self-
determination, one can understand how any overt expression of
"white man's burden" or sentiment of white superiority could
only be regarded as out of time and place. This image of their
world view should explain why they felt they must repudiate the
charge of racial partisanship. Only the 78-year-old mover of the
motion in the House of Lords, Viscount Finlay, was so bold as
to state explicitly that one ought to protect British lives before
those of Indians.

CHAPTER 9
The Roots and Resonance of the Jallianwala Bagh Massacre

It is not just a question of punishing General Dyer. I agree with Mr. Gandhi, the great Indian, representing, I think, all that is finest in India, when he said, "We do not want to punish General Dyer: we have no desire for revenge: we want to change the system that produces General Dyers." . . . What really matters is to change the system that produces crime.

—Colonel Wedgwood

The shots fired in Jallianwala Bagh did not cease to reverberate after the Dyer debate nor after the Government of India in 1920 paid compensation to those Indians whom they felt could prove that their relatives had died there. It was not hard to foretell what the Lords' repudiation would signify to the Indians, but one may still ask: What was their political response to that understanding?

Looking back, one wants to know whether we can now explain why these events occurred when they did despite the manifest intentions of the Government of India in 1919 to prevent violence by anticipating its outbreak. Why did the cycle of violence unfold in Amritsar? What have we learned about the preconditions for a massacre?

The Hunter Report resonated among Government of India officials as a fiasco that should never be repeated. One thing they learned was never again to appoint a public or binational committee to investigate violence perpetrated by their servants. Why did the Hunter Committee fail so miserably to fulfill its intended function, rendering a judgment acceptable to neither class and polarizing opinion? How would it still have failed if it was composed of its British majority only?

Regarding the debates, it has to be asked again what the Commons motion itself signified in terms both of the Dyer case and imperial policy. What would passage of the motion have implied?

This chapter will try to answer these questions in terms of the theory proposed—insofar as it has been confirmed—and tapping other sociological perspectives which complement it.

THE IMPERIALIST BACKLASH

Neither the general's partisans nor the Indian political class were satisfied with the results of the parliamentary debates of July 1920. Before the Commons debate, the *Morning Post* reiterated almost daily that it was Montagu—not Dyer—who stood on trial. On 6 July 1920, the day before the debate, this newspaper resorted to the ultimate ploy—alleging that Dyer's action was necessary to preserve the "honour of European women" which had been respected even in 1857, citing again the Lyallpur posters out of context and recalling the attack on Miss Sherwood.

Immediately after the Commons defeated the motion, the *Morning Post* announced a fund drive as a sign of appreciation to General Dyer as "The Saviour of India." Simultaneously, it continued its jibes at Secretary of State Montagu editorially, accompanying its announcement of the fund drive on 10 July 1920 with an editorial, "These Be Thy Gods, O Israel." On 12 July it began reprinting the fraudulent *Protocols of the Learned Elders of Zion* under the headline "The Cause of World Unrest (the Jews) . . . ," which were continued serially for two weeks. The fund accumulated £26,317 (exceeding the goal of £26,000) and mobilized a class- and race-conscious opposition that included lords and ladies, generals and colonels, as well as members (or admirers) of the imperial class in humbler circumstances. Often, they announced their identification and resentments publicly, as in the following sample of the £1 contributors from the *Morning Post*'s listing of 21 July:

> "Another Disgusted Sahib," Lieutenant-Colonel W. A. Harrison, "Sympathizer," . . . "One of the many wives who have to spend

most of their time in India," E. V. Richards, "8 Years in the East," "M. H. D.," "One who has never yet understood Chapter XIII, Manual of Military Law," "E. G. C.," "In Memory of Governor Eyre" (I. C. Giles), Sir Francis Stronge, "A Believer in the Jewish Peril," V. W. Wood, "Pogrom," Mrs. M. G. Roberts, "Colonel, Indian Army," "A British Officer and his wife who have spent several years in India," Lieutenant-Colonel J. R. Paul, "A protest against the condemnation of a loyal Soldier by the 'Gallipoli Gambler'" . . .

And from the 1 shilling contributors:

"A Widow's Mite" "Cy. S.," "Meerut," "A Working Housekeeper," "Patriotic and Disgusted Englishwomen," "A Small Token," "A West Country Widow," "B. S.," "Daily Breader," "A Daughter and Sister of Officers who have served in India," "Dare to be a Dyer" . . .

The Saviour of India was portrayed as a martyr, victimized before the Hunter Committee (by his own testimony), alleged to have been misquoted and denied counsel.[1]

The fund gathered one-third of its sum from India. More would probably have been raised there had not military officers and civil servants been informed by the Government of India that their contributions to such a fund would violate the law. Railway employees, schoolchildren, and Anglo-European societies remitted their contributions to the British-Indian newspapers, which relayed them to London; in most cases, individual contributions were under 10 rupees ($3.24). Some went further to express their indignation, such as the 6,250 British women of Bengal who forwarded a petition protesting the treatment meted out to General Dyer to the prime minister of Great Britain.[2]

THE INDIAN REACTION

As early as 26 July 1920, *The Times* (London) summed up Indian opinion in an article subtitled "Ground for Anxiety":

Whatever the basis of the decision reached by the Lords, it is impossible to contest the justice of the opinion of *The Times* [Bombay] as it has been telegraphed here that the debate will create the false impression that an important section of British opinion regards "preventive massacre" and the "degradation of subject peoples" as serviceable instruments of Imperial government. Feeling is running so high that it is impossible to combat this belief.

It will be infinitely more difficult now for sober Indians to join in combatting the non-cooperation movement even if, in the circumstances, many of them are willing to do so. I find a feeling of considerable apprehension among classes, usually removed from politics and entirely attached to the British connexion.

Before the recommendations of the Hunter Committee were issued and the parliamentary debate on the Dyer sanction, Gandhi had advocated cooperation with the reforms at the annual Congress session held in Amritsar in December 1919, seven months after the massacre there. One sign of the British desire to conciliate their subjects had been the king's pardon in December 1919 of many Indian prisoners convicted of political crimes (including Dr. Kitchlew and Dr. Satyapal) during the reign of martial law in the Punjab in 1919. Gandhi used all his influence then, including a threat of resignation, to get Congress to condemn categorically the collective violence by the Indian mob at Amritsar against the British on 10 April 1919: his motion was passed "amidst the whinings and whimperings of the bulk of delegates."[3]

By August 1920, Gandhi had changed course, advocating noncooperation as a policy of action for the Khalifat Committee to protest the terms of the preliminary peace settlement (announced in May 1920) which dismembered the Ottoman Empire claimed by the caliph on behalf of Islam. In Congress, Gandhi led a successful call for noncooperation in September 1920 to protest the exoneration of the perpetrators of the Amritsar massacre and Punjab terror and to support the pan-Islamic cause against the opposition of all previously established leaders. Although this was an auspicious occasion to initiate an anti-British campaign and cement Hindu-Muslim cooperation (on an artificial basis, it later turned out), Gandhi could not have justified such a radical turnabout had not the Hunter Committee obscured the issue of criminal culpability and the Lords repudiated the Dyer sanction.

The massacre and terror had altered Indian consciousness so that there could be no return to innocence, even among the nonpolitical classes who had trusted the British. Prakash Tandon records in his memoir of a *Punjabi Century: 1857-1947* how amazed nonpolitical Indians were by the events of April 1919:

> We were born to the "blessings of the British Raj" and accepted them as the natural order of life. . . .
> In Gujrat we felt the tremor only slightly. . . .
> When the news of Gandhi's *[sic]* arrest came there was trouble also in our Gujrat. A young handsome cousin of ours, grandson

of grand-uncle Thakur Das, led some young man to cut telegraph wires and march about the city, until they were picked up and put into the local jail. But in Lahore we heard that martial law was declared. . . .

All kinds of rumours floated out of Lahore of beatings and mass arrests, of people being made to crawl on their bellies on the roads, of students made to walk every day to Lahore Cantonment six miles away in the hot sun just to salute the flag. And then came the news of the Jallianwala Bagh at Amritsar. . . .

People in Gujrat were stunned and fumbled back in their memory to Nadirshah. But Nadirshah was just an adventurer, a bandit who claimed he had an excuse: some of his soldiers had been murdered after Delhi had capitulated, and the order of general massacre was the punishment he prescribed for Delhi breaking its word. But this Sarkar was different; it had been kind and benign, it had ruled for sixty years without the traditional marks of power. Why this sudden change?[4]

The effects of the Lords' repudiation of the most minimal sanction against Dyer negated further trust of the British. Rabindranath Tagore had renounced his knighthood earlier (in 1919) writing the viceroy that "the time has come when badges of honour make our shame glaring in their incongruous context of humiliation, and I for my part wish to stand shorn of all special distinctions, by the side of those of my countrymen who, for their so-called insignificance, . . . are liable to suffer degradation not fit for human beings."[5] Now Gandhi, too, returned the medals he had received for his wartime contributions to the British Empire, stating that

the punitive measures taken by Gen. Dyer . . . were out of all proportions to the crime of the people and amounted to wanton cruelty and inhumanity unparalleled in modern times. . . . Your Excellency's lighthearted treatment of the official crime, your exoneration of Sir Michael O'Dwyer and Mr. Montagu's despatch and above all your shameful ignorance of the Punjab events and callous disregard of the feelings betrayed by the House of Lords have filled me with the greatest misgivings regarding the future of Empire, have estranged me completely from the present Government and have disabled me from tendering as I have hitherto tendered my loyal cooperation.[6]

A less famous Indian, Braham Nath Datta Qasir, a resident of Amritsar, summed up the new situation in two lines of verse:

We know now what's good or bad,
We are no more yes-men.[7]

The noncooperation movement deflected the Indian National Congress from previous restriction to constitutional methods of agitation. It rejected the reforms advanced by Secretary of State Montagu and Lord Chelmsford, viceroy of India, which had been approved by Parliament when it passed the Government of India Bill in December 1919. Elections to fill the positions created for Indians by that bill were boycotted by the Congress in 1920.

More significantly, the classes not previously represented politically had emerged as actors. While before 1919 the movement had been limited to a westernized literate class of intellectuals, lawyers, and businessmen, now Gandhi had aroused mass support from workers and peasants, Hindus and Muslims (if joining the latter only temporarily). The British, then unable to discriminate between militant rhetoric and violent tactics, unwittingly had discredited the moderates, enabling Gandhi to rise to power because of his charismatic potential for galvanizing the populace.

Both in terms of British goals and Congress's goal, noncooperation was a failure. The refusal of many Indians to vote for the Indian representatives in the provincial legislatures of 1921 undermined the legitimacy of the new institutions and thwarted the aspirations of the many lawyers in Congress who could realized neither status nor profit from creating parallel institutions.[8] The potential for Hindu-Muslim unity was severely undermined in 1921 by the isolation of M. A. Jinnah, then a loyal and moderate congressman, who believed noncooperation would stir up the most reactionary Muslim elements. Jinnah, a brilliant tactician, was later credited as president of the Muslim League with being the "Father of Pakistan." The noncooperation campaign did not lead to swaraj (self-rule) within a year, as Gandhi had promised, but it did lead to a virtual pogrom against Hindus in Kerala initiated by the Moplahs, Muslim peasants of Arab descent who turned on their neighbors when they refused to join in rebellion against the British.[9] Gandhi and Congress were reluctant to see the connection.[10] Gandhi himself called off the noncooperation campaign after an Indian mob in a Congress procession at Churi Chaura (United Provinces) attacked and killed twenty-one Indian policemen on 5 February 1922. Although the noncooperation campaign was dead, so was the hope of cooperation between Indian representatives and the British executive.

In 1924, Lord Oliver, the secretary of state of India recently appointed by the new Labour Cabinet, recounted before the House of Lords the difficulties in India which were caused by the success of the noncooperation movement:

> One general cause of distrust in the minds of the Indian Home Rule Party is the Resolution passed by your Lordship's House on the Motion of the noble and learned Viscount, Lord Finlay, on the action taken by the Government of India in regard to Gen. Dyer. . . . I want to take this opportunity on behalf of myself and the Party to which I belong, to say that I believe the criticism of the Government of India's action passed by Your Lordship's House does not represent the opinion of the great majority of my fellow countrymen.[11]

WHY 1919?

In Chapter 1, I attempted to explain the dialectic of collective violence between political classes. I did not, however, attempt to predict how long or what preconditions were needed before class consciousness developed sufficiently to trigger threats to the governing class labeled as crimes which, in turn, would trigger new crimes. If collective violence was always latent given the political order of British India, one might ask why the massacre and riots preceding it occurred as late as 1919. How was it that the riot in Amritsar on 10 April 1919, which aroused the need for vengeance exhibited at Jallianwala Bagh, erupted when similar means of suppression (externing the leaders) had been successfully employed by the Punjab's governor in 1907 to avert riots? And why was British retaliation so massive at Jallianwala Bagh?

One answer to the first question lies in the general thesis that as opportunities are opened, discontented classes raise their expectations and, hence, are more frustrated when their expectations are not met. The "relative-deprivation" hypothesis, tested most systematically by T. R. Gurr, was proposed over a century ago by Alexis de Tocqueville in his observations of *The Old Regime and the French Revolution:*

> It is not always when things are going from bad to worse that revolutions break out. On the contrary, it oftener happens that when a people which has put up with an oppressive rule over a

> long period without protest suddenly finds the government relax-
> ing its pressure, it takes up arms against it. . . . Patiently endured
> so long as it seemed beyond redress, a grievance comes to appear
> intolerable once the possibility of removing it crosses men's
> minds.[12]

The grievance, in this case, was the Rowlatt Bills, seen correctly by the Indian political class as a sign of mistrust of their
capacity to rule and to distinguish crime from disloyalty to the
British raj. The government's insistence on forcing the Rowlatt
Act through despite unanimous Indian opposition invited a test
of strength between the British governing class and the Indian
political class. Gandhi perceived it as an opportune moment to
test his leadership on a national scale and unify Indians on a
mass basis.

This explanation is not inconsistent with that of Edwin Montagu, who wrote in 1920 that "the Dyer incident was [not] the
cause of the great racial exacerbation which is now in
existence"—it was the promise of advancement towards "responsible government" made by the Cabinet in 1917 that triggered it:

> As soon as the Indians were told that we agreed with them and
> they were to become partners with us, it instilled into their minds
> an increased feeling of existing subordination and a realisation of
> everything by which this subordination was expressed. Similarly,
> when the Europeans were told that, after driving the Indians for
> so many years, that regime was to be over and they might find
> themselves forced to cooperation with the Indians, or even forced
> to allow Indians to rule India, their race consciousness sprang up
> afresh.[13]

Regardless of whether one attributes this race consciousness of
the Indians to the British response to the massacre or to their expectations, one cannot explain the massacre at the Jallianwala
Bagh without tracing its roots into the racial consciousness of the
British officals in India. Montagu, of course, was in an excellent
position to observe how his evolving plans for Indian participation in the Government of India aggravated the race consciousness of the governing class. General Dyer, as a third-
generation Britisher in India, was schooled in the axioms of empire as well as the visceral fears that the mutiny of 1857 evoked
among his class. He expressed these axioms in an article in the
London *Globe* of 21 January 1921, in which, Furneaux recalls,

he declared the attempt to overthrow the British *Raj* in April 1919 was "well-planned." "She [India] would commit suicide and our politicians would be guilty of murder as associates in the crime." India did not want and did not understand self-government, he stated, and he gave his opinion that to the massed millions of India, "the *Raj* is immaculate, just, strong. To them the British officer is a Sahib who will do them right and protect them from enemies of all kinds. Of course, if the *Raj* suffers itself to be wantonly flouted and insulted, it is no longer the *Raj* at all. And it is when that happens that the extremists get their chance." Those in high places who paid attention to the demands of Indian extremists, he said, were either vote catching or frightened of long shadows. An Eleventh Commandment should be applied to India, he suggested, "Thou shall not agitate." . . . The Indians, he stated, would not be capable of self-government for generations, and if they made India unbearable for the British, then "Indians will wade through a sea of blood."[14]

Although they resented the Indian educated class and looked down on the uneducated masses, there is some evidence that the British military in India became less likely to assault ordinary Indians in the Punjab in the first decade of the twentieth century than they had been in the nineteenth century.[15] One may argue that this can be explained by the rise of political assassination against British political authorities by Indians: the previous unmeditated assault on one's coolie was now contemplated and mentally inhibited as not worth the risk. However, assassinations had been discrete and limited to specific political targets—viceroys, police superintendents, and officials. By 1919, the threat to the British by the terrorists had declined and been contained without eliciting unauthorized violence among the British military or civilians in India. The British governing class could plausibly believe that the terrorists were an ineffectual fanatical minority, isolated from the masses. By contrast, the Amritsar riot of 10 April 1919 was perceived and represented as a racial assault against the British by the Indians (representative of the mass rather than the political class alone)—an assault directed against Europeans qua Europeans and threatening the lives of every European if it were not answered by a counterattack. Where Indian rioting was not directed against British civilians in 1919—as in Delhi, Ahmedabad, and Viramgam—British officials managed to restore order by using firepower judiciously, over-

looking crowd shoving, taunts, and other reminders of their un-
popularity.

But can we explain the riot of 10 April 1919 at Amritsar
without reference to the especially repressive and ideological
nature of the Punjab's government, whose own control measures
were said to unify different classes against it and then precipitate
a riot by removing their leadership? Let us take Lt. Gov. Sir
Michael O'Dwyer's vantagepoint for the moment: as both a conservative and an empiricist, he would have argued that early
repression minimizes violence. His decision to intern Dr. Kitchlew and Dr. Satyapal in 1919 paralleled that of Governor Ibbetson in 1907 to deport Ajit Singh and Lajpat Rai from the Punjab then. Why did the 1919 internments provoke a riot and the
1907 ones effectively squash the urban opposition? Sir Michael
as a pragmatist was an exponent of the sociological perspective
that riots are caused by the failure of social control. To account
for the disorders, then, we must account not only for what he
had done to cause dissidence, but why the traditional techniques
of social control failed.

The government's last line of defense, the Indian police,
folded completely at Amritsar, as it folded in Kasur also. Although the Hunter Committee exonerated the British pickets who
fired into the crowd seeking access to the deputy superintendent's bungalow on 10 April, the committee did not assess the
responsibility of the police whose inactivity facilitated the murder
of the five Britishers. The committee judiciously refrained from
any imputation of disloyalty or cowardice in response to the Indian deputy police superintendent's ingenuous account of how he
hid for over two hours in a bank—an action which was intended
to justify the inactivity of seventy-five officers for three and a
half hours while buildings within view of the police station were
burning.[16]

But the breakdown of the police does not explain the anger
and thrust of the crowd before and after the British pickets shot
into them. The police were the last line of defense, not the
primary means of social control in the Punjab. One must explain
the crowd as a phenomenon itself, a product of an embracing
social movement that did not exist in 1907. One requirement for
such a social movement that existed in 1919 but not in 1907 was

communal unity. Communal and class disunity had been the principal means of social control then, but this was not always recognized by officals, even when disunity was instigated and exploited by the governing class.

Looking at this question more abstractly, we can relate it to the underlying relations among the Hindus, the Muslims, and the British (oversimplifying the situation by omitting the Sikhs and other groups) to explain both modern Indian nationalism and communal violence in British India.

Richard D. Lambert, studying communal rioting between Muslims and Hindus in India in the twentieth century, concludes that such riots were directly related to "the sharpness of major political tensions between the Indian National Congress and various Muslim political organizations."[17] They declined when spokesmen for both communites were united against the British and increased when parties representing different communities vied for shares of the power. Lambert has also noted evidence that Muslims sometimes believed the government would not punish them for looting Hindus: in some instances, they announced this publicly.[18]

Conflict with a common opponent, Simmel tells us, binds antagonists together.[19] But alliances, if they are to endure, also obligate partners to react correctly to their allies' enemy. This need is explained on the interpersonal level by Fritz Heider's "balance" theory, which postulates that the structure of a triad "is stable because it does not violate the universal expectations that my friend's friend is my friend, my friend's enemy is my enemy," as Theodore Caplow puts it.[20] There is a strain to balance sentiments and attitudes so that they are consistent with these expectations in role relations or group alliances. When a supposed ally refuses to aid in rebellion against an enemy, as Hindus refused to aid the irredentist drive of the Moplahs against the British in Kerala, one turns on the defectors to punish them for betrayal.

Whether in the Punjab or in other parts of India, when Muslim leaders depended on the raj for group advancement, the necessary consequence was enmity towards a noncommunal alliance with Hindus in Congress against the British. When Muslim and Hindu leadership united in a coalition to achieve transcendent national goals, an assault against members of either community was likely to be regarded as an assault against all Indians. Whether Muslim leaders elected to join with nationalist Hindus depended to a large extent on the contemporary definition of movement goals in Congress, the nature of Congress leadership, and existence of grievances transcending community and caste.

In 1907, there was no movement in the Punjab able to transcend caste, class, and community in appeal, and the political classes stood to lose permanently for their community more by opposition than each could gain by accommodation with the government. Consequently, the government of the Punjab could easily manipulate and divide communities by alternately threatening their representatives with loss of government jobs and cajoling them. The government falsely attributed its success to the internment of the two leaders in 1907, presuming a conspiracy between them when they were really enemies, without realizing how readily they could break the opposition (as they did) by accommodating the peasants and isolating the lawyers. Few people other than lawyers were involved in the nationalist movement in the Punjab in 1907. When the government of the Punjab threatened to discriminate in employment against politically suspect groups and stigmatized the members of the Arya Samaj (a Hindu revitalization movement) as conspirators, it effectively threatened not only the self-interest of the lawyers most involved in the Arya Samaj but the future of their whole community.

Because the caste system operated traditionally by reserving priority of access to certain occupations to certain castes, any community's or caste's superior opportunities would be regarded as the opening wedge toward establishing their monopoly over government jobs and freezing out other communities or castes. The life-chances of a group depend not on the nuclear family primarily but on the ranking of their subcaste, caste, and community. Moving up in status depended at this time not only on observance of the sacred rituals appropriate for the higher castes ("sanskritization") but on group opportunities to obtain new prestigious occupations.[21] Although Sikhs, Muslims, and Buddhists (like Christians and Jews) religiously reject the legitimation of the caste system—rooted in the Brahmins' interpretation of the Vedas—they operate as groups within the system and can be ranked in the status hierarchy. Therefore, each group had an ob-

jective interest both in aggrandizing its opportunities and protecting itself from other groups' self-aggrandizement. There was no
leadership then to elaborate an outlook transcending this. Thus,
in 1907, a potential coalition was thwarted by threatening any
group which aligned itself against the government with potential
loss of status, inducing members to hasten to official chambers
to assure the government of their loyalty. This competition led to
an increase in communal rivalry, rumors, and potentially
dangerous intergroup tension.

When the movement transcended these goals and Muslim and
Hindu leaders united, as they did during the anti–Rowlatt Bill
campaign, and attracted mass participation, such invidious
threats were ineffectual. This unity was achieved in Amritsar
because of the joint leadership of Dr. Kitchlew, a Muslim lawyer
of Kashmiri Brahmin ancestry, and Dr. Satyapal, a Hindu doctor who led an earlier successful campaign in 1919 to force the
railway authorities to continue issuing third-class tickets, a cause
appealing to the poorer class in all communities. Frequent mass
meetings were held before 10 April, and the cry of *"Hindu-
Musselman Kai Jai!"* (signifying Hindu-Muslim unity) was heard
in the streets during a joint celebration of Ram Naumi Day. On
this Hindu holiday, celebrated on 9 April, Hindus and Muslims
drank together, a sign of unusual solidarity. The deputy commissioner was fearful, realizing that Hindu-Muslim unity was an
ominous portent for the British. His decision to intern Dr. Kitchlew and Dr. Satyapal caused the crowd to gather, which provoked the pickets' killing twenty to thirty Indians, which in turn
provoked the murder of five Britishers. The pickets' firing was
the trigger arousing the assault to their common dignity in a way
that the Rowlatt Act alone could never have done. There is no
evidence that Gandhi, the doctrine of satyagraha, or prepara-
tions for civil disobedience (nonexistent in the Punjab) influenced this process.

Despite the aim of Lieutenant Governor O'Dwyer to repress
the educated classes and exploit the peasantry for recruiting, he
subverted his own objectives by facilitating creation of a movement on an ecumenical base. Had not a confrontation arisen
because of the misjudgment of the authorities in pursuing the
course of conventional wisdom, it is unlikely it would have
become violent. Analysis of the distribution of riots and protests

in the Punjab in 1919 shows that there was relatively less violence in towns and cities with an organized protest movement committed to a nonviolent campaign before 10 April 1919. The subsequent responsibility of Lt. Gov. Sir Michael O'Dwyer, his successor Sir Edward McLagan, and the Government of India in authorizing a reign of terrorism in the Punjab during martial law cannot be denied.

When Hindus and Muslims perceived an unequivocal assault against them collectively, even traditional violations of communal etiquette that often triggered communal rioting did not provoke distrust. Thus, responsibility for a dead calf discovered on the bridge in Gujranwala on 14 April 1919 was attributed to the police, rather than to the Muslims, and the crowd went on to riot and attack the railroad station, punctuating its progress with anti-British cries. Such an incident, involving a flagrant violation of the Hindu ban on cow-killing, illustrates that symbols which serve as provocations in one context do not necessarily trigger collective violence out of that context, despite the fact that most communal riots in India in the twentieth century have been associated with alleged religious violations or confrontations.[22] Evidently the perception of such violations itself is mediated by the state of underlying intergroup relations.

The social control perspective explains why collective violence cannot be attributed only to the violation of group mores or criminal violations but in the last analysis depends on the capacity of social control measures to deter violence or limit it. One of the more frequent findings of studies of collective violence is that most groups initiating violence are aided by the tolerance or participation of the authorities.

The social control perspective is usually used to explain rioters' behavior as contingent upon the acts or omissions of the authorities but seldom employed to explain the violence of the authorities. One may ask what social controls there were to limit General Dyer when he was vested with de facto powers of martial law and chose to disregard the minimum-force principle? Had Dyer been able to get his armored car through the entryway to the Jallianwala Bagh, he would have machine-gunned the crowd, he told the Hunter Committee, and casualties would have been greater. Few have noted that all the firing at the Bagh was done by fifty native Indian tribesmen (Gurkhas). This was indeed a tribute to Indian loyalty to the British Raj or the lack of solidarity among Indians that allowed the Indian Army to be able to count unhesitatingly on soldiers' loyalty provided they were stationed (as they were as a matter of policy) away from their province or community of birth. As long as there was no social control imposed by the civilian officials who abdicated responsibility at Amritsar (and conformity by his soldiers and officers), General Dyer could and did satisfy his need to make a "wide impression" with anomic lust.

Similarly, the officers in the Punjab who forced Indians to descend, salaam, salute, or march in the sun (often over 100°F in the Punjab in April) to show deference were undeterred by any social controls during martial law. They presumed that loyalty meant subordination and the absence of deference disloyalty: those who flouted their will today would be enemies tomorrow unless reformed by collective punishments. To "educate" them, British officers resorted to terror, humiliation, and coerced mechanical parodies of deference. Like General Dyer, who compelled Indians to crawl on the streets on which Miss Sherwood had been attacked in Amritsar, they hardly cared whether their acts evoked respect or cringing, for their object was apolitical. Their punishments were not intended to restore order, but to vent their rage against the outrage perpetrated against the British as a class. Looking back at the response to the Jamaica rebellion (Appendix C), we see the same phenomenon.

The debates on the Punjab "rebellion" and the debates on the Jamaica rebellion show how crimes committed by the natives are used to justify criminal reprisals by the authorities. Although such crimes (which are often explained by the administrators as punishments) may be later justified as self-defense, in Jamaica and the Punjab they occurred after the alleged rebellion had been suppressed or had run its course and when the population was subdued and unarmed.

Both at Amritsar and Jamaica it was the physical attack against members of the dominant class, rather than an attempt, however crude, to capture the machinery of government, which provoked such punitive reprisals. These "punishments" in which the victim is helpless to change the behavior of the executioner by avoiding violations are distinct from legal punishments, as they were in intent. They were correctly perceived by contemporary critics in 1920 as cases of terrorism" or "frightfulness"; in 1865 they were recognized as "atrocities." This inductive finding supports the thesis that it is the "outrage to morality" of the subject class's aggression which triggered the escalation of crime: the probable reason why the cycle did not spiral in the Punjab was not Gandhi's leadership but that the population was effectively terrorized by reports of the Amritsar massacre. Both the killings of Britishers at Amritsar on 10 April and of Indians at Jallianwala Bagh on 13 April were "outrages" against unarmed people, but the outrage by armed men drew eighty victims for every victim claimed by the unarmed mob. Because the authorities possessed a monopoly over the most effective means of violence in British India, Indians had no countersanctions against the violence of the authorities.

AMENDING THE THEORY

It was proposed, and confirmed in the case studied, that individual sanctioning of collective violence is a function of moral inclusiveness on the part of the judge and tolerance of its contrary, moral exclusiveness. However, tolerance of General Dyer's conduct was not one individual's act but was determined by a chain of organizational actions (or inaction).

General Dyer asked for and received the approval of his immediate superior, Major General Beynon, and the provincial lieutenant governor of the Punjab, Sir Michael O'Dwyer. The massacre was apparently overlooked by the Government of India for five months before it was debated in the Imperial Legislative Council in September 1919. At that time, they agreed to postpone judgment of General Dyer until after the Hunter Committee's hearing, even though the statement requested from Dyer by the commander in chief of the Indian Army had been received on 25 August 1919 and the Hunter Committee was not a judicial body qualified to make a legal indictment or judgment. This succession of lapsed opportunites for judgment led Lord Midleton, a "deviant" supporter of the motion, to denounce that government:

> After all the facts were known the Government of India extended his [Dyer's] autocratic power in the Punjab. A month later they sent him to the front. In October they promoted him, and in January this year they promoted him again; and then, in March,

they tell him that they cannot give him further employment.

If anybody is to be accused of favouring racial humiliation or frightfulness, it surely is those to whom all these facts were known, who took no action on them, and allowed it to be believed that they were condoned, so long as the emergency was hot, but are to be condemned now that public opinion has got cool. [PDL:257]

After the Hunter Committee's evidence was in, the Government of India had deliberately refrained from court-martialing Dyer out of fear of the effect of such an act on the military there. The Hunter Committee made it clear that Dyer had committed no crime but merely had had a "wrong conception of his duty."

Within the Hunter Committee, the cross-examination of British officers by the Indian Minority reinforced the class consciousness of the British Majority, increasing polarization within the committee. The majority sought a framework that could justify limiting the liability of the officers; the minority represented the class of victims. To placate Indian politicians whose cooperation he needed for passage of the reforms, Montagu had pressed the viceroy to create a committee which, ironically, daily enforced on the Indian members consciousness of their subordination, further negating its intended function.

The Hunter Committee was constrained by its limited mandate and its responsibility to the Government of India from going up the line from General Dyer and other officers to judge the responsibility of the government of the Punjab and the Government of India for the Amritsar massacre and Punjab terror of 1919, as had the parliamentary commission on Jamaica in 1866 which investigated the atrocities there and recommended the recall of Governor Eyre. By restricting judgment to the officers directly involved in administering martial law, the Hunter Committee's majority forestalled any conclusion regarding the responsibility of those sanctioning martial law. By neutralizing culpability (as they had by ascribing Dyer's action at Jallianwala Bagh to an "error" or "mistaken conception of his duty"), the Hunter Committee's majority made Montagu's later indictment of Dyer's firing as an example of "frightfulness" and "terrorism" seem incongruous. If Dyer's deed was an "error," it was an error that might be condoned because of his subsequent combat, as Lord Midleton argued, as readily as it might be censured.

If it was not an error, it was either the correct action or an offense for which he ought to have been court-martialed as soon as the government knew of it.

Reviewing the judgment and processing of the Dyer case illustrates above all that toleration or sanctioning against collective violence in bureaucracies is an organizational response; and organizations tend to sustain morale by protecting their members despite the rulebook and limits on their authority. An organization, such as the Government of India, indebted to the class which theoretically serves it, is bound by the class's universe of obligation. While individual violence against Indians was not formally condoned, rarely, as Curzon found during his viceroyalty, was it condemned and scarcely ever punished. Was it any wonder that when Dyer reacted at Jallianwala Bagh to express the rage of his class, they should support him?

On an organizational level, my original construction of the process of sanctioning was oversimplified. It is not a simple problem of approval or punishment; rather, there is a range of responses varying in prescriptiveness as in Figure 5. The region of indifference in which the massacre was originally placed is a region (like Dante's purgatory) with which many governments and bureaucracies are familiar besides the imperial Government of India. Indifference, of course, is a kind of toleration, as is the next social category they put it in, the class of role deviations—"a wrong conception of his duty." The government's subsequent sanction of unemployment—the general had failed to cooperate by resigning his commission—was inconsistent with the majority's exculpation and reinforced the imperial class's ire. Dyer was their surrogate: his deed was theirs. The debates in Parliament revolved not around whether to punish General Dyer but whether he ought to be exonerated by condoning his act and legitimating it: it was an open counterattack based on class solidarity.

The Government of India's policy in this case was neither to authorize slaughter nor to subject its servants to trial in either the military or civil courts, just as it had been toward the deputy inspector who shot the sixty-five captured Kuka rebels out of cannons in 1872. By evading the issue to placate the British-Indian bureaucracy, the government had made it possible for Dyer's defenders to attempt to legitimate a policy which *The*

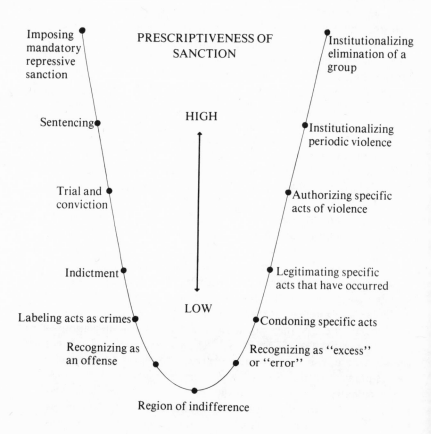

Figure 5 Stages in the sanctioning of collective violence

Times indicated was called by Indians "preventive massacre" in 1920. Dyer's defenders exploited the sympathy for him by focusing on the alleged denial of his rights of due process before the Hunter Committee (which was not a judicial body) and the antipathy to Secretary of State Montagu. They portrayed Dyer as a scapegoat. Their policy, known metaphorically by its supporters as one of the "firm" hand or "forceful" action, was contrary to both the prescriptions and the usual practices of the British military in India. Had it been approved, it would have marked a radical departure in British imperialism.

By the time the parliamentary debates opened, the British government was on the defensive against the left (an inconsequential assault) and the right. During the debates General Dyer received the obeisance to a tragic hero fallen from grace, even from his opponents. While Viscount Finlay, the mover of the motion repudiating the Dyer sanction, affirmed that Dyer "eminently possesses the qualities of tact and humanity," the Marquess of Crewe, an eloquent opponent of the motion, denied that Dyer could be characterized as "a bloodthirsty ogre" and concluded his judgment by saying that "I think we have to regard Gen. Dyer as a man who, having followed straitly and strictly the path of duty, as he saw it, took a wrong turning." [PDL:264] Even Secretary of State for India Montagu remarked "how gallant his record is—and everybody knows how gallant General Dyer's record is" in presenting his indictment.

In Chapter 1, while drawing out Durkheim's logic on crime and punishment, I proposed that offenses against persons outside the universe of obligation will not be labeled as crimes. Conversely, offenses not socially recognized and labeled as crimes are offenses against persons outside the universe of obligation. One must then conclude, as did the spokesmen for the unborn Indian nation in 1920, that the shooting down of 379 Indians (at the very least) was not a crime to the British governing class who ruled India because the Indians were not included in their universe of moral obligation. The debate analysis also confirmed this.

Those who opposed the motion (in effect repudiating the Dyer sanction) explicitly stated their inclusion of Indians within a common universe of obligation: the advocates do not talk about equity, justice, or common obligation but of "the authority of force." Had the motion passed in the House of Commons, it would have been correctly interpreted as a vote of no confidence, repudiating the Cabinet's imperial commitment and authorizing a policy of unveiled coercion and terror. Even so, it would not have altered the Government of India's and the War Council's decision not to offer Dyer new employment; similarly, his military status was unchanged by its failure. The Cabinet fought a defensive battle to prevent Commons from legitimating Dyer's policy and won a majority only because of the overwhelming support of Labour and Liberal M. P.'s, indicating how the limit on imperial policy was related to the political strength of the left in Britain.

The motion's opponents, understanding that Indians were not people toward whom many colleagues felt obligated, stressed British honor at least as much as Indian injuries in their speeches. The relative stress reflected their calculus of which arguments might move their colleagues. To uphold an obligation is a matter of duty; to uphold a promise toward the weak is a matter of honor. Some opponents explicitly recognized what this division between them and their colleagues signified. As Mr. Bennett said:

> Those who have looked too lightly and with approval, in too many cases, upon the action of Gen. Dyer have a scale of values of their own of human life, in which they place the Indian below the European. This is not a political question, but a question of human values, and until we get rid of that idea and recognize the sacredness of Indian life as on a par with the sacredness of European life, we shall be suspected by the people of India, our actions will be unfavourably coloured, and our policy in that country will be a failure. [PDC:1774]

The fact that the opponents chose to make a stronger affirmation of the minimum-force rule than positive defense of the equal value of human life may illustrate their understanding of the utility of relying on law and precedent as against the futility of appealing to values.

Similar themes and modes of argument condemning or justifying the actions of Jamaican officials were used in 1866 by speakers taking categorical positions as were used in 1920 by those assailing or defending in Parliament the action of General

Dyer at Amritsar. However, the officials' defenders, unlike Dyer's, explicitly appealed in Parliament to racial fears and spoke for racial solidarity with the British governing class in Jamaica exclusively. By contrast, Dyer's partisans in 1920 were anxious to deny prejudice or belief that British dominion in India had a racial basis. This difference was attributable to the fact that the world view of Dyer's partisans incorporated a new political map, hedged by British commitments to India which precluded assertion of any exclusive racial mission or superiority. The general's partisans were probably franker off the floor, but even in the columns of the *Morning Post* attacks on Indians were muted but attacks on Jews explicit. The ideology of anti-semitism elaborated against the background of accusation against the Jewish Secretary of State for India, Edwin Montagu, enabled them to displace their antagonism against the multitude of orientals to a less numerous group of aliens they conceived of as Asiatic. The belief that Jewish conspiracy was the source of unrest also enabled them to deny the generality of opposition to the British raj in India and avert precognition of the future. It was fortuitous and fortunate that when it was no longer acceptable to publicly attack the Indian educated class sneeringly, a new scapegoat became fashionable.

THE PROBLEM IN RETROSPECT

The problem that really ought to be pursued by Commons, said Colonel Wedgwood in 1920, did not relate to the judgment of General Dyer or other individual officers:

> What really matters is to change the system that produces crime.

One thing alone is certain: the problem cannot be reduced to the allocation of guilt at each time and place. It would be wrong to say that we have not made much progress. For we have not even begun.

Coding The Parliamentary Debates

THE CODE SHEET

I. Source Identification

    A. Name of speaker _____ Title _____
                 (last name, first initial)   (not gov't.)

    B. House in which speech was delivered (circle one):

Lords	1
Commons	2

    C. Status in Cabinet or Imperial Civil Service (circle one):

None	0
Present minister, secretary, undersecretary, or governor	1
Past minister, secretary, undersecretary, or governor	2

    D. Vote on motion first presented (circle one for members of both Houses):

No vote recorded	0
Yes	1
No	2

       Vote on second motion (House members only):

No vote recorded	0
Yes	1
No	2

    E. Serial order of speech within each House's sequence of debate—record number, 1st to 17th:_____

    F. Column identification in volume—insert number heading of first and last columns of speech: first_____, last_____

II. Paragraph theme summary

Tally each theme appearing in a paragraph (context unity) of given direction once only. Tally under M only if no evaluation is implied by another assertion regarding the same theme within the same paragraph.

	Approval	Disapproval	Mixed, narrative, or neutral
Total paragraphs	_____	_____	_____
Total columns	_____	_____	_____

A. Dyer's actions at JB

    PINs* ___ ___ ___   ___ ___   ___ ___

           ___ ___ ___   ___ ___   ___ ___

B. Dyer's Crawling Order

    PINs ___ ___ ___   ___ ___   ___ ___

          ___ ___ ___   ___ ___   ___ ___

C. Government of India and Hunter Committee

    PINs ___ ___ ___   ___ ___   ___ ___

          ___ ___ ___   ___ ___   ___ ___

D. British Cabinet evaluation and motives

    PINs ___ ___ ___   ___ ___   ___ ___

          ___ ___ ___   ___ ___   ___ ___

E. Army Council evaluation

    PINs ___ ___ ___   ___ ___   ___ ___

          ___ ___ ___   ___ ___   ___ ___

F. Behavior charged against other officers

    PINs ___ ___ ___   ___ ___   ___ ___

          ___ ___ ___   ___ ___   ___ ___

---

*PIN (paragraph identification number) is column number followed by numeral indicating ordinal position of paragraph in column in which it began.

	Approval	Disapproval	Mixed, narrative, or neutral

G. Political context of JB (present)

1. Gandhi and NV campaign

    PINs ___ ___ ___   ___ ___   ___ ___

           ___ ___ ___   ___ ___   ___ ___

2. Conspiracy asserted

    PINs ___ ___ ___   ___ ___   ___ ___

           ___ ___ ___   ___ ___   ___ ___

3. O'Dwyer policy blamed

    PINs ___ ___ ___   ___ ___   ___ ___

           ___ ___ ___   ___ ___   ___ ___

III. Affirmations

A. Definition of situation: political context of Jallianwala Bagh. Check if categorical affirmation (A), denial (D), ambiguous categorical or other assertion (M), or no statement (0) of:

	A	D	M	0
1. Response to British repression	—	—	—	—
2. Civil riot	—	—	—	—
3. Rebellion or insurrection	—	—	—	—
4. Conspiracy	—	—	—	—

B. Characterization of victims—check as many as apply:

	A	D	M	0
1. English men wounded or killed by Indians before arrival of Dyer	—	—	—	—
2. English missionary lady attacked on 10 April	—	—	—	—
3. English women and children in fort from 10 April	—	—	—	—
4. Inclusive or general reference to English	—	—	—	—
5. General Dyer	—	—	—	—
6. Crowd at the Bagh	—	—	—	—

C. Characterization of crowd at Jallianwala Bagh (circle one):

0 No judgment

1 Innocent of wrongdoing and/or helpless victims

2 Composed of many people who could not have known of order forbidding meeting

3 Composed of some people guilty of previous mob action and/or agitators

4 Guilty of conspiracy to rebel and/or willfully defying government decree

Last name of speaker _____

D. Selection of facts asserted

Check under letter corresponding to factual status alleged by speaker. If mixed or neutral statement is made along with affirmative (A) or negative denial (D), check under A or D only.

A Statement affirmed or contrary statement denied
D Statement denied or contrary statement affirmed
M Mixed statement without clear import or neutral statement
O No relevant statements at all

	A	D	M	0	Truth
a. The firing at the Bagh					
1. Dyer ordered fire on the crowd without warning.	—	—	—	—	T
2. Dyer did not cease firing when people began to leave.	—	—	—	—	T
3. Prior official orders in Amritsar forbade public meetings.	—	—	—	—	T
4. These orders were generally known to that crowd.	—	—	—	—	?
5. There were no women or children at that meeting.	—	—	—	—	F
6. The crowd at the Bagh was unarmed.	—	—	—	—	T
7. Dyer subsequently stated (August 1919) that his intent was not just to disperse the crowd.	—	—	—	—	T
8. The Crawling Order made dwellers on that street crawl to reach outer streets.	—	—	—	—	T

	A	D	M	0	Truth
b. What happened to Dyer later					
9. Dyer's action was defended by his immediate military and provincial civil superiors.	—	—	—	—	T
10. Dyer was promoted in rank by the Government of India after his testimony was taken.	—	—	—	—	F
11. Dyer had no legal counsel before the Hunter Committee.	—	—	—	—	T
12. Dyer's firing at the Bagh was found to have killed 379 Indians.	—	—	—	—	T
13. Dyer was sentenced without a trial.	—	—	—	—	F
14. Secretary of State Montagu knew the background of the firing at the Bagh at once (April 1919) from wires.	—	—	—	—	F
15. Montagu knew the background from conversation with Sir Michael O'Dwyer (Lt. Gov. of Punjab) in June 1919.	—	—	—	—	?
16. Under martial law, the civil authority had given up; all decisions were made by the military authorities there.	—	—	—	—	T

IV. Evaluation and judgment

  A. Evaluation of minimum-force rule (circle one):

   5 Rule taken as an imperative

   4 Rule accepted as correct but caveats made as to possibility of applying it reliably

   3 Rule acknowledged with indifference and/or not related to values or consequences

   2 Rule's application depends on political context: it ought not to be followed under all circumstances

   1 Counterrule (most effective means and/or any means necessary) asserted

   0 No evaluation of rule

B. Means-ends postulates of empire (circle as many as apply):

    0 None explicitly asserted
    1 Empire finally rests on force
    2 Empire depends on cooperation or partnership
    3 Empire rests on confidence in British fair play and/or belief in equal justice
    4 Only justification of empire is its ability to uphold standard of justice and equity

C. Justice postulates

Check under letter below if statement is categorically affirmed or contrary denied (A), denied or contrary affirmed (D), ambiguous or other (M), or missing (0):

	A	D	M	0
1. Rebellion is a crime.	—	—	—	—
2. All men are innocent unless proved guilty.	—	—	—	—
3. All men are entitled to a trial by a jury of peers.	—	—	—	—
4. Partisans are not peers.	—	—	—	—
5. Indian lawyers are partisans.	—	—	—	—
6. All men are entitled to be heard in their own defense.	—	—	—	—

D. Authority postulates

	A	D	M	0
1. Duty requires adherence of all officers and government servants to rules.	—	—	—	—
2. The government ought to support all officers doing their duty.	—	—	—	—

E. Consequences to be taken into account

Check under letter below if statement is affirmed or contrary denied (A), denied or contrary affirmed (D), ambiguous or other (M), or missing (0).

	A	D	M	0
1. Categorical past consequence: Dyer saved India (for us)	—	—	—	—
2. Categorical present consequence: Indian people distrust us	—	—	—	—

	A	D	M	0

3. Hypothetical future negative consequences avoided: if he had not fired, rebellion and massacre (of English) would have occurred — — — —

4. Hypothetical future negative action avoided: if he had not fired, subject peoples would be more apt to rebel — — — —

5. Hypothetical future consequences if sanction upheld: officers will be less apt to do duty — — — —

6. Hypothetical future consequences if sanction not upheld: Indians and other native people will lose faith in British justice — — — —

F. Selection of issues for judgment of General Dyer (circle one):

0 None covered
1 Firing at Jallianwala Bagh only
2 Crawling Order only
3 Both Jallianwala Bagh and Crawling Order
4 Both of above in context of other officers' actions
5 Jallianwala Bagh in context of other officers' actions during martial law

G. Judgment of Dyer's guilt for Jallianwala Bagh firing (circle one):

0 No judgment explicitly made
1 Action at Jallianwala Bagh correct and Dyer innocent
2 Correctness of continued firing impossible to assess
3 Firing at Jallianwala Bagh was an "error"
4 Firing at Jallianwala Bagh was a "grave" error or mistake and/or "massacre," "slaughter," "monstrous deed," etc., without explicit judgment on Dyer
5 Firing was a crime

H. Sanction against Dyer

1. Evaluation of sanction employed against Dyer:

0 No evaluation

1 Sanction unfair

  2 Sanction fair

  3 Stronger sanction recom-
     mended against Dyer alone

  4 Sanction against Dyer (same
     or stronger) and political
     sanctions against O'Dwyer
     and/or viceroy demanded

2. Consideration of procedural
   justice of sanctioning

  0 No evaluation

  1 Procedure proper and/or fair

  2 Procedure dilatory but fair

  3 Procedure unfair or lacking
     due process

I. Universalism value postulate

  X No assertions made
  0 Assertion some (or our) lives are more important than
     others (or theirs)
  1 Denial of charge of "racialism" or resentment at charge
     expressed
  2 Denunciation of belief (attributed to others) that Indian (or
     native) lives are less important or affirmation of equal
     value of all lives
  Y Affirmation that equal justice is due Indians or due all
     people or all British subjects in all places regardless of race

J. Terrorism

  0 Not mentioned
  1 Charge denied
  2 Acts deplored
  For coding: terrorism = frightfulness = intimidation =
  vengeance = Prussianism

V. Reference Groups

  A. Audiences and/or constituencies

     Tally number of paragraphs in which reference is made to each
     people or nation as parties to be taken into account (+), par-
     ties which ought not to be listened to (−), and neutral or am-
     biguous implications (?). Cite PINs in the lines below for each
     tally.

	(+)	(−)	(?)
Indians	_____	_____	_____
PINs	____ ____	____ ____	____ ____
	____ ____	____ ____	____ ____

British residents of Indian and/or British officers

	_____	_____	_____
PINs	____ ____	____ ____	____ ____
	____ ____	____ ____	____ ____

b. Testimonials* employed to confirm judgment on Dyer

Tally the number of testimonials cited from different individuals or groups within each paragraph (context unit).
General references ("all Englishmen agree") would be counted
once in each paragraph regardless of how often reiterated in
that paragraph. As many specific individuals or groups of individuals mentioned are tallied as are cited—the archbishop of
Simla, five English governesses, and Miss Sherwood, if all
mentioned as testimonial sources in one paragraph, would be
three testimonials. Cite PINs as above.

Testimonial direction on judgment of
Dyer's firing at Jallianwala Bagh

Source: Indians	Approval	Disapproval
	_____	_____
PINs	____ ____	____ ____
	____ ____	____ ____

Source: British residents of India and/or officers

	_____	_____
PINs	____ ____	____ ____
	____ ____	____ ____

---

*A testimonial is a citation supporting the speaker's conclusion which does not
necessarily assert that the opinion of the source of that statement is or ought to
be a criterion for the judgment to be made by the speaker's peers. If the statement directly asserts or clearly implies that the source is a reference group
positively to be taken into account, the statement is both a testimonial and an audience referent (+). Note the difference between counting instructions for audience referents and testimonials.

A NOTE ON RELIABILITY

The reliability of coding the debates was checked by having a second coder read and categorize ten of the thirty-three speeches, i.e., one-third of the thirty-one for whom the vote of the speaker was recorded. These ten were randomly selected within each House so as to include five in each House.

The principal second coder, Anne Weiss, is a former history graduate student, high school social science teacher, and an encyclopedia editor. Ms. Weiss read all the speeches in the debates to establish the meanings of the cross references and understand as much as possible about the issues in contention. I am deeply indebted to her for her curiosity and unremitting patience, qualities not explained solely by friendship and certainly not by any expected material compensation.

Since explicit coding rules were not formulated originally, we discussed the construction of code sheet items extensively. In general, items are construed loosely; that is, we accepted many linguistic variations as long as the speaker's implication was clear, taking into account the variations between American and British English. However, we purposely avoided making inferences as to what the speaker "really meant" when issues were evaded by rhetorical tactics. We did not discuss the hypothesis to be tested during these conversations.

Agreement was calculated by comparing the number of instances both coders agreed on an item for each item for the ten speeches: coder agreement among all items ranged from .5 to 1.0. In the case of items scaled on an ordinal scale (III.E, IV.A, IV.G, IV.H.1, IV.H.2), the extent of intercoder agreement as to whether a relevant assertion or judgment had been made was computed; for all cases in which there was a scale judgment made by both coders, the Spearman rank-order correlation between coders' rankings was calculated. Intercoder agreement as to the presence of an explicit judgment ranged from .8 to 1.0; among the cases both coders agreed that a judgment had been made, the rank-order correlation ranged from .89 to 1.00.

Items rated on a nominal scale for which intercoder agreement was less than .8 were not further analyzed. These items include justice postulates (IV.C), authority postulates (IV.D), and the paragraph theme summary. Originally, this summary included item V.A, "Audiences and/or Constituencies as Reference Groups," but an independent count by a third coder of these references after the exclusions had been explicitly defined produced a rank-order correlation of .85 with the count of the first coder (the author), correlating the net number of positive references.

The low agreement on the paragraph theme summary (II) was due to the ambiguity of speakers' references, the techniques of rhetoric, and the fact that one coder was much more familiar with the order of events than the others and so could infer the referent with more confidence. For instance, at each mention of the "government," the coder had to determine whether it was the Government of India or the Government of Great Britain (as represented by the Cabinet or India Office) that was being assailed or defended. Aggregating these categories would have increased reliability but would have obscured measurement of the thrust of the motion's supporters' argument that the Government of India had been at fault originally for not punishing General Dyer or that the sanction against Dyer was imposed on the Government of India for political reasons by the Secretary of State or the Cabinet.

Agreement on the assertions that "all men are entitled to a trial" and "all men are innocent unless proved guilty" was low because speakers adopted many variants of that position in order to rebut Churchill's declaration that the crown had the right to remove any servant at any time without even an administrative hearing and that no judicial guarantees were owed Dyer because no charges had been brought against him of a criminal or civil nature. Since both statements were historically true, a number of speakers hedged such assertions with preliminary caveats, leading to disagreement among coders as to whether a speaker had made an affirmative assertion of such a postulate or an ambiguous assertion of mixed implications. Authority postulates were seldom articulated in a generalized form in the debates, leading to similar disagreement as to whether the speaker had made such an affirmation or it was a coder's inference. Since the general rule of coding was to err on the conservative side in explicating the assumptions behind particular judgments, and these assumptions were explicated in the logical analysis summarized in Chapter 7, this category was also eliminated.

The Circle of Trust

Sociologists have often faltered in explaining the gap between values and norms—rules, laws, conventions, and customs of more transitory and less compulsive character—and practices. Judith Blake Davis has questioned the usefulness of the concept of values itself, regarding it as a higher-order neologism used tautologically to explain the behaviors from which it is abstracted.[1] The concept of values persists because it allows us to synthesize common elements of rules by inferring their objective and enables us to explain how people construct rules in new or ambiguous situations. But the concept has been misused as a catchall to explain differences between stated rules and actual practices as examples of competing values (or deviations), missing the point that the double standard of evaluation is the rule. Look, for example, at Robin M. Williams' remarks on values and beliefs in American society:

> We find emerging from the mass of detail a pattern indicating that democracy is a widespread focus of positive evaluation in America. . . . There have been complex and often contradictory variations . . . for example, the internment of Japanese. . . . The

greater is our awareness both of the persistence of democratic values and of the inadequacy of the summary characterizations of the culture as a whole.[2]

The discrepancy can be explained not only by distinguishing moral from legal obligations but by finding out to whom the obligation specified by the norm applies. Thus we ought to distinguish the substantive domain of the rules from the range of people to whom obligation is owed. These people constitute "the universe of obligation." If we look at it metaphorically from the viewpoint of the actor, we may call it a "circle of trust"—it encloses those whom one can count on being protected by with some certainty and toward whom one owes a duty. That is, it is the operative boundaries of Hillel's injunction not to do unto others what you would not desire they do unto you.

The circle of trust may be identical to the boundaries of group—class, collectivity, race, nation—or it may incorporate the whole human race. When the circle corresponds to the boundaries of the social system, we describe it as a circle characterized by moral inclusiveness—an inclusive circle. When it corresponds to that of the group only, the circle is exclusive. In a morally exclusive universe, trust is invested and professedly universal obligations tendered toward one's own kind only.

The range of the circle of trust radiating from a group need not correspond to the inclusiveness or exclusiveness of the criteria for belonging to that group. An exclusive group, such as an aristocratic estate, may remain exclusive to fulfill its reciprocal obligations toward other estates, as both Georg Simmel and Robert Merton have noted.[3] The range of the circle may be exclusive while the group from which the circle radiates stresses its inclusiveness: membership may be open to any believer in the true faith.

The most inclusive group, Simmel observed, is the modern territorial state. Within the state, the extension of loyalty to all citizens does not depend on the progressive homogenization of differences; individuals and groups have become increasingly differentiated by the multiplying array of cross-cutting group affiliations produced by the division of labor. Simultaneously with such differentiation, which, Simmel noted, led to greater individuation, he observed there was an increasing abstraction of the bases of potential self-identification which led to the formation of broader groups: persons who were not necessarily peers, colleagues, or role partners in a specific pursuit joined as members of "wage labor," the "mercantile class," and "women."[4] Karl Mannheim also believed that democracy led to "the self-discovery of social groups": the sociological frame of reference was the indispensable tool enabling groups to define their role and interests for themselves: "sociology has become the inescapable ground of self-validation for radicals, moderates and conservatives alike."[5] Groups tend to develop their own perspectives simultaneously as society attaches greater intrinsic value to "human-ness" abstractly. Exclusivist national ideologies which deny common human rights arose as an inexorable consequence of the process he described. Mannheim observed in the 1930s that

> Indeed, we witness the continued growth of nationalism rather than cosmopolitanism. The democratic process which enhances the general capacity for self-determination . . . awakens consciousness of kind on a national scale before it expands group consciousness to a global dimension. Nationalism is in this regard a phenomenon parallel to feminism and the German youth movement.[6]

SOME HEURISTIC ILLUSTRATIONS

The circle of trust is contingent on cultural assumptions about reality held in common by well-socialized group members of the same political generation.[7] The circle of trust is a property of the group, the basic element of the social system, rather than a product of individual circles.

Although few theoretical or empirical contributions have been made since Durkheim to clarify the problem of solidarity—as differentiated from explaining the causes of deviance—anyone adding to the overloaded sociological lexicon must inquire whether a novel concept is more than a neologism.[8] One may ask, therefore, what relation does the circle of trust have with other sociological concepts and how can it illuminate community or national cohesion?

The circle of trust may be mapped by defining boundaries of group identification and cohesion and symbolizing qualities of social relations within them. Several examples of such maps are depicted in Figure 6.

Figure 6a represents Harry Eckstein's analysis of modern Nor-

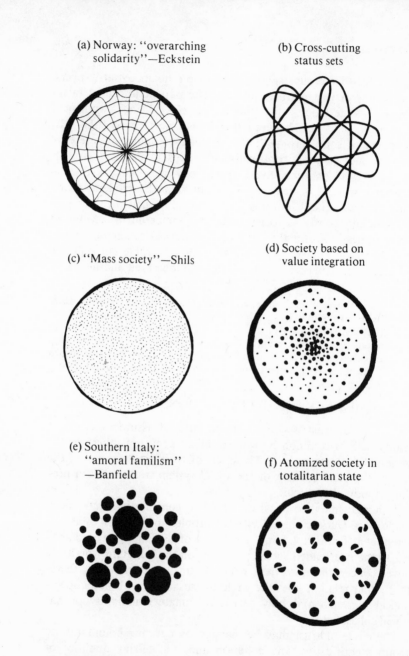

(a) Norway: "overarching solidarity"—Eckstein

(b) Cross-cutting status sets

(c) "Mass society"—Shils

(d) Society based on value integration

(e) Southern Italy: "amoral familism"—Banfield

(f) Atomized society in totalitarian state

Figure 6 Mapping the circle of trust

way, typified by "an overarching attitude of solidarity" toward "Norway as a community," reinforced by networks of organized groups within which patterns of accommodation and authority parallel the larger pattern of the state.[9] Figure 6b represents an ideal type of a society joined solely by cross-cutting status sets.

Figure 6c represents Edward Shils's concept of mass society, which is characterized thus:

> This dispersion of charisma from the center outward has manifested itself in a greater stress on individual dignity and in-dividual rights in all generations, in all strata, in both sexes, and in the whole variety of ethnic groups and peoples. . . . This con-sensus, which leans toward the interpretation of every living human being as a participant in the uniting essence which defines the society, has produced a wide distribution of civility.[10]

While individuals become increasingly diversified and groups less cohesive, the mass society is a consensual society: all members agree that each of them is due the same rights and obligations.

Such a minimal consensus can be differentiated from that in a society unified by a dominant value system, in which one would expect belief (and inclusion of all elements) to be attenuated as one goes from center to periphery, as exemplified in Figure 6d.

Figure 6e represents a homogeneous society lacking cohesion in collectivities, such as southern Italy, characterized by Edward Banfield as a society of "amoral familists" in which relation-ships outside the nuclear family or patron-client relation are unreliable and unregulated. Formal organizations such as church, party, labor union, or cooperative are shallowly rooted or find it difficult to endure, despite their correspondence with needs the peasants know they cannot fulfill alone; the man who is safe, people repeat continually, is "the man who plays alone."[11]

Figure 6f represents an atomized society similar to that in Figure 6e except that distrust among its members has increased. All have become fearful of the boundaries (defined by the regime) which segregate outsiders from insiders: this is the state theoretically induced by totalitarian terror.[12]

So far we can say that the circle of trust corresponds to either the most encompassing reference group or the in-group.[13] The perimeter of the circle of trust is the boundary within which group mores—whether universalistic or particularistic—apply.

Some groups' mores may obligate one toward a wider reference group or more inclusive universe of obligation.

The problem of a consensus of circle of trust in a multigroup or ethnically stratified society is more difficult to represent in two dimensions than the foregoing types. Let us assume there is a large but finite number of geometric possibilities of convergent circles out of an infinite variety of overlapping and non-convergent circles: how can the emergence of a common moral order of obligation be explained?

Pierre van den Berghe distinguishes between two types of race relations in biracial societies. The paternalistic type is character-ized by traditional bonds between the securely dominant race and the oppressed or subordinated race, accustomed to accommodate to its powerlessness with deference. By contrast, the competitive type is exemplified by conflict and more frequent unmasked violence. The dominant race bears no collective obligation to the other.

Van den Berghe believes that Mexico and Brazil are examples of societies which have evolved from paternalistic types, but Brazil, unlike Mexico, has an "appreciable amount of distinctly racial prejudices and discrimination" and is moving "toward the competitive model."[14] The United States and the Union of South Africa are examples of the competitive model which he calls "*Herrenvolk* (master race) democracies." Such societies are in-tegrated not by value consensus but "by a mixture of *political coercion* and *economic interdependence*."[15] Van den Berghe con-siders this model an example of organic solidarity, ignoring Durkheim's dictum that the division of labor in itself is not suf-ficient to produce solidarity between groups based on an ar-bitrary, ascribed characteristic, such as race is.

Where classes are bound by inclusive bonds within a homogeneous society but one group among them, discriminated by a real or mythical stigma, is completely ostracized and out of moral bonds, that group is a pariah caste. Such a status may ex-ist outside caste systems. The Tokushu Burakumin as described by Hiroshi Wagatsuma embody this status in Japanese society. One subgroup among them is known as *Hinin,* or nonhuman; their status was legally abolished in 1871. Herbert Passim remarks that when they first began to organize as a social movement demanding reform, "they could not decide whether to refer to themselves as the 'Jews of Japan' or the 'Negroes of Japan.' "[16]

PROPERTIES OF THE CIRCLE OF TRUST

These properties of the circle(s) of trust which differentiate social systems may lead to researchable questions if we can delineate them and observe their occurrence. Some readily discernible characteristics include:

1. Cohesion—the intensity of reciprocal obligations within the circle
2. Integration—the location of all membership groups and categories with which the dominant collectivity interacts inside the circle
3. Consensus—the agreement among all collectivities within the same social system on discrete and nonoverlapping circles of trust (pluralism) or the agreement on an inclusive perimeter encompassing them
4. Extent of solidarity—the agreement among all members on belonging together within the circle (signified by the joined perimeter bounding the circle) as contrasted to plural circles or societies sustained only by the mutual interest of diverse groups without any common identification (Figure 6b)
5. Out-group affect—whether the sentiment and obligations toward those outside the perimeter are characterized by acceptance, neutral affect, or exclusion and hostility

It is apparent that these characteristics are both logically and empirically related, but the range of potential combinations cannot be predicted here. Norway is a society which is integrated, consensual, highly cohesive, and solidary. Loyalty is focused on Norway as a community, as well as on classes and groups to which each member belongs. Eckstein describes modern Norwegian society as being permeated by a sense of "we-ness" or underlying solidarity. Social relations are characterized by consistent regard for diffuse obligations, taking into account the value of individuals apart from their instrumental utility relative to one's needs; community responsibility for the young, the dependent, and the deviant is freely acknowledged. The many voluntary associations in which people participate show a wide-spread acceptance of reciprocal obligations which are not motivated by material rewards.[17]

By contrast, Italian peasant society, similarly described by a visiting sociologist (Banfield) and its own members in response to dialogues initiated by a nonviolent activist attempting to organize that society (Danilo Dolci), has low cohesion (exemplified by mutual distrust), consensus, and solidarity, although it is also integrated. Reciprocal obligations outside the family are few and voluntary organizations difficult to sustain. The most successful nonpublic organization, the Mafia, both exploits and sustains the distrust of affiliation, exchanging protection for services. While the population is dense physically, social obligations (cohesion) are low.[18] Gabriel Almond and Sidney Verba's study of political culture shows that Italians have a low attachment to Italy as a nation-state. They remark that Italian political culture is composed of "unusually strong parochial, alienative subject and alienative participant components."[19] Luigi Barzini's observations clarify what this means in practice:

> Very few then are the rules which can help an Italian plot his course and steer a safe line in a country . . . in which society, the law and the state have feeble powers. . . . The first source of power is the family. The Italian family is a stronghold in a hostile land. . . . The strength of the family is not only . . . the bulwark against disorder, but, at the same time, one of its principal causes. . . . Most Italians still obey a double standard. There is one code valid within the family circle, with relatives . . . and there is another code regulating life outside.[20]

Both Italian and Norwegian societies are ethnically homogeneous, so that they do not show how such divisions affect consensus and solidarity. A stratified racial society, such as the Union of South Africa, provides an ideal example of nonconsensus. In that country, the legal privileges and rewards of each nonwhite class (Africans, Coloured, and Indians) is determined by the white governing class, which alone possesses political rights. How well is the political structure reflected by the moral universe of each racial class?

Evidence gathered in the 1950s from social distance scales and other questionnaires indicates the unwillingness of the white stratum to grant membership on equal terms to the nonwhites but the willingness of all nonwhites to grant such membership to whites if their racial disadvantages were removed. This was true of both English-speaking and Afrikaans-speaking subjects, representing the two major groups among the whites.[21]

One may justly object that social distance scales are an imperfect index of the circle of trust; it is conceivable that members of one group might refuse to associate on an intimate basis with members of another group and prefer to restrict them to subordinate roles, but might still consider themselves responsible to them as human beings. However, certain steps on social distance scales may be considered cutting points between social distance and moral distance. Thomas Pettigrew, for instance, administered a social distance questionnaire to white South African students in 1956 which contained the following option to which respondents could agree or disagree: "I wish someone would kill all of them." Among Afrikaans-speaking students, 26 percent expressed that preference toward the Indians, compared to 20 percent of English-speaking students.[22] It is unfortunate that Pettigrew did not ask the same question to Indian students regarding whites as preferred objects of annihilation.

Pettigrew's study also showed equal distaste among white South African students for Africans and Coloured: about half the English and three-fifths of the Afrikaner students expressed a wish to have nothing at all to do with them. H. F. Dickie-Clarke administered the same scale to a Coloured sample, enabling us to inquire whether the whites' desire to exclude them from any obligation is reciprocal. Only 1 percent of the Coloured surveyed expressed such distaste toward the English, and 10 percent toward the Afrikaners.[23]

It seems evident that the moral universes of South Africans of different colors diverge radically. There is no loyalty to the state or nation exhibited by the Africans, but an expedient conformity. Their lack of solidarity is shown resoundingly at soccer matches, where they are said to cheer invariably whatever nation's team opposes the white South African team. Feelings toward outsiders likewise depend on racial perspective and who the outsiders are.

The solidarity of citizens within the nation-state, as distinct from loyalty to the government, is also studied by political scientists from the perspective of political culture, national integration, and modernization. Polarity toward nations and groups outside the circle may be viewed in terms of nationalism and internationalism. It seems logical to infer that as a society moves toward greater exclusiveness, toward a definition of membership based on likeness, blood, or ideal characteristics of the true *Volk,* it ought to become more hostile toward outsiders among them.

The circle of trust comprehends, employing Weber's classification of relationships, those social relationships which are symmetrical within a social order, regardless of whether the basis of relatedness is associative or communal.[24] The bases for extending moral imperatives may be rational rather than sentimental, expedient rather than morally inspired. It ought to be reiterated that the circle of trust is not identical to the corpus of values and norms held in common but is the network of others toward whom obligations are owed and from whom reciprocity is expected.

The Jamaica Debate

It is illuminating to explore Brigadier General Surtees' comparison of the response to Dyer's action at Jallianwala Bagh with the response to the British officers' actions after the Jamaica rebellion of 1865. Were the patterns underlying these events significantly alike? And did the themes of arguments condoning or censuring the violence parallel each other?

In Jamaica in 1865, there was a brief uprising, during which period sixteen whites were killed and many more fled from the eastern coast, leaving their homes which were later looted. After this "rebellion," as it was construed by the government, had ceased, at least 350 Jamaicans were executed, 600 natives flogged, and 1,000 native huts burned during the month-long reign of martial law. Governor Eyre, who authorized the extension of martial law, was removed from his position after a royal commission documented these events and concluded "that the punishments inflicted were excessive; that the punishment of death was unnecessarily frequent; that the floggings were reckless, and at Bath positively barbarous; that the burning of 1,000 houses was wanton and cruel."[1]

The Jamaica Committee was formed to express Englishmen's

revulsion over these deeds. When the committee decided on a more radical course of strategy—to bring the accused officers and Governor Eyre up on charges in the criminal courts—its first chairman, Mr. Buxton, resigned and was replaced by John Stuart Mill.

The Jamaica debate was opened in the House of Commons by Buxton, who presented a four-part resolution, the first clause of which stated "that this House deplores the excessive punishments which followed the suppression of the disturbances of October last in the parish of St. Thomas, Jamaica, and especially the unnecessary frequency with which the punishment of death was inflicted."[2] The rest of the motion provided for compensation, amnesty of the remainder of the sentenced Jamaicans, and discipline of the officers involved.

According to Buxton, the chain of events was clear:

> [The] outbreak clearly arose from some violent local squabbles about the land on which the negroes had settled, and from which they were expelled. . . . The negroes, debarred from what they supposed to be their rights, were seized with a desire for vengeance . . . against Mr. Herschell and Baron Ketelholdt, who had taken an active part against them. . . . They came down a mere unorganized horde . . . armed only with the hooks used in cutting canes and bushes, and sticks and stones. . . . When they advanced upon the Court House, finding the Volunteers drawn up in front of them, they flung stones, wounding some of the company, and among others its captain, who thereupon, quite justifiably, for the Riot Act had been read, gave the order to fire. According to Corporal Marks some twenty negroes fell killed or wounded. This maddened the mob, and rushing upon the Volunteers before they could reload, they seized some of their rifles and drove them all inside the Court House. . . . It was a remarkable fact that those wounded in the Court House were shown in evidence to have been shot with gravel, not bullets. The negroes at last set the Court House on fire, overpowered the whites, of whom eight civilians and seven Volunteers, making a total of fifteen, were killed, besides three old pauper negroes said to have perished in the ruins. . . . They did not kill any other white or coloured persons, but went on along the east coast, plundering the houses which had been deserted on their approach.

Buxton denied that there had been any plans for a general massacre and that atrocities allegedly performed by the blacks had occurred. He refuted the charge of Governor Eyre's defenders that there had been a rebellion rather than a riot and that Eyre had saved the white population from the planned massacre. The issue, he claimed, was uncomplicated: "The question on which we shall divide is simply as to whether England will or will not sanction these butcheries."

A few speakers in that debate challenged Buxton's construction of the facts, but others, who accepted his judgment that these deeds were "atrocities" or "butchery," sided with John Stuart Mill in refusing to support the motion because, Mill asserted, Parliament could neither condemn nor condone crimes whose perpetrators had not been tried before a criminal tribunal. Mill insisted "that when such things have been done, there is a *prima facie* demand for legal punishment. . . . Neither the Government, nor this House, nor the whole English nation combined, can exercise a pardoning power without previous trial and sentence."

To Mill, the issue was not the intentions of those officers who had been "allowed to take the lives of the Queen's subjects improperly." He answered those who asked

> "How can we think of prosecuting anybody for putting people to death, when we cannot possibly suppose that those who did it believed them to be innocent?" Well, very probably they did not; though even this is by no means a thing which it is permissible to take for granted. But admitting the fact, it is an excuse that may be made for actions of still greater atrocity than I claim any right to attribute to these. Did the perpetrators of the massacre of St. Bartholomew think their victims innocent? On the contrary, did they not firmly believe them to be hateful to God and to all good men?

Mr. Adderley denounced both Buxton's and Mill's position, ignoring the question of the intentions of the officers accused or the necessity of the injuries they inflicted. Like the Hunter Committee's majority, he restricted the substantive issue to one of formal legality rather than lawfulness. Reviewing the evidence, he asserted that

> it was the opinion of the Commissioners . . . that martial law was fully and properly established, that it was fully justifiable, and proclaimed upon good reasons. If that were so, there can be nothing illegal, at all events, in the constitution of the tribunals, and the supposition of the hon. Gentleman to the contrary is opposed to the opinion of every authority on the subject. Nor can there have been anything illegally done by those who were bona fide engaged in the suppression of the insurrection.

Not all speakers who supported Buxton's first clause agreed

that there had been a riot, rather than a rebellion, or that the acts of the officers were offenses which could not be indemnified by proclamation of martial law, as Mill had asserted in contradiction to Adderley. The issue which Mr. Forster posed to his colleagues was the same as that hypothesized by the Marquess of Crewe in the Dyer debate of 1920: if such behavior was extended to a situation involving white men, would such violence against them be tolerated?

> Even if all of them had committed murder it would have been considered an outrageous thing to have executed them all. The murder of Mr. Hire was, no doubt, barbarous, but what would be said if for a murder in Ireland 130 persons were executed? . . .
> It was said that what had been done was in order to prevent the insurrection spreading to other parts of the island. If they were to apply that to Ireland, what would be said if 300 were executed in Tipperary for an insurrection that had broken out in Galway?

Forster concluded with a question:

> How was it that Gov. Eyre, whom he believed to be a humane and conscientious man, sanctioned proceedings of this kind, and how was it that British officers perpetrated atrocities from which they would have shrunk had the victims been white people? The reason was that they were not free, and he did not know that he himself or any Member of the House would have been free, from the race feeling—the feeling of contempt for what was regarded as an inferior race. This, however, only made it the more incumbent upon Parliament . . . to affirm that there ought not to be one code of morality for one colour, and another code for another.

Mr. Cochrane, an opponent of the motion on substantive grounds, confirmed that tolerance and sympathy for Governor Eyre depended on racial identification with the whites. He was "surprised that during this debate he had heard no sympathy expressed on the opposite Benches for the whites who were the first victims of this rebellion." Contrary to Buxton's representations, Cochrane recognized the Governor Eyre had to do what he did to prevent the whites from being murdered by the blacks:

> He held in his hand a letter written from Kingston, by Mr. Radcliffe, a minister of the Scotch Church, in which was the following passage:—
> "It has come to light that the insurrection was a portion, and only a portion, of an intended massacre of all the whites and respectable coloured people. The time was to be Christmas Day,

the directors the members of a secret society which has existed in
Kingston for some time, and the object the slaughter of the
whites and the seizure of their property. Surely the people of
England will at last have their eyes open to the character of the
negro; they have been petting panthers, who, not satisfied with
murdering their victims, mutilated them. We have been living on
a mine, and we wish the people of England to know it. We were
all to have been murdered on Christmas Day, and if the anti-
slavery people do not know it, we do." . . .

The truth was that a general insurrection was prepared, and
nothing but the energy of the Governor saved the white population from extermination.

And Colonel North pointed out

that those acts were done during a time of insurrection, when
there were but a few thousands of white people whom a handful
of troops had to protect from the mass of the population of the
island. Some hon. Gentlemen appeared to think that every negro
who was killed during these unhappy transactions was murdered,
while every white man who was butchered only got what he deserved.

The debate terminated inconclusively with the House passing
Buxton's first clause, which was supported by Conservative
Cabinet members for the same reason Mill had opposed it.
Disraeli, then chancellor of the exchequer, claimed that

the very phrase "punishment of death" implies a legal act, and
therefore there will be no ground whatever, in the event of the
Resolution being passed, for the assumption that we are necessarily called upon to act against individuals. The result of passing the
Resolution will, in fact, be quite contrary to that course which the
hon. Gentleman seems to imply will be the logical consequence. I
think that this is a Resolution very proper to pass, and one in
which all can join.

Buxton withdrew the remaining resolutions.

John Stuart Mill proceeded to seek justice in the courts. He
assessed the success of that campaign in his autobiography as
follows:

A bench of magistrates in one of the most Tory counties in
England dismissed our case: we were more successful before the
magistrates at Bow Street; which gave an opportunity to the Lord
Chief Justice of the Queen's Bench, Sir Alexander Cockburn, for
delivering his celebrated charge, which settled the law of the question in favour of liberty, as far as it is in the power of a judge's

charge to settle. There, however, our success ended, for the Old Bailey Grand Jury by throwing out our bill prevented the case from coming to trial. It was clear that to bring English functionaries to the bar of a criminal court for abuses of power committed against negroes and mulattoes was not a popular proceeding with the English middle classes. We had, however, redeemed, so far as lay in us, the character of our country, by showing that there was at any rate a body of persons determined to use all the means which the law afforded to obtain justice for the injured.[3]

While the executions in Jamaica had not been committed in a mass assembly as had General Dyer's massacre, they were akin in intent and function: both were acts of terrorist reprisal motivated by racial rage evoked by the natives' murders. That rage was further inflamed by false rumors of atrocities, confirmed by the governor, which justified officers to retaliate against any blacks, who were collectively identified as the enemy. According to Buxton:

> It was an actual fact that a girl . . . was tried by a court-martial and sentenced to be hung, but recommended to mercy. Brig.-Gen. Nelson officially informed Gen. O'Connor that he hung her in spite of this recommendation to mercy. He said . . . not because she had been proved to have perpetrated these atrocities, but because he was told . . . that women had committed atrocities; whereas, ten minutes' inquiry would have shown that no atrocities had been committed at all.

After narrating a score of such incidents, he asked rhetorically: "What could add to the blackness of this black story?" And then he adduced more instances of sham trials and sadistic tortures, such as that of the magistrate, Mr. Kirkland, who tied pianoforte wire amidst the cat-o'-nine-tails used for floggings.

Although the debate was obscured by the lack of agreement on the significance of Buxton's resolutions and differences on strategy determined by tactical as well as moral assessment of the culpability of Governor Eyre, those who deplored the governor's role were distinguished from those who exonerated him wholly by the same assumptions as those distinguishing opponents in the Dyer debate. Those censuring the officials' deeds did not all agree that there was only a riot, but either stated or implied that there ought to be only one rule of justice for blacks and whites alike. They referred to Jamaicans as "fellow-subjects" or the "Queen's subjects" and assumed that any punishment meted out to subjects of one race ought not to be tolerated if it would not be tolerated against another race.

The few defenders of Governor Eyre, like some of General Dyer's, claimed it was clearly a racial issue, but a case of self-defense rather than vengeance. They buttressed their claims by reference to testimonials from Englishmen in Jamaica, who, like the British imperial class in India, supported the actions taken in their self-defense and cited evidence of conspiracy and atrocities, reports of which were not verified by subsequent investigation. British-Indians supporting Dyer similarly claimed that he had prevented a massacre and that the Hunter Committee had ignored this. However, Dyer's defenders in Parliament dwelt more on the loss of authority in India than loss of lives.

Both the level of gore (alleged against the natives and documented against the British officers) and the level of fear and hostility seem higher in 1865 than in 1919. Mr. Cardwell, who sympathized with the first resolution of Buxton, reminded him that the natives' atrocities could not be judged so dispassionately at the time: "In dealing with Gov. Eyre we ought, I think, to remember the state of things at that time among the black population of the Southern States of America; that a civil war was going on in the neighboring island of Hayti." Besides racial fears being higher in 1865, there was no commitment to the self-development of Jamaican government, as there was to India in 1919, which would restrain Britons from expressing prejudices that would open them up to charges of hypocrisy in 1920. Their ideology of empire did not inhibit the expression of such prejudices and fears then as it did in 1920.

Forster's readiness (as well as that of other like-minded men) to transcend such prejudices was probably contingent not on a belief in racial equality but on a belief in the equality of moral obligations. Rather than the rights of the blacks, it was the "honour of England" which was at stake.

Notes

PREFACE

1. See especially Lewis Coser's *The Functions of Social Conflict* and Ralf Dahrendorf's *Class and Class Conflict in Industrial Society.*

2. Allen D. Grimshaw, "Factors Contributing to Colour Violence in the United States and Britain," *Race* 111 (May 1962):3–19.

3. Emile Durkheim, *The Division of Labor in Society.*

4. A. J. P. Taylor, *English History: 1914–1945,* p. 152.

5. Rajah Ram in *The Jallianwala Bagh Massacre—A Premeditated Plan* disputes this but presents no evidence, relying on tendentious inference to cover his own admission that "what actually transpired among the few top civil and military officers of the Government in the evening of the 9th of April, nobody can know" (p. 176). He is intent on demonstrating that this was a battle sought by both sides on the plain of Jallianwala Bagh—as in the following passage:

> It has been made out that people had gone to Jallianwala Bagh to attend the meeting without knowing the possible consequences, and that they were unknowingly trapped there. But to say this is to make a mockery of their supreme sacrifice. . . . People were well aware of the possible result of holding a meeting in defiance of military orders. . . . The fact is that they were not prepared to surrender themselves to the official dictates. Therefore, to say that innocent blood was shed is to belittle the importance of the supreme sacrifice made on that day by thousands of *Satyagrahi* soldiers, whose very presence in the Bagh amounted to an open defiance of authority.

CHAPTER I

1. Emile Durkheim, *The Division of Labor in Society,* p. 102.

2. Ibid., pp. 276–277.

3. Ibid., p. 281.

4. To be precise, these groups are categories which tend to be or become collectivities as Robert Merton has defined collectivities: "people who have a sense of solidarity by virtue of sharing common values and who have acquired an attendant sense of moral obligation to fulfill role-expectations." See *Social Theory and Social Structure*, p. 299.

5. Ralf Dahrendorf, *Class and Class Conflict in Industrial Society*, pp. 172–173.

6. Alvin W. Gouldner, "The Norm of Reciprocity: A Preliminary Statement," *American Sociological Review* 25 (April 1960): 161–177.

7. Both Dahrendorf and Simmel, working from different assumptions, propose this. For the development of Simmel's thought, see his *Web of Group Affiliations*.

8. *The Division of Labor*, p. 377.

9. Both Talcott Parsons and Erik Allardt have recognized that legitimacy is a function of solidarity. See Parsons' essay, "On the Concept of Political Power," in his *Social Theory and Modern Society*, p. 327, and Allardt's "A Theory of Solidarity and Legitimacy Conflicts" in *Cleavages, Ideologies and Party Systems*, ed. E. Allardt and Y. Littunen, p. 82.

10. The term "consciousness of kind" was first used by Franklin H. Giddings; see, for example, *Studies in the Theory of Human Society*.

11. George Herbert Mead's concept of the "generalized other" articulated in Mead's *Mind, Self and Society* has often been confounded with Harry Stack Sullivan's concept of the "significant other." Sullivan's notion is restricted to interpersonal processes, arising developmentally from the mother-child relationship, rather than a conception of emergent social structure (as is Mead's), Robert S. Perinbanayagam points out (*SSSI Notes*, September 1975). However, adapting the concept of the "significant other" enables us to explain why the child identifies with adults at the earliest stage of development, later enabling him to function in groups and internalize the "generalized other" in game-playing and other activities demanding differentiated role playing.

12. *The Division of Labor*, p. 430.

13. This hypothetical situation was true of cases going before the high courts before 1881 and was the background to the controversy over the Ilbert Bill described in Chapter 3.

14. This is Marx's term used as explicated by Ralf Dahrendorf, *Class and Class Conflict in Industrial Society*, p. 15.

15. This is the basis of Barrington Moore's alternative explanation to those of Tilly for counterrevolution in the Vendée. Moore believes that the complicity of the populace which "flocked to clandestine masses . . . was the break with the prevailing legality. . . . Through these acts a new crime becomes the basis for a new legality." See *Social Origins of Dictatorship and Democracy*, pp. 99–100. Moore's explanation differs from that of Frantz Fanon in *The Wretched of the Earth;* Fanon does not emphasize the instrumental role of illegality but the positive cathartic function of violence (rather than simply violating the law), which enables a powerless colonial class to transcend their feeling of impotence.

16. Allegations of crimes were made in fifty-two of seventy-six instances. If we add violations of the etiquette of white supremacy involved in their category of disputes over "civil liberties, public facilities, segregation, political events, and housing" to these, violations preceding the riots were alleged in sixty-six out of seventy-six instances. See "The Precipitants and Underlying Conditions of Race Riots," by Stanley Lieberson and Arnold J. Silverman, *American Sociological Review* 30 (December 1965): 887–891.

17. Allen D. Grimshaw, "Factors Contributing to Colour Violence in the United States and Britain," *Race* 111 (May 1962):3.

18. See Dahlke's "Race and Minority Riots—A Study in the Typology of Violence," *Social Forces* 30 (1952):419–425.

19. Norman Cohn, *Warrant for Genocide: The Myth of the Jewish World-Conspiracy and the Protocols of the Elders of Zion.*

20. Simmel's thought is developed by Lewis Coser in *The Functions of Social Conflict,* pp. 86–95.

21. See Hannah Arendt's *The Origins of Totalitarianism* for the most complete exposition of this thesis.

22. Coser, *The Functions of Social Conflict,* p. 110.

23. Durkheim, *The Division of Labor,* pp. 89–90.

24. Ibid., p. 172.

25. See Karl Mannheim, *Essays on the Sociology of Culture,* pp. 100–101, 176, 294.

26. Karl Mannheim, *Man and Society in an Age of Reconstruction: Studies in Modern Social Structure,* p. 53.

27. See Arthur Mitzman's *The Iron Cage: An Historical Interpretation of Max Weber.*

CHAPTER 2

1. V. N. Datta, *Jallianwala Bagh,* pp. 127–128.

2. See *The Other Side of the Medal.*

3. M. M. Ahliuwalia in *Kukas: The Freedom Fighters of the Punjab,* p. 87, concludes that the authorities were previously informed by the Kuka leader of the intention of undisciplined Kukas to attack but made no attempt to prevent them because they needed a display of "rebellion" in order to repress them as they previously had wished. He also notes that the Government of India's disapproval in that case was preceded by questions on the floor of Parliament on 29 February 1872, stimulated by a report of the execution in *The Times* (London) of 5 February; the undersecretary of state was forced to admit no trial had been given the Kukas. Ahliuwalia implies that the Government of India itself was not aware of the mode of execution imposed by Cowan (pp. 95–96). See also Fauja Singh Bajwa's *Kuka Movement,* pp. 100–108.

4. *Parliamentary Debates* (Commons), 3rd series, vol. 184 (31 July 1866), cols. 1767–1840; 3rd series, vol. 186 (21 March 1867), cols. 275–279; 3rd series, vol. 189 (13 August 1867), cols. 1437–1446; and John Stuart Mill, *Autobiography of John Stuart Mill,* pp. 207–210.

5. C. H. Philips, *The Evolution of India and Pakistan 1858 to 1947, Select Documents,* p. 264.

6. The Turkish costumes proclaimed their identification with the Pan-Islamic movement directed at ensuring the preservation of the Turkish Empire in order to protect the Islamic caliph situated there. The movement was joined by Gandhi and attained greater popularity in the Punjab than other parts of India, due to the Muslim predominance there (Datta, *Jallianwala Bagh,* p. 29).

7. Robert Bernays, *"Naked Fakir,"* p. 120.

8. Naidis accepted the Hunter Report's conclusion in "The Punjab Disturbances of 1919: A Study in Indian Nationalism" (unpublished Ph.D. dissertation, Stanford University, 1951, p. 62) while Datta rejected it in *Jallianwala Bagh,* p. 76. Replying to my personal inquiry, Datta explained (in a letter dated 22 February 1971) that he rejected the testimony of Deputy Commissioner Irving, whose report of seeing smoke from the banks before the second bridge firing was the basis of the Hunter Committee's conclusion, because Irving's recollection was not confirmed by other official witnesses who were at the bridge and his actions

that day were not explicable if he knew at that time that the banks were being burned down.

9. Datta, *Jallianwala Bagh,* p. 94.

10. Ibid., p. 96.

11. Rupert Furneaux elaborated a theory in *Massacre at Amritsar* that Dyer continued firing because he perceived the crowd rushing him due to effects of un-diagnosed arteriosclerosis distorting his perception. But Furneaux subsequently reverted to the conclusion that Dyer had, as he himself stated, deliberately ordered the firing protracted without any apprehension (see note 24). Furneaux based this conclusion on a letter from a noncommissioned officer with Dyer at the Bagh who stated (as reported by Furneaux in the *Times Literary Supplement,* 9 April 1964, p. 291): "I saw no sign of a rush towards the troops. After a bit, I noticed that Captain Briggs was drawing up his face as if in pain, and was pluck-ing at the General's elbow. . . . The General took no notice, and ordered fire to be resumed, directing it particularly at the wall."

12. Congress Report, vol. 2, pp. 116–118, quoted in Datta, *Jallianwala Bagh,* pp. 102–103.

13. Datta, *Jallianwala Bagh,* pp. 104–105.

14. Ibid., p. 163.

15. Ibid., p. 166.

16. Ian Colvin, *The Life of General Dyer,* p. 186.

17. M. R. Jayakar relates in *The Story of My Life* that he and other Punjab Subcommittee members believed Dyer had set a trap but does not mention Hans Raj's role at all (pp. 323–324).

18. Datta, *Jallianwala Bagh,* p. 164.

19. The royal proclamation commuted or reduced 85 of the death sentences and 258 of the life sentences: the average sentence before reduction was 5¼ years and after reduction 1¾ years.

20. E. V. Walter, "Violence and the Process of Terror," *American Sociological Review* 29 (April 1964): 251, 256.

21. HC:112–113. General Dyer later claimed to have been misquoted by this printed line; however, at least two members of the Hunter Committee, one English general and one Indian member, recalled his saying this.

22. Dyer's testimony from Hunter Report, 1920, vol. 6, p. 68, as reported by Datta, *Jallianwala Bagh,* p. 156. In his earliest report to his superior, Major General Beynon, on 14 April 1919 and in his subsequent defense before the Army Council in 1920 (for which he had engaged counsel), Dyer made statements con-tradictory to this regarding the possibility of his being rushed by the crowd and his intent to adhere to the minimum-force principle. However, by the time of his 25 August self-report, Dyer had been assured by Beynon and Lt. Gov. Sir Michael O'Dwyer of approval for his action in firing and had been commended by the army commander in chief for his conduct of the Afghan campaign. Thus he considered himself out of danger of any sanctions and did not consider the possibility of self-incrimination, as he had before and would do later. O'Dwyer, in his secret testimony before the Hunter Committee, repeated that "the sugges-tion that the appearance of the crowd was as if they were going to intercept him or rush at him has never been made by Dyer." This remark was based on his in-terview with Dyer shortly after the event (Dyer's testimony from the Hunter Report, 1920, as cited above). See note 11 also.

23. George Orwell, *A Collection of Essays,* p. 159.

24. J. Nehru, *An Autobiography,* p. 43; this has also been cited by Mark Naidis in *India,* p. 153.

25. The extent of extortion may have been much more widespread than

documented by Congress because individuals were reluctant to make public charges which would necessarily implicate them as well. Extortion was agreed to out of fear of being falsely accused and imprisoned.

CHAPTER 3

1. Vincent A. Smith, *The Oxford History of India,* pp. 579-580.

2. Josselyn Hennessy, "British Education for an Elite in India (1780-1947)," in *Governing Elites: Studies in Training and Selection,* ed. Rupert Wilkinson, p. 143, citing Pannikar, *Survey of Indian History* (London: Asia Publishing House, 1947).

3. Thomas R. Metcalf, *The Aftermath of Revolt: India, 1857-1870,* pp. 310-313.

4. Ibid., p. 318.

5. Ibid., p. 326.

6. My calculations are based on the numbers of candidates and vacancies reported between 1870 and 1914 by Sir Verney Lovett in *The Cambridge History of India,* vol. 6, ed. H. H. Dodwell, p. 370; he attributes the figures to civil service commissioners.

7. H. L. Singh, *Problems and Policies of the British in India, 1885-1898,* cites Parliamentary Command Paper 4956 as his source; Philip Mason [Philip Woodruff] bases his figures on anonymous official records reported in *The Men Who Ruled India,* vol. 2, *The Guardians,* p. 363.

8. Cited in C. H. Philips (ed.), *The Evolution of India and Pakistan, 1858 to 1947: Select Documents,* p. 548.

9. Public Service Commission statistics for 1887 are cited by Anil Seal in *The Emergence of Indian Nationalism: Competition and Collaboration in the Later Nineteenth Century,* pp. 116-118.

10. Ibid., p. 165.

11. Philips, *Evolution of India and Pakistan,* p. 124.

12. Ibid., p. 125.

13. M. N. Das, *India under Morley and Minto: Politics behind Revolution, Repression and Reforms,* p. 24.

14. Mason, *The Guardians,* p. 174.

15. Norman Gerald Barrier, "Punjab Politics and the Disturbances of 1907" (unpublished Ph.D. dissertation, Duke University, 1966), pp. 153-154.

16. Das, *India under Morley and Minto,* p. 220.

17. Seal, *Emergence of Indian Nationalism,* p. 19.

18. B. Pattabhi Sitaramayya, *History of the Indian National Congress,* vol. 1, pp. 11-17; L. R. Rao, "The Early Phase of Indian Nationalism, Part 2," *Journal of Karnatak University* 6 (June 1962):115-127, documents Hume's fear of revolution, which he hoped could be prevented by an alliance of the British and Indian educated middle classes.

19. R. R. Sethi, *The Last Phase: 1919-1947,* p. 609.

20. Seal, *Emergence of Indian Nationalism,* pp. 280, 329.

21. Ibid., pp. 333-334.

22. Ibid., pp. 296-297.

23. Pattabhi Sitaramayya, *History of the INC,* vol. 1, p. 66; Seal, *Emergence of Indian Nationalism,* p. 279.

24. S. Gopal, *British Policy in India: 1858-1905,* pp. 268-271.

25. Stanley A. Wolpert, *Tilak and Gokhale: Revolution and Reform in the Making of Modern India,* pp. 49-60.

26. Ibid., pp. 67-71; and Pansy Chaya Ghosh, *The Development of the Indian National Congress: 1892-1909,* pp. 71-73.

226

NOTES

27. Ghosh, *Development of the INC,* p. 77.
28. Wolpert, *Tilak and Gokhale,* p. 87.
29. Gopal, *British Policy in India,* pp. 269–270.
30. Das, *India under Morley and Minto,* p. 36.
31. Ghosh, *Development of the INC,* p. 132.
32. Wolpert, *Tilak and Gokhale,* p. 214.
33. Das, *India under Morley and Minto,* pp. 162–174.
34. Pattabhi Sitaramayya, *History of the INC,* vol. 1, pp. 89–90; Das, *India under Morley and Minto,* pp. 91–104.
35. Pansy C. Ghosh examines the evidence on this issue in some detail in *The Development of the INC.* Some quantitative index of the breadth of protest is provided by Banarjea's estimate, before the Congress convention of 1906 over which he presided, that "out of 259 anti-partition demonstrations held in the country since October 1905, in 135, the two communities had unitedly protested against the measure" (p. 122). There was a similar split among the Muslims regarding the boycott. One public meeting of 30,000 Muslims was held in 1906 in support of the boycott, as reported in the newspaper *The Pioneer* (p. 153).
36. Philips, *Evolution of India and Pakistan,* p. 194.
37. Pattabhi Sitaramayya, *History of the INC,* vol. 1, p. 69.
38. Smith, *Oxford History of India,* p. 771.
39. Das, *India under Morley and Minto,* pp. 50–55.
40. Allan Greenberger's *The British Image of India* analyzes themes in British novels about India and finds a distinct preference for the "martial races" and a marked antagonism toward the educated Hindus of Bengal, which expressions parallel the convictions expressed in the correspondence of Curzon and Lansdowne (see Philips, *Evolution of India and Pakistan,* pp. 564–568). Greenberger ascribes this preference to the British affinity for "men of action" (p. 128) but does not explore the intensity of hostility expressed toward the more educated Hindus.
41. Barrier, "Punjab Politics and the Disturbances of 1907," pp. 129–130. Arya members alone constituted one-third of Congress delegations from the Punjab between 1904 and 1906 (app. D, p. 354).
42. Ibid., pp. 135–138.
43. Ibid., pp. 180–189.
44. Ibid., p. 127, citing *Panjabee* of 3 October 1904, p. 2.
45. Ibid., pp. 170–171, 201–203.
46. Ibid., pp. 209–232.
47. Ibid., p. 233.
48. Ibid., p. 216.
49. Ibid., pp. 240–247.
50. Ibid., pp. 273, 278.
51. Ibid., pp. 279–280.
52. Ibid., pp. 258–263.
53. Ibid., p. 325.
54. Wolpert, *Tilak and Gokhale,* p. 220
55. Ibid., p. 223.
56. Ibid., pp. 224–225.
57. Das, *India under Morley and Minto,* pp. 113–115.
58. Uma Mukherjee and Haridas Mukherjee, "Sri Aurobindo and Bande Mataram," *Modern Review* (Allahabad) 114 (August 1963):126.
59. *Sandhya,* 25 September 1907, cited by Mukherjee and Mukherjee, "The Story of Bande Mataram Sedition Trial, 1907," *Modern Review* 106 (October 1959):288.

60. Das, *India under Morley and Minto*, p. 114; also Cmd. 9190, pp. 15-18.
61. Sethi, *The Last Phase*, p. 682.
62. Pattabhi Sitaramayya, *History of the INC*, vol. 1, p. 80.
63. Das, *India under Morley and Minto*, p. 85.

CHAPTER 4

1. Joan Bondurant, *Conquest of Violence: The Gandhian Philosophy of Conflict*.
2. M. K. Gandhi, *Non-violent Resistance*, pp. 74-76.
3. H. H. Dodwell, *The Indian Empire*, pp. 483-484.
4. For an explanation of the convolutions of Gandhi's concept of nonviolence at the time see P. Giuliano, "The Rejection of Violence in Gandhian Ethics of Conflict Resolution," *Journal of Conflict Resolution* 12 (1965):197-213.
5. Khushwant Singh, *A History of the Sikhs*, vol. 2, pp. 178-181.
6. Ibid., vol. 2, pp. 168-185.
7. C. H. Philips, *The Evolution of India and Pakistan, 1858 to 1947: Select Documents*, p. 264.
8. Ibid., p. 265.
9. B. Pattabhi Sitaramayya, *History of the Indian National Congress*, vol. 1, p. 129.
10. *Parliamentary Papers* (Commons), 1918, vol. 8 (*Reports*, vol. 4), Cmd, 9198, "Report of Sir N. Chandavarkar and Mr. Justice Beacroft on Detenues and Internees in Bengal," pp. 1-6.
11. Pattabhi Sitaramayya, *History of the INC*, vol. 1, p. 146.
12. *Parliamentary Papers* (Commons), 1918, vol. 8 (*Reports*, vol. 4), Cmd. 9190, "Report of Committee Appointed to Investigate Revolutionary Conspiracies in India," p. 226.
13. Khushwant Singh, *A History of the Sikhs*, vol. 2, pp. 186-188.
14. Cmd. 9190, p. 75.
15. Pattabhi Sitaramayya, *History of the INC*, vol. 1, p. 170.
16. *The Statesman* (Calcutta), 14 March 1919, p. 6.
17. Dodwell, *The Indian Empire*, p. 586.
18. Philip Mason, *The Guardians*, p. 228.
19. Pattabhi Sitaramayya, *History of the INC*, vol. 1, pp. 161-162.
20. S. D. Waley, *Edwin Montagu*, p. 235.
21. Mason, *The Guardians*, pp. 228-229.
22. *The Statesman* (Calcutta), 14 March 1919, p. 6.
23. M. K. Gandhi, *My Experiments with Truth*, pp. 561-562.
24. *The Statesman* (Calcutta), 19 March 1919, p. 6.
25. H. F. Owen, "Organizing for the Rowlatt Satyagraha of 1919," in *Essays on Gandhian Politics: The Rowlatt Satyagraha of 1919*, ed. R. Kumar, pp. 77-90; and D. E. U. Baker, "The Rowlatt Satyagraha in the Central Provinces and Berar," in same collection, pp. 119-123.
26. *The Statesman* (Calcutta), 5 April 1919, p. 8.
27. Government figures reproduced in Michael O'Dwyer's *India As I Knew It: 1885-1925*, p. 419, cited in Datta, *Jallianwala Bagh*, p. 10; see also Indian National Congress Punjab Subcommittee, *Report of the Commissioners*, vol. 1, pp. 4-5, 20-21.
28. Datta, *Jallianwala Bagh*, pp. 14-19.
29. Ibid., p. 55.
30. Ibid., p. 40.
31. Personal letter from V. N. Datta dated 22 February 1971.
32. Disorders Inquiry Evidence (*Reports*, vol. 6), vol. 4, p. 340, cited in Mark

Naidis, "The Punjab Disturbances of 1919: A Study in Indian Nationalism" (unpublished Ph.D. dissertation, Stanford University, 1951), p. 94.

33. Ralf Dahrendorf, *Class and Class Conflict in Industrial Society,* pp. 226, 239.

CHAPTER 6

1. Rupert Furneaux, *Massacre at Amritsar,* p. 181.

2. Ian Colvin, *The Life of General Dyer,* p. 121.

3. *A History of the Sikhs,* vol. 2, p. 167.

4. Colvin, *Life of General Dyer,* cited in Furneaux, *Massacre at Amritsar,* p. 181.

5. V. N. Datta, *Jallianwala Bagh,* p. 109.

6. Ibid., p. 136.

7. Ibid.

8. Datta, *Jallianwala Bagh,* p.137.

9. Colvin, *Life of General Dyer,* cited in Furneaux, *Massacre at Amritsar,* p. 113.

10. See Datta, *Jallianwala Bagh.* The contents of vols. 6 and 7 did not lead to any new findings on the direct responsibility for the massacre, but they do bear on the validity of charges against Sir Michael O'Dwyer of terrorism in wartime recruiting that were raised in the O'Dwyer vs. Sankaran Nair trial (see note 20 below) of 1924.

11. Great Britain, War Office, *The Manual of Military Law.*

12. Sir Michael O'Dwyer later claimed that the reason the Hunter Committee had been unable to find a conspiracy was that Montagu had proscribed investigation of the disturbances in Peshawar from their scrutiny, which disturbances would have linked the Afghan attack of May 1919 with the "Punjab risings." Sir Michael imputes at least three conspiracies: the conspiracy with the Afghan tribesmen, Gandhi's conspiracy, and the conspiracy in the name of Gandhi. See O'Dwyer's *India As I Knew It: 1885-1925,* pp. 280, 290, 313.

13. Datta, *Jallianwala Bagh,* pp. 161–167.

14. *Manual of Military Law,* Ch. 13, Sec. 9, p. 218.

15. Ibid., Ch. 13, Sec. 13, p. 219.

16. Ibid., Ch. 13, Sec. 32, p. 224.

17. Ibid., Ch. 13, Sec. 33, p. 224.

18. Ibid., Ch. 13, Sec. 35, pp. 224–225.

19. The logic of this citation does not compel us to follow their comparison, because the expectation the report tests—to expect more protest from communities raising more soldiers—is only one of the plausible hypotheses. If resistance prevailed earlier, there might be fewer recruits but more protest in 1919, contradicting the expectations behind their comparison.

20. These charges are documented by official memoranda which were not disputed by O'Dwyer, as were later charges by Sankaran Nair. O'Dwyer's 1924 libel suit against Nair was inspired by Nair's charges that terrorism was used by recruiters. Nair produced Indian witnesses to testify to men being captured from villages, subjected to torture by thorns and brambles, and stripped naked and to women being abused by local Indian officials. O'Dwyer denied any knowledge at the time of such activities by subordinates but did acknowledge having heard of such charges before the Hunter Committee in 1920: this testimony, contained in the heretofore unavailable vol. 6 of the Disorders Inquiry Committee is summarized by Datta, *Jallianwala Bagh,* pp. 14–18.

21. Datta, *Jallianwala Bagh,* p. 53.

22. B. Pattabhi Sitaramayya, in *History of the Indian National Congress,* vol. 1, p. 180, reports on the Congress convention of December 1919 in Amritsar:

> The atmosphere of the Congress was charged with electricity. Punjab and its atrocities naturally claimed the greatest attention. Gandhi was anxious that the mob violence in the Punjab and Gujrat should be condemned. The Subjects Committee threw out the resolution. Gandhi was disappointed. . . . He firmly, but politely and respectfully, expressed his inability to be in the Congress if the Congress could not see its way to accepting his view-point. The next morning, amidst the whinings and whimperings of the bulk of delegates, Resolution V was approved which, "while fully recognizing the grave provocation that led to a sudden outburst of mob frenzy, expressed the deep regret of the Congress at, and its condemnation of, the excesses committed in certain parts of the Punjab and Gujrat resulting in the loss of lives and injury to persons and property during the month of April last."

23. C. V. Setalwad, *Recollections and Reflections* (Bombay: 1946), p. 311, cited in Datta, *Jallianwala Bagh,* p. 118.

CHAPTER 7

1. Great Britain, *Parliamentary Debates* (Commons), 5th series, vol. 131 (28 June–16 July 1920), cols. 1705–1820; (Lords), 5th series, vol. 41 (6 July–16 August 1920), cols. 223–380.

2. O'Dwyer's counterattack on the government held it to be disloyal to its own servants as well as covering up evidence of conspiracy behind the rebellion: "What makes the action of the Coalition Government, of whom Mr. Montagu professed to be the only mouthpiece, the more deplorable is that neither the Government of India nor the Secretary of State expressed any detestation or condemnation of the acts of the rebels or murderers. . . . Their thunder was reserved for their own loyal but unfortunate servants." See Michael O'Dwyer, *India As I Knew It: 1885–1925,* pp. 298–302.

3. Great Britain, *Parliamentary Papers* (Commons), 1920, vol. 8 (*Reports,* vol. 4), Cmd. 771, "Statements of Brig.-Gen. Reginald E. Dyer," pp. 7–8.

4. Ibid., p. 11.

5. Colonel Wedgwood responded in 1918 to the Montagu-Chelmsford report in Commons by saying, "I am glad I have lived to see the day when a fellow countryman of mine in an official position, not only puts these views forward but has been able to get them received unanimously by the House of Commons as the right thing to do. I regret . . . that he is a Jew and not an Englishman. In doing the right thing by the world the Englishman has been left behind, and the Jew has come first." See Eugene F. Irschik, *Politics and Social Conflict in South India,* p. 147. Even today, the *Oxford Universal Dictionary* (1955) persists in defining a Jew as "a person of Hebrew race" and retaining derogatory meanings.

6. Ibid., p. 145.

7. See Norman Cohn's *Warrant for Genocide* for analysis of the sources and distribution of "The Myth of the Jewish World-Conspiracy and the Protocols of the Elders of Zion"; English publication and response are described on pp. 149–156.

8. Reprinted in *The Statesman* (Calcutta), "Political Storms," 22 August 1920, p. 12.

9. Allan Greenberger, *The British Image of India,* p. 109, quoting Gordon Casserley, *The Elephant God* (London: P. Allan & Co., 1920), pp. 127, 130–133.

10. "West and East," *The Times of India* (Bombay), 10 August 1920, p. 10.

11. Irving M. Copi, *Introduction to Logic,* chaps. 5–10.

12. Gandhi wrote: "In Amritsar innocent men and women were made to crawl like worms on their bellies. Before this outrage the Jallianwala Bagh tragedy paled into insignificance in my eyes, though it was this massacre principally that attracted the attention of the people of India and the whole world." See *My Experiments with Truth,* p. 576.

13. Lord Carmichael said: "What I feel about Gen. Dyer is that I cannot believe that the 'Crawling Order,' and one or two things of that sort, show that he is a man whose judgment is as correct as it could be. . . . I really do not believe that any Englishman, Scotsman, or Irishman, or anyone approves of the feeling that lies at the basis of the Crawling Order" [PDL 300, 304].

14. A minority of the motion's supporters—Major General Davidson and Lords Lamington and Midleton—do not advance any of these arguments. Lords Lamington and Midleton both claim that if Dyer was guilty, the government is responsible for authorizing his action because they did not censure or court-martial him immediately. Therefore, the government rather than Dyer ought to be censured. Both their arguments rely on an implicit premise that if the government is responsible, Dyer is not responsible for the massacre. This premise precludes their holding that perhaps both Dyer and the Government of India were responsible.

CHAPTER 8

1. Inconsistent premises and conclusions—such as affirming that "all men are innocent unless proved guilty" (IV.C.2A) and that "the crowd was guilty of conspiracy to rebel and/or willfully defying government decree" (IIIE.4)—can be interpreted as evidence of a double standard, which is a sign of moral exclusiveness. (This is corroborated by contextual analysis, which shows that the former is consistently associated with references to General Dyer or the rights of Englishmen.) Unfortunately, justice postulates (IV.C) were discarded from further analyses because of low intercoder agreement on these items: the reason for such disagreement is discussed in "A Note on Reliability" in Appendix A.

2. See note 1 above.

3. Lord Lamington's letter to the editor of *The Times* (London), published on 23 July 1920, p. 10, reiterates this point:

> The more that Gen. Dyer's conduct is open to criticism, the more culpable is the Government for having taken no action till it was desirable to make a sacrifice to appease the clamour of the extreme party in India. I spoke and voted for Lord Finlay's motion not to show approval of Gen. Dyer's action, but to show disapproval of the Government.

During the debate in Lords, Lord Lamington made the same argument:

> Where I really come to my difficulty, and why I feel I ought to follow the terms of the Motion, is with regard to the long delay before any action was taken. The Lord Chancellor talked about the hot weather and asked how the Government could take any action before knowing the facts. I should not think of matching my brains against those of the Lord Chancellor, but it seemed to me a very trivial excuse for the Government's not taking some action. You do not shoot 200 Indians every day. General Dyer was under Military Law and you could have held a Court Martial at once. [PDL:306]

4. The tendency among partisans of Dyer to displace the blame to the

bureaucracy might be probed by comparing the proportion of partisans' speeches devoted to attacking the government on procedural issues and to defending Dyer's action to parallel counter-themes (procedural defense/substantive attack) in the speeches of Dyer's opponents. It was originally intended to test this question by classifying the central theme of each paragraph in each speech and comparing the ratio of all paragraphs relating to the procedural issue and the substantive question in the speeches of partisans and opponents of Dyer. However, this was impossible because the paragraph theme count was too unreliable. Reasons for lack of reliability are discussed in "A Note on Reliability" in Appendix A.

5. Only one or two other lords joined Lord Ampthill in opposing the bill, which was passed without a division. Lord Midleton, one of the "deviant" supporters of the motion, spoke in favor of the bill; Lord Lamington, the other "deviant" supporter, voted for a key provision of the reforms on a vote taken on an amendment, the passage of which would probably have defeated the whole scheme. Besides Lords Ampthill and Midleton, six speakers in the Lords debate on that bill were also speakers in the Dyer debate: all supported the bill and also, except for Lord Carmichael, who finally abstained, spoke out vigorously against General Dyer on the motion in the Dyer debate.

6. *Parlimentary Debates* (Lords), 5th series, vol. 38 (15 December–23 December 1919), cols. 112–114.

CHAPTER 9

1. Furneaux reviews the evidence for such assertions and concludes that, except for the charge that Dyer did not receive a copy of the Hunter Committee's report prior to publication, they are false. Dyer's friends, realizing his "excitability," urged him to produce counsel before testifying, which advice he rejected. However, the English members of the committee might be said to have played a substitute role by employing certain leading lines of questioning in the cross-examination, cueing him in to rationales which he failed to exploit. See *Massacre at Amritsar*, pp. 119–127.

2. "British Women and Gen. Dyer," *The Statesman* (Calcutta), 24 August 1920, p. 7.

3. B. Pattabhi Sitaramayya, *History of the Indian National Congress*, vol. 1, p. 180.

4. *Punjabi Century: 1857–1947*, pp. 120–123.

5. Datta, *Jallianwala Bagh*, p. 170.

6. Ibid., p. 171.

7. Ibid., p. 173.

8. Only one-third of the eligible voters had voted in certain provinces. See the official figures in L. F. Rushbrook Williams' *India in 1920*, p. 65.

9. See witnesses' testimonials collected by Sir Sankaran Nair in *Gandhi and Anarchy*, p. 40.

10.. M. K. Gandhi, *Collected Works*, vol. 21, p. 466; vol. 22, pp. 200–202.

11. *Parliamentary Debates* (Lords), 5th series, vol. 56 (1924), col. 324.

12. *The Old Regime and the French Revolution*, pp. 176–177. See also T. R. Gurr, "A Comparative Study of Civil Strife," in *Violence in America*, ed. H. D. Graham and T. R. Gurr, pp. 568–572.

13. S. D. Waley, *Edwin Montagu*, p. 235.

14. See Furneaux, *Massacre at Amritsar*, p. 164.

15. Barrier, in "Punjab Politics and the Disturbances of 1907," cites unpublished statistics collected by Lord Curzon showing that "European attacks upon Punjabis diminished sharply after 1900" (p. 153). While it is unlikely that

Lord Curzon, during his tenure as viceroy, collected such figures solely for the Punjab, to my knowledge they have never been published for all of British India or each province, so this generalization cannot be definitely confirmed.

16. *Parliamentary Papers* (Commons), 1920, vol. 14, Cmd. 681, p. 25.

17. Richard D. Lambert, "Hindu-Muslim Riots" (unpublished Ph.D. dissertation, University of Pennsylvania, 1951), p. 79.

18. Ibid., p. 149.

19. See discussion of Georg Simmel's thesis as enunciated in *Conflict* in Lewis Coser, *The Functions of Social Conflict,* chap. 8.

20. Fritz Heider, paraphrased by Theodore Caplow in *Two Against One: Coalitions in Triads,* p. 73.

21. M. N. Srinivas, *Social Change in Modern India,* chap. 1.

22. Lambert, in "Hindu-Muslim Riots," analyzes the recorded causes of twentieth-century riots in India. He shows that the majority (68 of 116) occurred after a violation of religious norms or rituals sacred to one community: these involved altercations about the route of religious processions, playing music before a mosque, and alleged cow-killing. Only 11 of the 116 riots were triggered solely by economic or political causes.

APPENDIX B

1. Judith Blake Davis, "Values, Norms and Sanctions," in *Sociology Today,* ed. Robert E. Faris.

2. Robin M. Williams, Jr., in *American Society,* devotes chap. 11 to values and beliefs in American society and establishes the following criteria for determining the values of a social system: extensiveness, duration over a period of time, intensity with which the value is sought as indicated by various verbal reactions and sanctions when it is violated, and prestige of the value carriers (pp. 409–410). He omits only the question of to whom it is believed to pertain and thus leads to summations which must either negate or ignore the evidence he has presented.

3. See Simmel's *The Sociology of Georg Simmel,* p. 95, and Merton's *Social Theory and Social Structure,* p. 292.

4. *The Web of Group Affiliations,* pp. 172–185.

5. *Essays on the Sociology of Culture,* p. 294.

6. Ibid., pp. 100–101.

7. This usage of ideology—to comprehend the assumptions ordinary men (rather than political strategists or philosophers) make to interpret their position in the existing order and make that order seem tolerable, as opposed to a well-integrated belief system—is similar to the usage of Robert Lane in *Political Ideology: Why the American Common Man Believes What He Does.* Similarly to Mannheim's usage in *Ideology and Utopia,* pp. 55–59, it connotes ideas which function defensively to rationalize the present social order.

8. The *International Encyclopedia of the Social Sciences,* 1968, has no entries for either Solidarity or Social Order. The article "Social Cohesion" by Stanley Schacter (vol. 2, pp. 542–546) discusses theory and research on cohesion in small groups. Robert Angell, author of the article "Integration," concludes that both theory and research are deficient on all levels regarding this question in the discipline (vol. 7, p. 385).

9. Harry Eckstein, *Division and Cohesion in Democracy: A Study of Norway,* pp. 180–182.

10. Edward Shils, "The Theory of Mass Society," *Diogenes* 39 (1962):45–66.

11. Edward C. Banfield, *The Moral Basis of a Backward Society;* Danilo Dolci, *The Man Who Plays Alone.*

12. Carl J. Friedrich and Z. K. Brzezinski, *Totalitarian Dictatorship and Autocracy,* pp. 290-298.

13.The concept of the in-group was contributed by William Graham Sumner in *Folkways,* pp. 12-13. Merton distinguishes its empirical and logical relations to membership groups and reference groups in *Social Theory and Social Structure,* pp. 297-299, observing that "Sumner too soon and without warrant concluded that deep allegiance to one group generates antipathy (or, at the least, indifference) toward other groups. Coming out of the evolutionary tradition of social thought, with its emphasis on society as well as nature being red in tooth and claw, Sumner described an important but special case as though it were the general case."

14. Pierre van den Berghe, *Race and Racism,* p. 69.

15. Ibid., p. 139.

16. Dialogue recorded in the CIBA symposium *Caste and Race: Comparative Perspectives,* ed. Anthony de Reuck and Julie Knight, p. 141.

17. Eckstein, *Division and Cohesion in Democracy,* chap. 5.

18. See especially pt. 1 of Dolci's *The Man Who Plays Alone.*

19. Gabriel Almond and Sidney Verba, *The Civic Culture: Political Attitudes and Democracy in Five Nations,* p. 36; see also pp. 131 and 139.

20. Luigi Barzini, *The Italians,* pp. 186, 191, 194.

21. Helen Fein, "Ideology and Belief: Its Theoretical Relevance to the Question of Caste in South Africa Today" (unpublished paper, Columbia University, May 1969).

22. Thomas I. Pettigrew, "Social Distance Attitudes of South African Students," *Social Forces* 38 (1960):29-42.

23. H. F. Dickie-Clarke, *The Marginal Situation: A Sociological Study of a Coloured Group,* p. 220.

24. Max Weber, *The Theory of Social and Economic Organization,* pp. 118-128.

APPENDIX C

1. *Parliamentary Papers* (Commons), vol. 30 (*Reports,* vol. 14), Cmd. 3683, "Report of the Jamaica Royal Commission (1866), Part 1," p. 41.

2. *Hansard's Parliamentary Debates* (Commons), 3rd series, vol. 184 (1866). All following references are to this debate.

3. John Stuart Mill, *The Autobiography of John Stuart Mill,* p. 209.

Bibliography

GENERAL METHODS, RESEARCH, AND THEORY

Books

Allardt, Erik. "A Theory of Solidarity and Legitimacy Conflicts." In *Cleavages, Ideologies and Party Systems,* edited by Erik Allardt and Y. Littunen. Helsinki: Academic Bookstore, 1964.

Almond, Gabriel, and Verba, Sidney. *The Civic Culture: Political Attitudes and Democracy in Five Nations.* Princeton: Princeton University Press, 1963.

Anderson, Eugene, and Anderson, Pauline. *Political Institutions and Social Change in Continental Europe in the Nineteenth Century.* Berkeley: University of California Press, 1964.

Angell, Robert. "Social Integration." In *International Encyclopedia of the Social Sciences,* vol. 7, edited by D. E. Sills. New York: Macmillan, 1968.

Arendt, Hannah. *The Origins of Totalitarianism.* 2nd enlarged ed. New York: Meridian Books, 1958.

Banfield, Edward C. *The Moral Basis of a Backward Society.* Glencoe, Ill.: Free Press, 1958.

Barzini, Luigi. *The Italians.* New York: Atheneum, 1964.

Caplow, Theodore. *Two Against One: Coalitions in Triads.* Englewood Cliffs, N. J.: Prentice-Hall, 1968.

Cohn, Norman. *Warrant for Genocide: The Myth of the Jewish World-Conspiracy and the Protocols of the Elders of Zion.* New York: Harper & Row, 1969.

Copi, Irving M. *Introduction to Logic.* 2nd ed. New York: Macmillan, 1961.

Coser, Lewis. *The Functions of Social Conflict.* A Free Press Paperback. New York: Free Press, 1956.

Dahrendorf, Ralf. *Class and Class Conflict in Industrial Society.* Stanford: Stanford University Press, 1957.

Davis, Judith Blake. "Values, Norms and Sanctions." In *Sociology Today,* edited by Robert E. Faris. Chicago: Rand McNally, 1964.

Dickie-Clarke, H. F. *The Marginal Situation: A Sociological Study of a Coloured Group.* London: Routledge & Kegan Paul, 1966.

Dolci, Danilo. *The Man Who Plays Alone.* Translated by Antonia Gowan. London: MacGibbon & Kee, 1968.

Durkheim, Emile. *The Division of Labor in Society.* Translated by George Simpson. A Free Press Paperback. New York: Free Press, 1933.

Eckstein, Harry. *Division and Cohesion in Democracy: A Study of Norway.* Princeton: Princeton University Press, 1966.

Fanon, Frantz. *The Wretched of the Earth.* Translated by C. Farrington. New York: Grove Press, 1963.

Feldman, Arnold. "Violence and Volatility." In *Internal War,* edited by Harry Eckstein. New York: Free Press, 1964.

Finlay, David J.; Holsti, Ole R.; and Fagen, Richard R. *Enemies in Politics.* Chicago: Rand McNally, 1967.

Friedrich, Carl J., and Brzezinski, Z. K. *Totalitarian Dictatorship and Autocracy.* 2nd ed., revised by Carl J. Friedrich. Cambridge: Harvard University Press, 1965.

Giddings, Franklin H. *Studies in the Theory of Human Society.* New York: Macmillan, 1922.

Gurr, Ted Robert. "A Comparative Study of Civil Strife." In *Violence in America: Historical and Comparative Perspectives.* A Report to the National Commission on the Causes and Prevention of Violence, June 1969. Prepared under the direction and authorship of Hugh Davis Graham and Ted Robert Gurr. A Signet Book. New York: New American Library, 1969.

Hilberg, Raul. *The Destruction of the European Jews.* London: W. H. Allen, 1961.

Holsti, Ole R.; Loomba, Joan K.; and North, Robert C. "Content Analysis." In *The Handbook of Social Psychology,* vol. 2, 2nd ed., edited by Gardner Lindzey and Elliot Aronson. Reading, Mass.: Addison-Wesley, 1969.

Janowitz, Morris. "Patterns of Collective Racial Violence." In *Violence in America: Historical and Comparative Perspectives.* A Report to the National Commission on the Causes and Prevention of Violence, June 1969. Prepared under the direction and authorship of Hugh Davis Graham and Ted Robert Gurr. A Signet Book. New York: New American Library, 1969.

Lane, Robert. *Political Ideology: Why the American Common Man Believes What He Does.* New York: Free Press, 1962.

Lipset, Seymour M. *Political Man.* Anchor Books. New York: Doubleday, 1960.

Mannheim, Karl. *Ideology and Utopia.* Translated by Louis Wirth and Edward Shils. New York: Harcourt, Brace, 1936.

———. *Man and Society in an Age of Reconstruction: Studies in Modern Social Structure.* New York: Harcourt, Brace, 1940.

———. *Essays on the Sociology of Culture.* Edited by Ernest Manheim in cooperation with Paul Kecskemeti. London: Routledge & Kegan Paul, 1956.

Mead, George Herbert. *Mind, Self and Society.* Chicago: University of Chicago Press, 1934.

Merton, Robert. *Social Theory and Social Structure.* Revised and enlarged ed. New York: Free Press, 1957.

Mitzman, Arthur. *The Iron Cage: An Historical Interpretation of Max Weber.* New York: Grosset & Dunlap, 1969.

Moore, Barrington. *Social Origins of Dictatorship and Democracy.* Beacon Paperback. Boston: Beacon Press, 1966.

Morris, Charles. *Signification and Significance.* Cambridge: MIT Press, 1964.

Nieberg, Harold L. *Political Violence: The Behavioral Process.* New York: St. Martin's Press, 1969.

Parsons, Talcott. *Social Theory and Modern Society.* New York: Free Press, 1967.

Reuck, Anthony de, and Knight, Julie, eds. *Caste and Race: Comparative Perspectives.* London: J. & A. Churchill, Ltd., 1967.

Rubenstein, Richard E. *Rebels in Eden: Mass Political Violence in the United States.* Boston: Little, Brown, 1970.

Rudé, George F. *The Crowd in History: A Study of Popular Disturbances in France and England, 1730–1848.* New York: Wiley, 1964.

Schacter, Stanley. "Social Cohesion." In *International Encyclopedia of the Social Sciences,* vol. 2, edited by D. E. Sills, New York: Macmillan, 1968.

Simmel, Georg. *The Sociology of Georg Simmel.* Translated and edited by Kurt Wolff. Glencoe, Ill.: Free Press, 1950.

———. *Conflict.* Translated by Kurt Wolff. New York: Free Press, 1955.

———. *The Web of Group Affiliations.* Translated by Reinhold Bendix. New York: Free Press, 1955.

Smelser, Neil. *Theory of Collective Behavior.* New York: Free Press, 1963.

Sorel, Georges. *Reflections on Violence.* Translated by T. F. Hulme. New York: Peter Smith, 1941.

Speier, Hans. *Social Order and the Risks of War.* New York: G. W. Stewart, 1952.

Sullivan, Harry Stack. *The Collected Works of Harry Stack Sullivan.* New York: W. W. Norton and Company, 1953.

Sumner, William Graham. *Folkways.* Boston: Ginn, 1907.

Tilly, Charles. "Methods for the Study of Collective Violence." In *Problems in Research on Community Violence,* edited by Ralph W. Conant and Molly Apple Levin. New York: Praeger, 1969.

Tocqueville, Alexis de. *The Old Regime and the French Revolution.* Translated by Stuart Gilbert. Anchor Books. New York: Doubleday, 1955.

Van den Berghe, Pierre. *Race and Racism.* New York: Wiley, 1967.

Waskow, Arthur I. *From Race Riot to Sit-In, 1919 and the 1960s.* Anchor Books. New York: Doubleday, 1966.

Weber, Max. *From Max Weber: Essays in Sociology.* Translated and edited by H. H. Gerth and C. Wright Mills. Oxford University Press Paperback. New York: Oxford University Press, 1946.

———. *The Theory of Social and Economic Organization.* Translated by A. M. Henderson and Talcott Parsons. A Free Press Paperback. New York: Free Press, 1947.

Williams, Robin M., Jr. *American Society.* 2nd ed., rev. New York: Knopf, 1960.

Articles and Papers

Caplan, Nathan S., and Paige, Jeffrey M. "A Study of Ghetto Rioters." *Scientific American* 219 (August 1968): 15–21.

Dahlke, Otto. "Race and Minority Riots—A Study in the Typology of Violence." *Social Forces* 30 (1952): 419–425.
Fein, Helen. "Ideology and Belief: Its Theoretical Relevance to the Question of Caste in South Africa Today." Unpublished paper, Columbia University, 1969.
Gouldner, Alvin W. "The Norm of Reciprocity: A Preliminary Statement." *American Sociological Review* 25 (April 1960): 161–177.
Grimshaw, Allen D. "Factors Contributing to Colour Violence in the United States and Britain." *Race* 111 (May 1962): 3–19.
Hughes, Everett G. "Good People and Dirty Work." *Social Problems* 10 (Summer 1962): 3–10.
Lieberson, Stanley, and Silverman, Arnold J. "The Precipitants and Underlying Conditions of Race Riots." *American Sociological Review* 30 (December 1965): 887–891.
Lipsky, Michael, and Olson, David J. "Riot Commission Politics." *Transaction* 6 (July/August 1969): 8–21.
Mack, Raymond W., and Snyder, Richard C. "The Analysis of Social Conflict." *Journal of Conflict Resolution* 1 (1951): 213–247.
Oberschall, Anthony. "Group Violence: Some Hypotheses and Empirical Regularities." Paper delivered at 1969 American Sociological Association Convention. Mimeographed.
Perinbanayagam, Robert S. "Concepts and Their Misuse: Significant Others and Generalized Others." *SSSI Notes* 1 (2) (July 1975): 6–7.
Pettigrew, Thomas I. "Social Distance Attitudes of South African Students." *Social Forces* 38 (1960): 29–42.
Shils, Edward. "The Theory of Mass Society." *Diogenes* 39 (1962): 45–66.
Turner, Ralph H. "The Public Perception of Protest." *American Sociological Review* 34 (December 1969): 815–831.
Walter, E. V. "Violence and the Process of Terror." *American Sociological Review* 29 (April 1964): 248–257.
———. "Power and Violence." *American Political Science Review* 58 (June 1964): 350–360.
Westley, W. "Violence and the Police." *American Journal of Sociology* 29 (August 1953): 34–41.

GREAT BRITAIN

Documents

Great Britain, Parliament. *Parliamentary Debates* (Commons), 5th series, vols. 115–148 (29 April 1919–10 November 1921).
———. *Parliamentary Debates* (Lords), 5th series, vols. 37–56 (23 October 1919–27 March 1924).

Newspapers and Periodicals

Blackwood's Magazine. "Amritsar: By an Englishwoman," vol. 1254 (April 1920) pp. 441–446.
Morning Post (London). 1 December 1919–31 August 1920.
The Nation. "Peril of the Military Mind," vol. 26 (20 December 1919), pp. 412–413.
———. "Whitewash: Report of the Gov't. of the Punjab on the Disturbances in the Province," vol. 26 (7 February 1920), pp. 632–633.

____. "Mr. Montagu's Gesture," vol. 26 (29 May 1920), pp. 288–289.
____. "Choice in India," vol. 27 (17 July 1920), pp. 488–489.
The Nineteenth Century. "The Prelude to Amritsar," vol. 88 (June 1920), pp. 1066–1073.
The Times (London). 1 April 1919–31 July 1920.
The Times Literary Supplement. Letters to the editor on the Dyer case, 9 January 1964–14 May 1964.

INDIA

Documents

Great Britain, Parliament. *Parliamentary Papers* (Commons), 1918, vol. 8 (*Reports*, vol. 4), Cmd. 9190, "Report of Committee Appointed to Investigate Revolutionary Conspiracies in India."
____. *Parliamentary Papers* (Commons), 1918, vol. 8 (*Reports*, vol. 4), Cmd. 9198, "Report of Sir N. Chandavarkar and Mr. Justice Beacroft on Detenues and Internees in Bengal."
____. *Parliamentary Papers* (Commons), 1920, vol. 8 (*Reports*, vol. 4), Cmd. 771, "Statements of Brig.-Gen. Reginald E. Dyer."
____. *Parliamentary Papers* (Commons), 1920, vol. 14 (*Reports*, vol. 6), Cmd. 681, "Report of the Committee Appointed by the Government of India to Investigate the Disturbances in the Punjab, etc."
____. *Parliamentary Papers* (Commons), 1920 vol. 14 (*Reports*, vol. 6), Cmd. 534, "District Accounts Submitted by the Government of the Punjab."
Great Britain, War Office. *The Manual of Military Law.* London: His Majesty's Stationery Office, 1914.
Indian National Congress Punjab Subcommittee. *Report of the Commissioners.* 2 vols. Bombay: Karnatak Press, 1920.
Philips, C. H., ed. *The Evolution of India and Pakistan, 1858 to 1947: Select Documents.* London: Oxford University Press, 1962.
Williams, L. F. Rushbrook, ed. *India in 1920.* Calcutta: Government of India, 1921.

Newspapers

The Pioneer (Allahabad). 1–31 December 1919 and 1 July–31 August 1920.
The Statesman (Calcutta). 1 March–30 April 1919, and 1–31 August 1920.
The Times of India (Bombay). 1–31 December 1919 and 1 July–31 August 1920.

Biographies and Autobiographies

Colvin, Ian. *The Life of General Dyer.* London: Blackwood, 1929.
Gandhi, M. K. *My Experiments with Truth.* Ahmedabad: Navajivan Publishing House, 1948.
____. *Non-violent Resistance.* New York: Schocken Books, 1951.
____. *The Collected Works of Mahatma Gandhi.* Vols. 20–22. Delhi: Government of India, 1967.
Jayakar, M. R. *The Story of My Life.* Vol. 1. Bombay: Asia Publishing House, 1958.
Nehru, J. *An Autobiography.* London: Lane, 1936.
O'Dwyer, Michael. *India As I Knew It: 1885–1925.* London: Constable, 1925.
Sankaran Nair. *Gandhi and Anarchy.* Indore, n.d.

Tandon, Prakash. *Punjabi Century—1857-1947.* New York: Harcourt, Brace & World, 1961.
Wayley, S. D. *Edwin Montagu.* London: Asia Publishing House, 1964.

Historical Works: Books

Ahliuwalia, M. M. *Kukas: The Freedom Fighters of the Punjab.* Bombay: Allied Publishers Private Limited, 1965.
Bajwa, Fauja Singh. *Kuka Movement.* Delhi: Kuka Research Centre, 1965.
Bernays, Robert. *"Naked Fakir."* London: Gollancz, 1931.
Bondurant, Joan V. *Conquest of Violence: The Gandhian Philosophy of Conflict.* London: Oxford University Press, 1958.
Das, M. N. *India Under Morley and Minto: Politics behind Revolution, Repression and Reforms.* London: G. Allen, 1964.
Datta, V. N. *Jallianwala Bagh.* Ludhiana: Lyall Book Depot, 1969.
Dodwell, H. H., ed. *The Indian Empire.* The Cambridge History of India, vol. 6. Delhi: S. Chand & Co., 1964.
Furneaux, Rupert. *Massacre at Amritsar.* London: G. Allen, 1963.
Ghosh, Pansy Chaya. *The Development of the Indian National Congress: 1892-1909.* Calcutta: Firma K. L. Mukhopadhyay, 1960.
Gopal, S. *British Policy in India: 1858-1905.* Cambridge: Cambridge University Press, 1965.
Greenberger, Allan. *The British Image of India.* London: Oxford University Press, 1969.
Hennessy, Josselyn. "British Education for an Elite in India (1780-1947)." In *Governing Elites: Studies in Training and Selection,* edited by Rupert Wilkinson. New York: Oxford University Press, 1969.
Irschik, Eugene F. *Politics and Social Conflict in South India.* Berkeley: University of California Press, 1969.
Kumar, R., ed. *Essays on Gandhian Politics: The Rowlatt Satyagraha of 1919.* Oxford: Clarendon Press, 1971.
Mason, Philip [Philip Woodruff]. *The Men Who Ruled India.* Vol. 2. *The Guardians.* New York: Schocken Books, 1964.
Metcalf, Thomas R. *The Aftermath of Revolt: India, 1857-1870.* Princeton: Princeton University Press, 1964.
Naidis, Mark. *India.* New York: Macmillan, 1966.
Orwell, George. *A Collection of Essays.* Anchor Books. New York: Doubleday, 1971.
Pattabhi Sitaramayya, B. *History of the Indian National Congress.* Vol. 1, *1885-1935.* Delhi: S. Chand & Co., 1969.
Ram, Rajah. *The Jallianwala Bagh Massacre—A Premeditated Plan.* Chandigarh: Punjab University Publishing Bureau, 1969.
Seal, Anil. *The Emergence of Indian Nationalism: Competition and Collaboration in the Later Nineteenth Century.* Cambridge: Cambridge University Press, 1968.
Sethi, R. R. *The Last Phase: 1919-1947.* Bound with vol. 6, The Cambridge History of India. Delhi: S. Chand & Co., 1964.
Singh, Hira Lal. *Problems and Policies of the British in India, 1885-1898.* Bombay: Asia Publishing House, 1963.
Singh, Khushwant. *A History of the Sikhs.* Vol. 2, 1839-1964. Princeton: Princeton University Press, 1966.
Smith, Vincent A. *The Oxford History of India.* 3rd ed., edited by Percival Spear. Oxford: Clarendon Press, 1958.

Srinivas, M. N. *Social Change in Modern India*. Berkeley: University of California Press, 1966.
Taylor, A. J. P. *English History* 1914-1945. New York: Oxford University Press, 1965.
Thompson, Edward. *The Other Side of the Medal*. New York: Harcourt, Brace, 1926.
Wolpert, Stanley A. *Tilak and Gokhale: Revolution and Reform in the Making of Modern India*. Berkeley: University of California Press, 1962.
Woodruff, Philip [pseud.]. *See* Mason, Philip.

Historical Works: Articles

Ganguly, Satyendra Nath. "A Glimpse on the Original Revolutionary Societies of Bengal." *Modern Review* (Allahabad) 116 (November 1963): 382-384.
Giuliano, P. "The Rejection of Violence in Gandhian Ethics of Conflict Resolution." *Journal of Conflict Resolution* 12 (1965): 197-213.
Gordon, Leonard A. "Portrait of a Bengal Revolutionary." *Journal of Asian Studies* 27 (February 1968): 197-216.
Joshi, V. S. "Tilak and the Revolutionaries." *Modern Review* (Allahabad) 117 (January 1965): 29-33.
Mukherjee, Uma, and Mukherjee, Haridas. "The Story of Bande Mataram Sedition Trial, 1907." *Modern Review* (Allahabad) 106 (October 1959): 286-288.
____. "Sri Aurobindo and Bande Mataram." *Modern Review* (Allahabad) 114 (August 1963): 125-129.
Prasad, Varma V. "Lokamanya Tilak and Early Indian Nationalism." *Patna University Journal* 16 (1961): 1-35.
Rao, L. Raghavendra. "The Early Phase of Indian Nationalism, Part 2." *Journal of Karnatak University* 6 (June 1962): 115-127.

Historical Works: Dissertations

Barrier, Norman Gerald. "Punjab Politics and the Disturbances of 1907." Unpublished Ph.D. dissertation, Duke University, 1966.
Lambert, Richard D. "Hindu-Muslim Riots." Unpublished Ph.D. dissertation, University of Pennsylvania, 1951.
Naidis, Mark. "The Punjab Disturbances of 1919: A Study in Indian Nationalism." Unpublished Ph.D. dissertation, Stanford University, 1951.

JAMAICA

Great Britain, Parliament. *Hansard's Parliamentary Debates* (Commons), 3rd Series, vol. 184 (1866).
____. *Parliamentary Papers* (Commons), vol. 30 (*Reports,* vol. 14), Cmd. 3683, "Report of the Jamaica Royal Commission (1866), Part 1."
Mill, John Stuart. *The Autobiography of John Stuart Mill*. New York: Columbia University Press, 1924.

Index

Copi, Irving C., 138
Coser, Lewis, viii, 15
Crawling Order. *See* Dyer, Brigadier
General Reginald E., Crawling Order
of
Crewe, Marquess of (M.P., House of
Lords, 1920), 140–142, 158, 187
Crime, functions of, 11–13, 15, 222 n.15
Crime–punishment–crime cycle, ix,
10–15, 182–183, 189
Crimes of British against Indians, 56–
57, 66, 176. *See also* Jallianwala Bagh
massacre
Crimes of Indians against British, 61,
67–68. *See also* Amritsar, 1919,
government reaction, shooting, and
riot in
Curzon, Earl of Kedleston (M.P.,
House of Lords, 1920): actions of,
during viceroyalty, 56–57, 60, 62,
185, 231–232 n.15; role of, in debate,
22–23, 138–140, 143, 158

Dahlke, Otto, 14
Dahrendorf, Ralf, viii, 4, 91
Das, M. N., 62, 64, 70
Datta, V. N., 31, 33–34, 87, 90, 107,
124, 223–224 n.8
Davidson, Major General Sir J. H.
(M.P., House of Commons, 1920),
158, 230 n.14
Davis, Judith Blake, 203
Debates in Parliament on Dyer sanction: analysis of, 138–167; backgrounds of speakers, 136–138; conclusion on motions, 132, 136–138;
defense mechanisms used in, 101,
155, 164–165; meaning of motions,
xii, 97–99, 129, 133–134, 136–138,
150, 187–188; methods of analysis of,
99–101; rhetorical tactics in, 165–167,
187–188; speakers tabulated by assumptions, 158. *See also* Dyer sanction, response to
Defense of India Act, 25, 75–76, 119
Definition of the situation: altered in
Dyer's testimony, 131–132; in debates, 98, 146–150, 159–160; in disorder reports, 95–96, 109–112,
125–126. *See also* Axioms of empire
Delhi, 82–83, 176–177
Devi, Rattan (Indian witness cited), 32
Dickie-Clarke, H. F., 211

Disorder reports compared, xi–xii,
95–96, 106–128
Disraeli, Benjamin, 6
District reports. *See* Punjab, Govern-
ment of 1919, district reports of
Division of Labor. See Durkheim,
Emile
Dodwell, H. H., 78
Dolci, Danilo, 210
Doveton, Captain (British army officer, Punjab, 1919), 41
Durkheim, Emile: cited, 11–13, 187–
205; critique of theory of, 3–4, 13,
15–17; quoted, 1–2, 6–7, 15–16; revision of theory of, 17–19, 93; theory of
Division of Labor, ix, 1–3, 6, 17
Dyer, Brigadier General Reginald E.
(British army officer, Punjab, 1919):
bans Amritsar meetings, 30; career
of, after massacre, 45, 103–104, 106,
129–132, 183–184; Crawling Order
of, 20–21, 40–42, 117, 122, 144, 154,
163–164, 170–172, 230 nn.12, 13;
described by J. Nehru, 44–45; enters
Amritsar, 31; inferred motives of, 20,
33–34, 182, 224 n.11; judgment of,
by Indians, 105, 117, 171–172; judgment of, by officials, 96–98, 105, 112,
114–118; knowledge of military law
of, 112–113; orders shooting in Jallianwala Bagh, xi–xii, 20–21, 31–34,
181–182; testifies on motives, 20–21,
43–45, 104–105, 124, 131–132, 224–
225 n.22; sanctions against, xii, 94–
95, 97, 105–106, 129, 132–133, 136,
150, 185–189; views quoted, 175–176.
See also Debates in Parliament on
Dyer sanction
Dyer fund drive, 135, 169–171
Dyer sanction, response to, 168–173,
187–188

Eckstein, Harry, 205–207, 209–210
Empathy, indices of, 100, 156–157
English radicals, 69–70. *See also* British
political parties' division on India
Equal justice tree, 138–144
Ethnic stratification: breeds crime, ix,
8–11; within Government of India,
52–55; and political order, 4–6, 48,
208; recognized in debate, 100–108; in
South Africa, 208, 210–211
Exploitation, 5, 66

About the Author

Helen Fein, a political sociologist concerned primarily with the problem of collective violence, holds an M. A. degree (1958) from Brooklyn College and a Ph.D. degree from Columbia University (1971). The documentary research for *Imperial Crime and Punishment* included a study of contemporary British newspapers found in the British Museum Newspaper Library. Dr. Fein also spent a year (1971–1972) in India where she lectured at the University of Kurekshetra (near Amritsar) and visited Jallianwala Bagh. At present she is completing a study, "The Calculus of Genocide," analyzing the causes of national differences in the magnitude of Jewish victimization during the Holocaust. Her other publications include articles in *Patterns of Prejudice* and the *Jewish Spectator*.